INVENTING
THE
AMERICAN
WOMAN

SECOND EDITION

ARTHUR S. LINK
General Editor for History

INVENTING THE AMERICAN WOMAN

An Inclusive History

SECOND EDITION

Volume 2: Since 1877

GLENDA RILEY
Ball State University

Harlan Davidson, Inc.
Wheeling, Illinois 60090-6000

Library of Congress Cataloging-in-Publication Data

Riley, Glenda
   Inventing the American woman : an inclusive history / Glenda
Riley. — 2nd ed.
      p. cm.
   Includes bibliographical references and indexes.
   Contents: v. 1. To 1877 — v. 2. Since 1877.
   ISBN 0-88295-922-0 (v. 1) — ISBN 0-88295-923-9 (v. 2)
   1. Women—United States—History.   2. Sex role—United States—
History.   I. Title.
HQ1410.R55   1995
305.4' 0973—dc20   94-39761
                                                                CIP

Poetry extract on p. 340, © 1983 by Elena Avila, used by permission.

Cover design: DePinto Graphic Design

Manufactured in the United States of America
99 98 97 96   4 5 BC

CONTENTS

REFERENCE
CONTENTS IN BRIEF

INTRODUCTION
Gender Expectations Across Cultures

Since the first edition of *Inventing the American Woman* appeared in 1986, the study of women's history has penetrated the curriculums of most American high schools, colleges, and universities. The widespread response to *Inventing*, as well as subsequent requests for its revision and updating, further demonstrate the tremendous thirst that Americans have developed for knowledge concerning the nation's women and their historical experiences.

Like the first edition, this one presents an overview of the history of women in the United States. Intended for use as an introductory textbook supplement in U.S. history or a core text in women's history courses, it combines factual knowledge with a thesis intended to provoke discussion and further thought. More specifically, this volume tracks the evolution of gender expectations and social constructs concerning the essence of womanhood that have played, and continue to play, a critical role in directing and shaping American women's behaviors, responses, and dissatisfactions.

American Indians were the first to establish gender expectations in what is today the United States, but when European settlers reached early America they disregarded or rejected native people's ideas regarding women. Instead, European settlers established their own beliefs which soon became dominant and reflected the thinking of a society that argued for the acceptance of certain enduring "truths" regarding women. A real American woman supposedly was, among other things, a devoted mother, a domestic individual who labored most happily and productively within her own home, an unusually virtuous person who had to remain aloof from the corruption of politics, and a weak-minded, physically inferior being who needed guidance from wiser and stronger people, namely men. Once established as principles, these tenets were embodied in a series of intricate images and prescriptions that defined and limited women's roles. In other words, people invented an ideal American woman.

On one hand, this model of womanhood might be judged innocuous. Generally, white middle- and upper-class women best fulfilled its mandates. In turn, it rewarded and honored them. If they remained domestic and unassertive, such women could expect the plaudits of family members, friends, and clergy. Often, such women felt grateful and even revered; they gained satisfaction from meeting their society's expectations of women. For other groups of women, especially Native American, African American, Spanish-speaking, and Asian American women, as well as women employed outside their homes and poor women, this model simply appeared irrelevant.

On the other hand, the model should not be underestimated as a form of social control, for it provided a comfortable substitute for careful thought. People generally found it was easier to believe that both women and men had a well-defined "place" than to deal with the full complexities of human society and personality. Such thinking also helped perpetuate an economic system based upon the usually greater physical strength of men, who for centuries had performed the heavy labor involved in hunting, farming, and manufacturing, while women often remained behind to bear and raise children and perform lighter tasks. And it reinforced a political system in which men made more of the public decisions and women more of the private, or domestic ones.

Gender expectations and social constructs also kept in force power imbalances. Prevailing beliefs regarding women translated into sanctions, which in turn undergirded policies and legislation regulating families, schools, churches, politics, and the workplace. Too often, these resulting prescriptions robbed all women of the opportunity to cultivate their talents and deprived the developing nation of women's nondomestic skills and labor. Such constraints frequently caused women's education and socially acceptable literature to be narrow, often puerile, and limiting to the mind. And they encouraged women's clothing and pastimes to be impractical, sensuous, and physically restrictive.

Consequently, during the 1600s, 1700s, and early 1800s, thousands of women resisted being molded into the idealized American woman. Although middle- and upper-class women were generally the first to speak against and challenge tenets of American womanhood, women of other social classes soon expressed their discontent as well. Typically, women dissidents drew upon women's culture and its varied resources both to help them endure the system and to reform it. At the same time, such forces as early industrialization, urbanization, and national expansion not only tested customary prescriptions but demonstrated their unsuitability to a modernizing society.

By the mid-1800s, the idealized American woman sustained open attack. Women's participation in women's rights activism, reformism, religious revivalism, and paid employment all helped erode the model. During the late 1800s and well into the twentieth century, such other developments as Progressivism, world wars, civil rights, contemporary feminism, and the emergence of double-income families forced many Americans to continue to rethink their beliefs, recasting their ideas in a mold that better fits the reality of all kinds of women in the present-day United States, including professionals, poor women, lesbians, full-time homemakers, divorced women, and those of color.

Now, as the United States moves into the twenty-first century, its people will continue to struggle with, and redefine, expectations of women and societal constructs regarding them—and increasingly those affecting men as well. Understanding the historical development of both the nation and its women is essential to these undertakings. Thus, this book considers women and the changes they experienced during various epochs of American history. At each chapter's conclusion is a list of suggested readings to provide the interested reader with additional factual information, varied interpretations, and methodological perspectives regarding women's issues and themes for particular eras.

About terminology: A special attempt has been made in this text to respect sensitivities regarding the labels and language that carry great freight in such issues as racism, sexism, ageism, and classism. Some of the relevant style choices and definitions observed include referring to so-called minorities as *peoples of color*; virtually interchangeable references to *African Americans* and *blacks;* use of the term *Anglos* to mean white Americans; and preferred use of the term *Chicanos/Chicanas* for *Mexican Americans* and *Latinos/Latinas* for the broader group of Americans with heritage from any Spanish-speaking country. Upper-case *Native Americans* is used interchangeably with *American Indians* or, where unmistakable, *Indians*. Especially in precolonial and colonial context, the term *native Americans* (lower-case *n*) identifies indigenous Spanish-speaking as well as American Indian peoples. Except where hyphens are truly necessary to avoid misreading, this text also prefers not to hyphenate groups of people, even when such compounds as African American and Asian American are used as adjectives.

Such choices in terminology and style remain an especially important effort in a book that braves generalizations regarding the complex historical experience of so many kinds of people—in this case, over half the people of the United States. This book, after all, is about more than

American women's past. By implication it is also about their collective present and future, periods that will witness the emergence of a long overdue development—a reinvented, and far more inclusive, American woman.

"Reordering Women's Sphere"
The Gilded Age and Progressive Era, 1878 to 1914

6

The Gilded Age, which took its name from a Mark Twain novel, was supposedly gilt on the outside and base metal underneath—more style than substance. Characterized by economic expansion and growing agrarian discontent, it lasted until approximately 1890. Then, the founding of the Populist Party in 1890 and a debilitating depression between 1893 and 1897 caused Americans to rethink their values.

During the mid- and late-1890s, people began to recognize that hard work did not automatically guarantee success. Instead, governmental welfare and social justice programs had to redress the inequities of an imperfect economic structure. As the nation turned from the excesses of the so-called Gilded Age to Progressive Era reform, women both implemented massive change and benefited from it. Women, especially those of the middle and upper classes, used their energy and will to alter ideas, including those regarding gender.

THE GILDED AGE, LATE 1870S TO APPROXIMATELY 1890

Industrialization

Four major developments characterized the period that bridged the Reconstruction and Progressive eras. The first of these, industrialization, affected American women in a number of ways.

Certainly, the proliferation of technological devices and convenience goods altered the nature of women's work within the home. At the same time, the rapid expansion of the industrial work force opened a growing number of employment opportunities to women outside the home. As a result of mass production and early assembly lines, jobs once done by skilled male workers could be performed by any unskilled workers willing to work for low wages.

In addition, the marginal wages that many married men brought home forced their wives to take paid employment to earn supplemental income. Immigrant families also expected their daughters to contribute economically, while an increasing number of single women, many of them migrants from rural areas, needed to support themselves.

Despite women's increasing entry into the labor force, old ideas held sway. Thus, women found themselves generally segregated in "women's" jobs, meaning those that required minimal training and garnered little respect. In the textile industry, for example, men served as managers and such skilled operatives as fabric cutters, while women worked as machine-operators, trimmers, and finishers. In bakeries, men held the position of baker and women that of packer. In breweries, men labored as brewers and women as bottle washers.

Women themselves reinforced gender segregation in the workplace by flocking to industries that would employ them—textile, garment, tobacco, printing, and food processing—thus insuring by their continued availability that they would remain ghettoized and poorly paid. Typically, unskilled women earned considerably less than skilled men, but even skilled women earned only about one-half the wage commanded by their skilled male counterparts. Black women earned only one-half the pay of white women.

A growing number of women sought to redress their situation by organizing Working Girls' Clubs, which began to meet in New York during the 1880s and addressed practical issues, including wages, insurance, employment bureaus, and lunch programs. Women also joined such men's labor organizations as the Knights of Labor. After 1881, when the Knights of Labor voted to open membership to women, female workers joined formerly male assemblies and organized female assemblies. Black women workers also participated in this movement, especially by founding assemblies of laundresses, chambermaids, and housekeepers. The Knights soon chartered 130 locals that included both men and women, and approximately 270 "ladies' locals." By 1887, the Knights counted sixty-five thousand women among its members.

The Knights of Labor encouraged the efforts of its female members by organizing a woman's department. The Knights also blended the domestic values of fairness, cooperation, and social service with labor activism by supporting the causes of equal pay for equal work, woman suffrage, and temperance. Such paid organizers as one widow with two children, Leonora Barry, who lectured, inspected factories, and organized labor assemblies throughout the 1880s, furthered such programs. As the Knights declined during the late 1880s after several unsuccessful strikes and Barry resigned from her post as general investigator in 1890, the union abandoned much of its women-oriented agenda.

Anglo women (but not women of color) were also eligible to join the American Federation of Labor (AFL) from its inception in 1881. But it was not until 1888 that AFL president Samuel Gompers urged the active recruitment of women workers. Women soon found union dues too high for their limited wages and the reception given them by male members decidedly cool. Still, in 1888 Elizabeth Morgan became a prime mover in the formation of the Ladies Federal Labor Union, and in 1890 Mary Burke of the Retail Clerks International served as the first woman delegate to an AFL convention. In 1891, the AFL created the office of National Organizer for Women and, in 1892, appointed bindery worker Mary E. Kenney to the post.

Despite these changes, resistance to the idea of women working outside the home remained strong. Most male workers clung to the long-standing ideology of women as wives and mothers, while refusing to recognize the new attitudes and the economic necessity that propelled women into the labor force. Many men also feared that women's willingness to accept low wages devalued their own earning power.

The situation of working women of color was even more discouraging. They faced double jeopardy—discrimination on the basis of both gender and race. Thus, only a minuscule number of black women, Latinas, and Asian women held factory employment. The widespread belief that people of color were best at menial labor further helped confine these women to such jobs as laundry workers, scrubwomen, cooks, field-workers, crop pickers, tobacco strippers, and other unskilled labor. In the South, black women workers were also used predominantly in tenant farming and sharecropping, while black women prisoners performed mainly convict labor in field- and roadwork. In 1890, census figures indicated that 975,530 nonwhite (black, Indian, and Asian) women were employed, but 30.83 percent were servants and 15.9 percent were laundresses; only 2.76 percent worked in manufacturing.

In addition, office and sales work virtually excluded women of color. Native-born Anglo women increasingly filled these jobs, which had once been the province of white men. In 1870, nineteen thousand women held office jobs, a figure that jumped to seventy-five thousand by 1890. Women also rapidly replaced men as telegraph and telephone operators and sales clerks.

Both white and black employed women, however, moved into the professions in growing numbers. While their status was slightly higher than that of other employed women, nurses and teachers also endured low wages, long hours, and poor working situations. Still, women were attracted to the professions. Especially in urban areas, where hospitals and clinics existed, of course, many women entered nursing. Similarly, in cities where school enrollments were high and teachers in great demand, the employment of women teachers grew rapidly. In 1883, Alabama's superintendent of public instruction noted that "members of the most elegant and cultivated families in the State are now engaged in teaching." In response to the demand, in 1886 Lucy Craft Laney founded the Haines Institute in Augusta, Georgia, a school dedicated to training blacks as nurses and teachers. In addition, far more black women than men entered teaching, while black nurses rapidly increased in number.

Women also entered law and medicine in greater numbers during the Gilded Age. In 1879, Belva Ann Lockwood became the first woman attorney to practice before the U.S. Supreme Court. In 1884 and again in 1888, Lockwood ran on the National Equal Rights party ticket for the presidency of the United States, thus drawing national attention to the issue of woman suffrage. Meanwhile, in 1883, at age sixty-three, black reformer Mary Ann Shadd Cary received a law degree from Howard University and soon became a successful lawyer in Washington, D.C. In 1897, Lutie Lytle received admission to the Tennessee state bar and became the first black woman to practice law in that state.

By 1880 the number of women doctors had grown to 2,312. A number of black and interracial institutions trained women as doctors, including Howard University Medical School, New England Female Medical College in Boston, and Women's Medical College of Pennsylvania. In 1893, Meharry Medical College in Nashville, Tennessee, graduated its first black women physicians, Annie D. Gregg and Georgiana Esther Lee Patton.

Other women of color also began to practice medicine. In 1896, Dr. Kong Tai Heong became the first woman doctor in Hawaii. She had trained at the Canton Medical School in China and relocated in Hawaii with her husband, Dr. Li Khai Fai. After they founded Honolulu's first Chinese hospital, in 1910 Dr. Kong and her husband entered private practice. She soon achieved renown as an obstetrician in Honolulu's Chinese community.

Overall, by 1890 nearly four million women worked for wages outside their homes. Approximately one out of every seven women held a job. The overwhelming number of these women were single, only slightly over 14 percent were married, and nearly 18 percent were divorced or widowed.

Urbanization

The second major trend of the Gilded Age, urbanization, also deeply influenced women's lives. During the 1870s and 1880s America's urban population grew far more rapidly than did its rural population. Such cities as New York and Chicago served as magnets, drawing immigrants from abroad and migrants from rural areas. They also functioned as major marketplaces and manufacturing centers, while contributing to a widespread upheaval in American ideas and values.

Consequently, urban women spearheaded new approaches to women's issues. Increasingly, they rejected traditional thinking regarding large families. During the late 1870s and 1880s, a wide variety of women supported the concept of voluntary motherhood, including suffragists, moral reformers, and women who desired freedom from continual pregnancies and childcare. Because the Comstock Law of 1873 restricted the mailing and advertising of birth-control devices, women relied upon abstinence, male continence (the avoidance of ejaculation), and *coitus interruptus*. Occasionally, people could obtain rubber condoms and pessaries (female prophylactics) through subtle advertising that avoided the term birth control. Manufacturers of the Gem Pessary, for example, claimed that it would prevent and cure "uterine disease."

In reaction, those who feared women's control over childbirth and imagined such ramifications as medical complications and population decrease launched a crusade against planned parenthood and abortion. Such groups as the American Medical Association and the Young Men's Christian Association (YMCA) initiated national anti–birth control programs. Still, for many reasons, family size did decline, especially among native-born, middle-class, well-educated, urban white women who, during the 1880s, bore an average of between two and three children.

Black women's fertility, which had begun to decline somewhat even before the Civil War, also continued to drop during the 1880s, but at a slightly slower rate than did Anglo women's. First-generation immigrant women hesitated to embrace Voluntary Motherhood. Instead, they tended to cling to traditional ideas of family size and limited roles for women, at least until second-generation women introduced new beliefs.

Besides reshaping ideas regarding family size, urban women helped alter customary thinking regarding marriage. They divorced their spouses at higher rates than did rural women, obtained divorces in greater numbers than urban men, and quickly adopted such catchall grounds as cruelty.

Opposition to the rising divorce rate proved swift and vocal. When the New England Divorce Reform League, organized in 1881, became the National Divorce Reform League in 1885, it initiated the first divorce reform movement in the United States. It especially lobbied the U.S. Congress, asking Congress to fund a statistical study of U.S. marriage and divorce.

When in 1889 the U.S. Census Bureau released its first statistical study of divorce, it confirmed many Americans' fears. Not only was the divorce rate rising, but people in states with restrictive laws, such as New York and South Carolina, sometimes took advantage of permissive laws in such areas as South Dakota and Oklahoma Territory by temporarily migrating there. Also, American marriages failed at the rate of one in every thirteen to fifteen, while women obtained two-thirds of divorces and men one-third. Despite Victorians' emphasis on romance, love, and family, the U.S. divorce rate increased at a rate of approximately 30 percent every five years and held the record as the highest in the world.

The National Divorce Reform League continued its crusade, asking now for uniform divorce laws in every U.S. state and territory, which would, they hoped, at least halt migratory divorces. But Congress maintained that divorce legislation fell under states' rights rather than federal power. Also, numerous women's rights leaders opposed uniform divorce laws. Elizabeth Cady Stanton explained that prevailing liberal divorce laws were "for oppressed wives . . . what Canada was for Southern slaves." In 1913, the Divorce Reform League collapsed and Americans continued to seek migratory divorces, especially in the newest divorce capital, Reno, Nevada.

Meanwhile, urban women put increasing pressure on other American conventions. Middle- and upper-class Anglo women especially insisted that institutions of higher education admit them. By 1879, Columbia College in New York City permitted women to enroll in selected courses, and in 1889 established Barnard College for women. Barnard utilized Columbia's professors, library, and course standards. Nine women graduated in the first class with educations equivalent to male students attending Columbia. Meanwhile, in 1888 Hunter College of the City University became the first U.S. college to provide free education for both white women and women of color.

It was also in cities that women first began to discuss the problems plaguing American Indians and other peoples of color. After listening to Ponca leader Standing Bear speak in Boston in 1879, Helen Hunt Jackson began to write about Native American rights. In 1882, Jackson's *A Century of Dishonor* chronicled duplicitous U.S. government relations with Indians. Two years later, Jackson's romantic novel *Ramona* achieved best-seller status. At the same time, a Paiute chief from Nevada named Sarah Winnemucca traveled to American cities in an attempt to save her people from the ravages of white conquest and settlement. As a public lecturer dressed in beautiful native garb and author of *Life Among the Paiutes: Their Wrongs and Claims* (1883), Winnemucca alerted the nation to the cause of decimated and poverty-stricken American Indians.

In another city, San Francisco, Shanghai native Mary Tape exposed discriminatory policies against Asians. As a young immigrant, Mary had lived for five years at the Ladies' Relief Society near San Francisco's Chinatown and later taught herself painting, photography, and telegraphy. When the San Francisco schools denied Mary and Joseph Tape's daughter Mamie admission, Mary sued the Board of Education. The court supported Tape, but the school board circumvented the ruling by establishing a separate Chinese school. Mary wrote the head of the board: "May you . . . never be persecuted like the way you have persecuted little Mamie Tape . . . [who] will never attend any of the Chinese schools of your making!"

Immigration

The third trend of the Gilded Age, immigration, also altered women's situations. Massive immigration of the late 1870s and the 1880s added thousands of women of varied backgrounds and cultures to the U.S. population. German and Scandinavian women and men immigrated at approximately equal rates, although single people formed the majority. Jewish men and women also came to the United States in similar numbers, but married couples and families among them outnumbered single people. Irish women, especially single ones, outnumbered Irish men after the potato famine of 1846; they particularly did so during the 1880s and the 1890s, the last great decade of Irish immigration.

Of the Irish, most single and some married women joined the U.S. labor force in positions ranging from factory operatives to domestics. Besides laboring, immigrant women often thought, wrote, and worked for labor reform. Irish women were especially active in reform causes. Irish women Religious, including the Sisters of Mercy, the Presentation Sisters, and the so-called gray nuns, established schools and hospitals, as well as providing myriad social services to immigrant and working women.

Beginning in 1880, another Irish immigrant, who was a dressmaker, Mary Harris "Mother" Jones, became in her words "totally engrossed in the labor movement." Jones employed Socialist rhetoric to organize workers in the coal, western mining, and southern cotton industries, and to stir up strikes. Mother Jones participated in all the fiery labor confrontations of the era, developed ideological eccentricities that annoyed everyone from Socialists to industrial managers, and later helped found the Social Democratic Party and the Industrial Workers of the World. Tramping through mining camps, this diminutive, white-haired woman wielded her umbrella like a sword and soon became an American legend.

During the Gilded Age, the background of new immigrants also began to broaden. Although the largest immigration continued to originate in northern and western Europe, the United States now gradually drew peoples from southern and eastern Europe, Asia, and Latin America. Among these groups, Italian, Greek, and Chinese male immigrants vastly outnumbered females, but among Spanish-speaking peoples, women held their own. Because Mexico experienced continued political upheaval during the 1880s and 1890s, especially under the dictatorship of Porfirio Díaz, numerous women migrated to the United States. In 1892, for example, Díaz deported dissident leader Teresa Urrea, who went first to Arizona and later to New York.

Agrarian Dissatisfaction

Finally, agrarian dissatisfaction also affected women during the Gilded Age. Beginning in 1884, five years of agricultural prosperity gave way to a decline in farm prices. When the drought of 1887 further complicated matters, farmers founded such organizations as the Farmers' Union, the Farmers' Mutual Benefit Association, and the National Colored Farmers' Alliance. Out of these came two regional groups, the Southern Alliance and the National Farmers' Alliance of the Northwest; both hoped for regulation of railroads and big business, the abolition of national banks, and cheap currency.

Women were not expected to take activist positions in such organizations, but thousands of rural women decided to contribute to the Southern Alliance and the National Farmers' Alliance in whatever ways they could. They often joined women's auxiliaries, which urged the inclusion of women's programs in the larger groups' agenda. One especially active and vocal woman was Annie La Porte Diggs, columnist for the *Kansas Liberal,* who during the late 1880s supported the Farmers' Alliance. Then, as associate editor of a Topeka newspaper called the *Alliance Associate,* Diggs built a reputation as a proponent of agricultural reform. When the Populist Party formed in Kansas in 1890, Diggs mounted the speakers' platform and used her eloquence on behalf of both the National Farmers' Alliance and the infant Populist Party.

THE PROGRESSIVE ERA, 1890s AND EARLY 1900s

Women and Social Ills

Beginning with such diverse yet pivotal events as the founding of the Populist (People's) Party in 1890 and the Panic of 1893, discontent began to spread over America. In 1894, populist leader Jacob Coxey marched on Washington, D.C., with a group that grew to about five hundred jobless people demanding much-needed relief. They inspired similar "armies" of the jobless to become "living petitions" to the U.S. Congress.

The word "reform" was once again heralded across the land; transformations had to occur, people said, in industry, business, education, government, race relations, the family, and women's roles. In the face of increasing labor violence, multiplying urban slums, spreading disease, and growing poverty, Americans soon exchanged a national fascination with the pursuit of wealth and the creation of gigantic corporations for an incipient concern with consumers' rights and trustbusting.

Young, educated, middle- to upper-class women and men formed the vanguard of the Progressive movement of the 1890s and early 1900s. As a result of the excesses of the Gilded Age, thousands of women stood poised and ready to support various reform causes. Also, out of these women's discontent with the limitations on their private lives came a pent-up energy and a determination to mend, heal, and improve American society. Of course, women had long participated in reform movements, notably abolitionism, temperance, and women's rights, but now middle- and upper-class women backed voluntary reform associations in greater numbers than ever before.

Women's Clubs

Reformers's age, ethnicity, gender, race, region, religion, and social class affected their thinking concerning reform. Thus, as with any other episode in human history, people held very different beliefs regarding which reforms should take priority, when they should be implemented, and how they should be accomplished.

Many middle- and upper-class women chose to work for reform through their long-established, and increasingly politicized, women's clubs. By 1890, the women's club movement had grown to such proportions that individual clubs joined into a national association. Called the General Federation of Women's Clubs (GFWC), it encompassed two hundred clubs and twenty thousand women.

Typically, women's clubs focused on cultural and literary activities, improving social conditions within their own communities, opening new jobs and careers for women, and the achievement of woman suffrage. They also actively supported the conservation of the environment. As Marion Crocker told the GFWC convention in 1912, "if we do not follow the . . . most modern discoveries of how to conserve and propagate and renew wherever possible those resources which Nature in her providence has given Man for his use but not abuse, the time will come when the world will not be able to support life."

In other words, club members devoted their energies to "municipal housekeeping," meaning that women had special talents and moral responsibilities which allowed them to understand and solve civic problems. As one commentator explained in 1912: "Woman has a special function—her power to make, of any place in which she may happen to live, a home for all those who come there. Women must now learn to make of their cities great community homes for all the people."

It can be argued that the philosophy of the women's club movement verged on feminism. It is often called, in fact, "domestic feminism," meaning the enlargement of women's interests and sphere through reform activities. By providing a basis for women's organized voluntarism and legitimizing women's participation in civic affairs, the club movement helped women enter the public arena so long dominated by men. In 1914, these clubs even formally endorsed woman suffrage. Although clubwomen did not yet demand equality, they made it clear that women's proper place was no longer restricted to the home.

The club movement may have been largely middle- and upper-class, but it reached beyond native-born Protestant women. For instance, the National Council of Jewish Women, founded in 1893 by Hannah

Greenbaum Solomon in New York City, offered a wide variety of social services. Jewish women also organized local synagogue sisterhoods and staged demonstrations to deal with local problems, including anti-Semitism. In 1902, Jewish women picketed against sharp rises in the price of kosher meats. Lasting almost a month, the kosher-meat protests confirmed Jewish women's growing militancy.

Jewish women also comprised a strong constituency in the Educational Alliance of New York's Jewish community. Julia Richman, a member of the board between 1893 and 1912, worked to Americanize Jews and to uplift Jewish women through women's activities and feminism. Esther Luria, a Polish Jew and writer for the Yiddish socialist press in New York during the Progressive years, campaigned for woman suffrage and the unionization of women workers.

After 1900, many additional Jewish women's groups organized on behalf of the Zionist movement, which worked to establish a Jewish homeland in Palestine. These women had a dream, perhaps best described by Emma Lazarus, whose poem "The New Colossus" was inscribed in 1903 on the Statue of Liberty's pedestal. Lazarus's poem called for freedom from oppression, while her essays in popular journals championed Jewish nationalism. In 1912, women's support for Jewish nationalism culminated in the founding of Hadassah, the Jewish women's Zionist group dedicated to funding medical and other services in Palestine.

This is not meant to suggest that the club movement encompassed all types of women. Anglo clubwomen had not yet added racial discrimination to their list of potential reforms, nor did they actively recruit black members. Although the General Federation of Women's Clubs eventually admitted black clubs, it admitted them only as segregated local chapters.

A strong but separate club movement did develop among black women, who were largely middle- and upper-class women interested in pursuing educational, philanthropic, and welfare activities. Rather than copying white clubwomen's priorities, however, black women often found it necessary to focus on improving the lives of black Americans. In 1895, under the leadership of Josephine St. Pierre Ruffin, founder and president of Boston's Woman's Era Club, a convention established the National Federation of Afro-American Women. Like its rival association, the Colored Women's League, the new group dedicated itself to initiating social and race-oriented reforms. Then, in 1896 Mary Church Terrell founded the united National Association of Colored Women (NACW), which provided a network for black women's clubs by bringing together thirty-six clubs, including the National Federation of Afro-American Women and the Colored Woman's League.

An urban woman, Sudie Rhone of Cheyenne, Wyoming, remarked that black women had little desire to join white women's clubs. She noted that black women preferred to join the Searchlight Club, founded in 1904 by African American women, even though it was the only service club for black women in Cheyenne. Rhone maintained that widespread prejudice kept the two groups of women essentially segregated.

Although racial reforms tended to receive first priority, black clubs, much like white clubs, often added woman suffrage to their list of worthy causes. Adella Hunt Logan, principal of Tuskegee Institute, argued that black women needed the vote to secure a fair share of public school funds for black schools, while Margaret Washington, dean of women at Tuskegee and wife of Booker T. Washington, reasoned that black women could use suffrage to further social reform. In addition, through their publications and speakers, such groups as the College Alumnae Club vigorously supported women's right to vote.

These and other groups of clubwomen inadvertently cooperated in revising the image of women as helpless and passive creatures. Women's impact on community problems, social structures, and power bases demonstrated that women were effective shakers and movers who provided crucial services to a highly industrialized, urbanized, and complicated nation.

Yet the effect of clubwomen's activities on the customary view of American women proved somewhat limited, for clubwomen usually cast themselves in the traditional role of moral keepers. Like women of the pre–Civil War era, reformers and clubwomen of the 1890s and early 1900s emphasized their womanly virtue. By characterizing themselves as a unique group vested with special attributes, they segregated themselves and continued to cast men as potential objects of reform rather than as colleagues in reform endeavors.

Education

As in earlier eras, education played a key role in Progressive women's reform efforts. An increasing number of middle- and upper-class Anglo women now attended such women's colleges as Barnard, Bryn Mawr, Mount Holyoke, Radcliffe, Smith, Vassar, and Wellesley. Affected by the theory of the day, which claimed that higher education might debilitate women mentally and physically, women's colleges dedicated themselves to educating women without destroying health and femininity in the process. Consequently, women's colleges combined academics, physical and health education, and training in domestic values and skills.

Such programs produced many successful women, including Alice Freeman Palmer, second president of Wellesley and in 1892 the first dean of women at the newly founded University of Chicago. For generations of female college students, Palmer exemplified the educated woman who combined intellect, service, and domesticity. But the question remained unanswered whether to perpetuate domestic ideas and beliefs or to break with them.

Under the presidency of M. Carey Thomas between 1894 and 1922, Bryn Mawr, a Quaker women's college, took the lead in challenging concepts of domesticity. Thomas, the first woman in the world to earn a Ph.D. degree, believed that women had the full capability to achieve serious scholarship, and she disdained those who sacrificed careers for "suffocating" marriages. In 1913, Thomas wrote that women "may have spent half a lifetime in fitting themselves for their chosen work and then may be asked to choose between it and marriage." She added that "no one can estimate the number of women who remain unmarried in revolt before such a horrible alternative." To Thomas, marriages could be happy only if the partners were equally involved in careers and home.

Thomas herself chose not to marry. Instead, she established a long-term romantic relationship with a female partner. Other women made a similar choice. Actress Charlotte Cushman, for example, lived, worked, and traveled with sculptor Emma Stebbins for twenty years. At the time, people sometimes called such relationships "Boston Marriages." Because most of these female couples hedged-in their personal lives with great privacy, it is not known if their liaisons were lesbian in nature.

Ultimately, women's colleges failed to resolve the question of how women could combine career and family, or even if they should attempt to do so. In 1910, approximately 5 percent of college-age Americans, of whom 40 percent were female, attended college. Also in 1910, 67 percent of Bryn Mawr graduates married, as compared with only 45 percent before 1900. These Bryn Mawr women bore a larger number of children than their predecessors, while fewer entered graduate schools and professions. A decade after her 1900 graduation, a Radcliffe graduate described the dilemma of such a college-trained woman: "I hang in a void midway between two spheres. A professional career puts me beyond reach of the average woman's duties and pleasures, but the conventional limitations of the female lot put me beyond reach of the average man's duties and pleasures."

At the same time, many coeducational colleges and universities faced their own problems. After 1900, the percentage of women in their student bodies rose to 50. Fearing the encroaching feminization of higher education, these schools limited female admissions, developed special curricula to attract more male students, and relegated women to normal schools (teacher-training) or home economics departments. Along with many other Americans, administrators at these schools feared the effect of low marriage rates among college-trained women.

At the large research universities that emerged during the 1890s and early 1900s, female students also faced restricted opportunities. Still, after 1900, female enrollments, especially in the social sciences, climbed dramatically at such schools as the University of Chicago and Columbia University. As a result, the number of women faculty members increased and research on gender differences began. At Chicago, psychology graduate student Helen Thompson pioneered intelligence tests of undergraduates, which demonstrated that men and women students differed only slightly in intellect. At Columbia, psychology graduate student Leta Hollingworth confirmed that male and female intellectual capabilities were indeed similar.

During the 1890s and early 1900s, other feminist scholars explored additional areas. Sociologist Mary Roberts Coolidge and physician Cielia Mosher conducted studies of sexuality that refuted myths about women's "natural" inhibitions. Emily Putnam, first dean of Barnard College, analyzed women's roles throughout history, most notably in *The Lady: Studies of Certain Significant Phases of Her History* (1910).

As a result of such developments, colleges and universities increasingly offered athletic opportunities to their women students. Beginning in the 1880s, tennis became the most popular sport for college women. During the 1890s, after Smith College's pioneering sponsorship of basketball for women, basketball challenged tennis for top position. By the mid-1890s, college athletic associations sponsored women's competitions in aquatics, field hockey, rowing, track and field events, and winter sports. Golf achieved widespread popularity because it seemed well-suited to the supposedly delicate, genteel nature of women. Similarly, when educator and temperance reformer Frances Willard started the bicycle craze for women, she explained that she rode attired in a "simple, modest suit" composed of a tweed skirt and jacket, a straw hat, and walking-shoes with gaiters (to keep the skirt down).

Of the era's sports-minded women, Louise Pound provides an outstanding example of a woman who thrived on both scholarship and sports. In 1900, Pound earned a Ph.D. degree at the University of Heidelberg. Pound also gained widespread attention through her prowess in lawn tennis during the 1890s and in golf between 1900 and 1927. She later remarked that she had long played golf without a set of matched clubs: "Most women at that time would use their husbands' clubs cut off. When I got a set of matched clubs . . . I cut six strokes off my game." Pound also became a humanities professor at the University of Nebraska, where she supported women's basketball and organized a female military company replete with 1880 Springfield rifles.

Women were also drawn to the excitement surrounding the coming of the automobile. Between 1905 and 1909, Joan Newton Cueno reigned as an auto racing champion, while Alice Huyler Ramsey captured the distinction of being the first woman to drive across the United States.

During the 1890s and early 1900s, black women's education also experienced drastic alterations. Although relatively few black women received higher education before 1890, after that year a growing number sought advanced training, especially as teachers. By 1900, 13,524 black women taught school as opposed to 7,734 black men. By 1910, 22,547 of the nation's 29,772 black teachers were female.

These women attended such integrated schools as Oberlin in Ohio and such black schools as Wilberforce University, also in Ohio. Black schools often diverged sharply from their white counterparts in curriculum. Anxious to meet the practical needs of the black community rather than provide a rigorous, classical education, black women's schools frequently offered training primarily as homemakers and teachers. By World War I, nearly one hundred black colleges and universities admitted women. Of these, Scotia Academy, Spelman, and Bennett admitted only black women.

An exceptional role model for black woman teachers was Maria Louise Baldwin of Cambridge, Massachusetts. Beginning in 1887, she taught at the interracial Agassiz Grammar School. Two years later, Baldwin received appointment as principal, a post she held for more than thirty years. She also continued her own education by taking classes at Harvard University and Boston University. An inspiring lecturer, Baldwin spoke against racial prejudice and for tolerance and in 1897 became the first woman to give the George Washington Birthday Address at the Brooklyn Institute.

Racial Issues

During the Progressive era, racial reform usually focused on the difficulties facing black Americans. Reformers were just becoming aware of American Indian problems and generally overlooked those of Latinos and Asians. Although Chicanos (especially those with dark skin or those who clung to their own language and culture) also suffered from such evils as lynching, and Asians from such ills as employment discrimination, these groups had yet to command public attention.

In fact, the critical issue of the lynching of black men and women was just gaining exposure during the early 1890s. Beginning in 1892, a Memphis, Tennessee, newspaper editor, Ida Wells-Barnett, organized a national antilynching crusade. Wells-Barnett's exhortations to black women to defend their race from violence led to the founding in 1892 of the Women's Loyal Union in New York.

In addition, black clubwomen attacked a plethora of other race-related problems. The black women's club movement in Indiana during the 1890s and early 1900s provides a case study of the national pattern. Although black women in Indiana were few in number, they created myriad organizations. Two of the earliest were the Sisters of Charity (1874) and the Alpha Home Association (1883), which helped blacks ravaged by age, illness, and poverty.

During the 1890s and early 1900s, increasing black migration to Indiana and the growth of urban social problems stimulated the organization of additional clubs and societies. In 1903, for example, Lillian Thomas Fox founded the Woman's Improvement Club (WIC) in Indianapolis. Committed at first to the self-improvement of its members, the WIC soon turned its attention to eradicating tuberculosis among black Americans. Then, in 1911, Anna C. Moore founded the Thursday Coterie to rescue young black Indiana women from prostitution.

Other African American women's groups had initiated similar reforms across the nation. In 1897, Victoria Earle Matthews founded the White Rose Industrial Association of New York to help migrant women from the South obtain housing, employment, and training. In 1908, Lugenia Burns Hope organized the Atlanta Neighborhood Union to provide playgrounds for black children, as well as health and other services to Atlanta blacks. And in 1910, the College Alumnae Club of Washington, D.C., formed to establish reading clubs for children, encourage black girls to attend college, and establish a scholarship program.

Urban Problems

By the 1890s, urbanization and massive immigration had created cities rife with tenements, crime, disease, and despair. By 1900, six American cities numbered over a half-million people; three of them contained over one million people. In all six, officials demonstrated a notorious inability to halt and to solve proliferating social problems.

Women reformers responded by attacking numerous issues. For one, they assailed prostitution in a "Social Purity" crusade. Branding prostitution a "Social Evil" that constituted a moral problem and a national menace, reformers urged government control. But making prostitution a criminal offense only created new problems. Even with the 1910 passage of the White-Slave Traffic Act (Mann Act) which forbid transporting a woman across state lines for immoral purposes, prostitution continued to thrive. The streetwalker replaced the brothel, while pimps and crime syndicates took over the organizing and marketing of prostitutes.

Other women reformers, notably Jane Addams, believed that something more fundamental was needed. Born in Illinois in 1860, Addams graduated from Rockford College; in 1883 she left medical school due to poor health. While recuperating in Europe, Addams observed a number of social experiments, especially in England. Enthused about settlement houses, Addams returned to Chicago where in 1889 she and her friend, Ellen Gates Starr, established Hull House. In her 1910 autobiography, *Twenty Years at Hull-House*, Addams explained that she and Starr intended "to provide a center for a higher civic and social life; to institute and maintain educational and philanthropic enterprises, and to investigate and improve the conditions in the industrial districts of Chicago."

The founders of Hull House, and of the approximately fifty other settlement houses that patterned themselves on its model, had been heavily influenced by the social sciences while in college and now sought an outlet for their ideas, energies, and even their sense of social guilt. In flocking to the settlement house movement they wrought a revolution in social service. Reformers now lived among the people whom they served, thus experiencing and understanding their problems. As a result, they offered to their clients a panoply of programs, including vocational training, childcare and kindergartens, youth clubs, immigration reform, and health education and care. They also attacked slum conditions by campaigning for better garbage collection, public health programs, and the establishment of branch libraries and museums. And they fought poverty by crusading for such labor reforms as the eight-hour day, the minimum wage, and unionization, as well as advocating welfare programs, unemployment compensation, and an early form of social security.

Settlement houses also served as training schools for women activists, giving them experience in local politics and ways to attain power. Florence Kelley, a strong opponent of child labor and the leader of the National Consumers League for thirty-two years after its founding in 1899, had begun her social-reform career in 1891 at Hull House. Edith and Grace Abbott also began at Hull House. Edith produced a number of classic books on social welfare and, beginning in 1924, served as dean of the School of Social Service Administration at the University of Chicago, while from 1921 to 1934 Grace headed the U.S. Children's Bureau.

Similarly, the Henry Street Settlement House on New York's East Side spawned many female reformers. Lillian Wald, a settlement worker on Henry Street during the 1890s and one of the first public health nurses, became a leader of the child-welfare movement. In 1904, Wald joined Florence Kelley and others in founding the National Child Labor Committee. In 1912, Wald and Kelley convinced the Department of Commerce and Labor to establish the Children's Bureau in the Department of Commerce and Labor. Julia C. Lathrop, who worked for the Illinois Board of Charities helping the state's 102 almshouses and insane asylums, was appointed by President William Howard Taft as the Bureau's first head.

In addition to training women reformers, settlement houses gradually extended support to woman suffrage. Because they lacked the right to vote and thus had little political influence, settlement workers soon recognized the importance of suffrage. Thwarted in their efforts to ease what Addams described as "unsanitary housing, poisonous sewage, contaminated water, infant mortality, adulterated food, smoke-laden air, juvenile crime, and unwholesome crowding," these women added the suffrage message to their speeches, articles, and petitions. How could women, they argued, fully exercise their moral obligations to American society without political participation and power?

Temperance

A similar pattern developed among women determined to abolish alcohol consumption. Seeing alcoholism as a causal factor in the disruption of American family life and a detriment to the advancement of the working classes, women thronged to the temperance movement. During the 1890s, the Women's Christian Temperance Union (WCTU) became the largest women's organization yet. By the turn of the century, it counted over 176,000 members, with chapters in every state and county.

Because the WCTU owned newspapers, office buildings, temperance hotels, and other related businesses, it provided a practical training ground for female leaders, business executives, speakers, and writers. The WCTU also taught generations of women to value the benefit of their moral sensibilities to an increasingly troubled society.

Under the aggressive leadership of Frances Willard, the WCTU also added woman suffrage to its multifaceted program. As president of the WCTU between 1879 and 1898, Willard maintained that women's political influence was crucial to the achievement of temperance goals. Willard's slogan— "Do Everything"—included not only the support of alcohol-free restaurants, boys' clubs for orphans, industrial schools for girls, homes for alcoholic women, and paid temperance organizers, but the support of woman suffrage speakers, the production and dispersion of suffrage literature, and the gathering of names on suffrage petitions.

Willard also recognized that women's leverage depended on their unity. Unlike other reformers who overlooked women of color, immigrant women, and regional women, Willard urged the WCTU to reach across racial, ethnic, social class, and regional lines. Thus, she not only attracted women of many backgrounds and persuasions to temperance but to woman suffrage as well.

After Willard's death in 1898, however, the WCTU moved away from its strong suffrage stance. Because liquor interests already feared that women, if given suffrage, would vote for national prohibition, the WCTU hoped to disassociate temperance and suffrage in people's minds. The WCTU also worried that people might construe its advocacy of woman suffrage as feminism, a "radical" cause at the turn of the century. Still, many temperance proponents continued to advocate woman suffrage.

Woman Suffrage

In 1890 the suffrage movement had entered a renewal phase when the National Woman Suffrage Association and the American Woman Suffrage Association united into the National American Woman Suffrage Association (NAWSA). Elizabeth Cady Stanton served as the organization's first president, but many suffragists feared that Stanton's extreme views—for example, favoring divorce—would turn public sentiment against their organization. In addition, with suffragist Matilda Joslyn Gage, Stanton was hard at work on the controversial *Woman's Bible*, which demonstrated religion's role in the oppression of women. Thus, in 1892 the NAWSA elected Susan B. Anthony to replace Stanton.

During the 1890s and early 1900s, NAWSA sought support state-by-state, arguing that women voters would "clean up" politics. In 1910, Washington State approved woman suffrage. But antisuffragists disagreed with NAWSA's argument; they believed political involvement would taint women. In 1911, an antisuffrage group called the National Association Opposed to the Further Extension of Suffrage to Women organized; it soon claimed a membership larger than that of NAWSA.

Between 1904 and 1915, newly elected NAWSA president Anna Howard Shaw dealt with such opposition by staying in the middle of the road, trying to offend no one. Rejecting militancy, NAWSA relied instead on the education of women and state suffrage campaigns to advance its cause. It also increasingly replaced the argument that women had a *right* to vote with the declaration that women *needed* the vote to become effective reformers and caretakers.

To further avoid provoking public enmity, NAWSA also supported white supremacy and generally abstained from recruiting black women as members. One exception, however, was light-skinned Adelia Hunt Logan of Alabama. A member of both the National Association of Colored Women and the NAWSA, Logan wrote in 1905 one of the most comprehensive arguments in support of woman suffrage. Logan insisted that "government of the people for the people and by the people is but partially realized so long as woman has no vote."

More typically, black women formed separate suffrage associations. The Tuskegee Woman's Club of Alabama and the Colored Woman's Suffrage Club of Los Angeles were two examples of black women's suffrage groups during the 1890s and early 1900s. Unlike their white counterparts, black women suffragists developed broader programs and tended to see woman suffrage as both a gender and a racial issue. They argued that they needed the vote for themselves as female citizens *and* to enhance their effort to uplift and liberate black Americans. In the view of black reformer and suffragist Anna J. Cooper, black women activists had no choice but to fight for women's rights and black rights at the same time.

Family

Wives and mothers during this time were urged to foster harmonious human relations within the family, especially by providing a moral example, solace and support, and instruction. Among the middle and upper classes, women also had to devote increasing time and energy to home care and supervising servants, for Victorian homes now had different rooms for every function, such as sewing and music, as well as separate bedrooms for each member of the family. In 1900, an essayist in *Harper's Bazaar* extolled the virtues of home life for women: "We American women all take our 'public works' too seriously, toil and strive too unremittingly, give too little heed to the trivial round of home life, which we expect to maintain itself unaided."

Despite such nostrums, women continued to assert their independence and individuality. During the 1890s and early 1900s, approximately

10 percent of women chose not to marry. And, even though in 1900 the federal Comstock Law and similar state laws continued to restrict the dissemination of birth-control information and devices, while strong anti-abortion laws denied women the right to have a foetus surgically removed, in that year the birth rate stood at 3.5 children per mother, a drop from 7 or 8 children per mother a hundred years earlier.

Also in 1900, the divorce rate rose to one out of twelve marriages; a decade later it stood at almost one out of nine. Women still obtained nearly two-thirds of divorces and men one-third. That women stood in the forefront of the growth of divorce suggests, among other things, that their expectations of marriage had risen; that they believed they too had a right to liberty, happiness, and personal satisfaction; and that they were willing and able to find means of economic support other than spouses.

Women also displayed a growing concern for children's rights. They supported such groups as the Massachusetts Society for the Prevention of Cruelty to Children and the Society for the Prevention of Child Cruelty, which attempted to defend battered children. Too, they joined the National Parent-Teacher Association, founded in 1897, which served as a child-advocate in the nation's schools.

The "New Woman"

It appeared that American women had reached a new pinnacle. In 1893, the World's Columbian Exposition not only featured women's art and other work, but included three buildings designed by and for women. Outside the Exposition gates, Buffalo Bill Cody's Wild West drew thousands to its tents, where they watched women shoot, rope, and ride broncs. Of these, Annie Oakley claimed center stage; by becoming a better shooter than most men, Oakley won the hearts of millions and helped open Wild-West and rodeo arenas to women performers.

Generally, "new women," as Americans called women who acted differently than their mothers, were Anglo, college-educated, single, and self-supporting. They, and sometimes married women as well, cycled, skated, played golf and lawn tennis, and, following Oakley's model, took up hunting and match shooting. Others loosened their corsets or, like Alice Roosevelt, smoked in public. When President Theodore Roosevelt was criticized for his daughter's behavior, he responded that he could do only one of two things—be President or control Alice.

Charles Dana Gibson's portrayals of modern women further characterized this "new" American woman. Created by Gibson for *Life* magazine during the 1890s, the "Gibson Girl" was a healthy, sensual, and rebellious young woman. Dressed in a simple shirtwaist and skirt, or in a one-piece bathing suit, the provocative Gibson Girl appeared on magazine covers, in advertisements, and in prints hung on the walls of homes and public places.

But "new women" developed even more daring ventures. In 1911, Harriet Quimby became the first licensed female pilot in America, and, in the following year, was the first woman pilot to fly across the English Channel. Also in 1912, Katherine Stinson began setting aviation records, including being the first woman to loop a plane, fly nonstop across the United States, and fly in Asia.

New women also dared to extend their social behavior. Working girls strutted around Coney Island amusement park, picnic grounds, beaches and lakes, and the dance halls that dotted every major city. Here, they met men who bought them drinks, then chatted and danced with them. In 1912, the dance craze promoted such risqué frolics as the bunny hug, the turkey trot, and the tango. Two years later, the Massachusetts Vice Commission reported that a significant number of young women willingly let themselves be picked up by men and had sexual relations with them. What, Americans wondered, would become of these new women?

Employed Women During the Progressive Era

Continuing Problems

During the 1890s, women entered the work force in growing numbers, yet experienced little improvement in hours and working conditions. In 1893, Helen Campbell described in *Women Wage-Earners* the horrible conditions the Massachusetts Bureau of Labor had discovered: "employees packed 'like sardines in a box'; thirty-five persons, for example, in a small attic without ventilation of any kind." Campbell added that "there are no conveniences for women; and men and women use the same closets [bathrooms], wash-basins, and drinking cups. . . . In another case, a water-closet in the center of the room filled it with a sickening stench."

Campbell's report also detailed health hazards to women workers. Lung and bronchial diseases assaulted women who labored with such dust-laden materials as feathers, fur, and cotton. Caustic soda ate at soap workers' hands, which became raw and bleeding by the end of the day, while phosphorus destroyed match workers' jaws. Button and pin workers regularly suffered jammed and caught fingers which, after the first three injuries, they had to treat at their own expense.

Still, by 1900 five million women, or one out of every five, held paid employment outside their homes. Four times as many women as in 1870 now worked in industry, largely in manufacturing textiles, shoes, hats, gloves, stockings, and collars, but also in such "heavy" industries as tobacco production, canning, bookbinding, meat packing, and laundries. Three out of four women working in industry were under twenty-five, while nearly 75 percent were single, Anglo women living in urban areas.

Yet other women worked in sales, especially in the large department stores that increasingly characterized urban consumerism. In 1899, an investigator for the Chicago Consumers' League posed as a department store clerk and subsequently disclosed that shopgirls received $2.00 to $3.00 a week, supplemented by a sales commission of 5 percent. Shopgirls' total wages averaged $3.00 to $5.00 per week, or about $.06 to $.10 per hour. In addition, managers expected female clerks to stand constantly without rest breaks, to take only a thirty-minute lunch period, and to always protect the store's goods from shoplifters. The investigator added that many clerks limped by afternoon and made sales "under positive physical agony."

Other employed women worked as office clerks. Although in 1870 men had accounted for 97.5 percent of clerical laborers, by 1890 women constituted 17 percent of the clerical work force. The new typewriter, which posed no threat to men's customary occupations, eased women's entry into clerical labor. In fact, typing soon became known as "woman's work"; by 1910 women comprised 80.6 percent of all stenographers and typists. Another factor that facilitated women's dominance of clerical work was the widespread belief that women's "feminine" qualities, including manual dexterity, attention to minor details, and talents as caretakers, especially suited women to office work. Thus, by World War I, women comprised 50 percent of clerical workers.

Still other working women toiled at such domestic employment as housekeeper, maid, nursemaid, and dressmaker. Largely immigrants and women of color, domestic servants tended to leave their jobs as soon as other employment appeared. In 1910, servants accounted for 31 percent of employed women. The following year, a government study discovered that people preferred even such exhausting labor as commercial laundry work over domestic service. An African American woman and an Irish woman both cited more time to themselves and better pay as advantages of their laundry jobs. They could also avoid sexual harassment; in 1911 an African American cook explained that she lost her job when she refused to let her employer's husband hug and kiss her.

Insurgency and Protest

During the 1890s and early 1900s, journalists known as muckrakers exposed the harsh conditions that working women and children endured. Marie Van Vorst, for example, campaigned against child labor. In her book, *The Woman Who Toils* (1903), Van Vorst exposed the dangerous working conditions in southern mines. Investigatory bodies discovered that women tolerated dangerous working conditions because they had to support themselves and help their families. For similar reasons, garment workers tolerated sweatshops, as garment factories were known, as well as tyrannical bosses called sweaters.

Gradually, reformers began to ask penetrating questions. Did the economic system lie at the base of America's industrial troubles? Would economic reforms solve most of women's problems? Writer and speaker Charlotte Perkins Gilman thought so. In her most important work, *Women and Economics*, published in 1898, and in articles and speeches presented well into the 1900s, Gilman called for a "reordering of woman's sphere."

Gilman maintained that women's total economic dependence on men destroyed the female personality. She argued that economically independent women made happier and more effective wives, mothers, and individuals, but that they must have efficient and professional services, including communal kitchens and daycare centers. Gilman wrote that "this is the true line of advance, making a legitimate human business of housework; having it done by experts instead of by amateurs; making it a particular social industry instead of a general feminine function." To further explore feminist and social-justice issues, in 1909 Gilman created a journal called *The Forerunner*. Although many Americans read Gilman's work or listened to her speeches, her ideas were generally regarded as extremely radical and were thus seldom adopted.

Meanwhile, socialist women leaders demanded their own brand of change. During the socialist women's movement, which peaked between 1870 and the First World War, Tejana Lucy González Parsons wrote for such journals as the *Socialist* and the *Labor Defender*, and crusaded for a suffrage plank in the socialist labor platform. In her well-known article, "Cause of Sex Slavery," Parsons maintained that women's exploitation derived from capitalism. Parsons argued, much like Gilman, that "it is woman's economical dependence which makes her enslavement to man possible."

Other socialist women expanded upon these arguments. Russian-born Emma Goldman crisscrossed the country lecturing on anarchism and women's rights. Goldman also edited the radical monthly, *Mother Earth,* from 1906 to 1917. Between 1900 and 1920, Kate Richards O'Hare, an avowed feminist, supported such issues as woman suffrage and maternity benefits for working women. Widely known as a lecturer and writer, O'Hare carried socialist and feminist messages across the nation and especially to the Great Plains states.

Helping Oneself

Meanwhile, the thousands of women pouring into the labor force, especially immigrant women, needed assistance and reform. Now originating in southern and eastern Europe, including Italy, Lithuania, Poland, Russia, and Yugoslavia, and even Syria, as well as in Mexico and other Spanish-speaking countries, immigrant women initially lacked knowledge of American language and culture. Also, because their families expected them to help out financially, these women took jobs, thus becoming targets of exploitation by employers and others eager to benefit from their ignorance.

Often victimized by unusually low wages, long hours, piecework in the home, seduction into prostitution, unwanted pregnancies, grinding poverty, and lack of welfare services, immigrant women turned to such organizations as the Immigrant Protective League of Chicago, directed by reformers Sophonisba Breckinridge and Grace Abbott. This and other similar groups offered help with employment, housing, and health care. They also attempted to protect immigrant women from falling, or being lured, into prostitution, sometimes the only thing that would allow them and their families to survive such things as homelessness, malnutrition of their children, and even starvation.

Employed women themselves worked on their own behalves by collaborating with women reformers through the auspices of the National Women's Trade Union League. Under the leadership of such women as Margaret Drier Robins, president of the National Women's Trade Union League beginning in 1907, the NWTUL founded successful programs to help immigrant women, provide health care for working women, and bring working women together to discuss their grievances. The League also attempted to organize women into unions and to gain membership and active roles for them in already existing unions of the AFL. The NWTUL supported strikes and pickets, lobbied the federal government to conduct investigations and pass labor legislation, and worked diligently for woman suffrage. Through its journal, *Life and Labor*, published between 1911 and 1921, the NWTUL also informed the public about the situation of employed women.

The NWTUL failed to resolve internal divisions between laboring women and nonlaboring women, as well as between unionism and feminism, yet its contributions proved significant. In addition to its programs, the League trained rank-and-file labor women who later promoted labor organization and reform for working women. For instance, Rose Schneiderman, who joined the NWTUL in 1905, later served as a paid union organizer and NWTUL president. Because Schneiderman believed that woman suffrage would lead to labor legislation, she also led the industrial unit of the New York Woman Suffrage Party.

Immigrant women workers did not sit and wait, however, for changes to filter down from middle- and upper-class reformers nor for society to embrace Gilman's, the NWTUL's, and others' ideas. Rather, they themselves campaigned and organized; immigrant women turned to other immigrant women for help, which in turn led to the formation of ethnic women's organizations. The largest of these was the Polish Women's Alliance, founded in 1898, and dedicated to the education of Polish women. Finnish domestics established another group in 1910, which used pooled funds to rent a communal apartment. This venture turned into a self-help cooperative known as the Finnish Women's Cooperative Home, a venture that counted 400 shareholders and housed more than forty women.

Between 1910 and 1915 alone, more than a half-million non-English-speaking females under the age of thirty entered the United States and gradually Americanized themselves. Young employed women provided a bridge between their traditional mothers and the larger world into which they daily ventured. In addition, women who could not understand English could grasp and enjoy the new silent picture films increasingly available in urban areas. These films, which largely attracted immigrant and working-class audiences, acculturated old and new generations of women, especially in American clothing styles, behavior, and values.

Strikes and Violence

Other working women believed that the solution to labor problems lay in unions. Around the turn of the twentieth century, Cuban women workers in the cigar-making industry in Tampa, Florida, organized especially in the Cuban union "La Resistencia." In addition, Lucy González Parsons helped found the Industrial Workers of the World (IWW) well before it held its first congress in 1905, and supported the International Labor Defense (ILD), which assisted laborers and dissidents. Elizabeth Gurley Flynn served as a fiery orator for the "Wobblies," nickname for the IWW, after 1905, while Harriet Stanton Blatch, daughter of Elizabeth Cady Stanton, in 1907 helped organize what became the Equality League of Self-Supporting Women. Two years later, Pauline Newman, a veteran shirtwaist striker, became the first female organizer of the International Ladies' Garment Workers' Union.

Besides organizing unions, speaking, writing, and lobbying, such women also utilized pickets and strikes. One of these was the 1898 strike of glove workers against assembly-line techniques. Also, in 1905 some eight thousand laundry workers in Troy, New York, protested new regulations and machines. And in 1909, twenty thousand shirtwaist workers surged out of factories in New York and Philadelphia to launch the largest women's strike in U.S. history.

Still, none of these efforts at labor reform averted the tragic 1911 fire at the Triangle Shirtwaist Factory, which occupied two floors high up in a New York City building. As flames ripped through the lofts and set piles of material afire, female workers rushed to the doors only to find them locked to prevent workers from walking out with goods. Fire escapes and sprinkler systems were nonexistent, even though leaders of the 1909 shirtwaist workers' strike had demanded them. As a result, 146 women perished either in the fire or by jumping or falling out of windows ten stories up. Labor leader Rose Schneiderman later proclaimed to a mass meeting that "this is not the first time that girls have been burned alive in the city. . . . Every year thousands of us are maimed."

Despite a public outcry and a mammoth strike of textile workers in 1912 in Lawrence, Massachusetts, employers continued to thwart protests and strikes by using the courts, public opinion, police, blacklists, fines, and dismissal. Women found it difficult to unionize extensively enough to combat such techniques. More specifically, long hours and heavy home responsibilities kept women from union meetings, while low wages were inadequate to pay union dues and the hostility of male union members intimidated potential women members. Consequently, in 1913 only 6 percent of women workers belonged to unions as compared to 3 percent in 1900.

Protective Legislation

Gradually, a number of reformers came to the conclusion that rather than unions and strikes, protective labor laws would provide a partial answer to women's labor-related problems. They especially hoped for state legislation guaranteeing safe working conditions, reducing health hazards, establishing a minimum wage, shortening hours, and compensating workers for on-the-job accidents. In the 1908 case *Muller v. Oregon,* the U.S. Supreme Court confirmed that women's child-bearing abilities and physical weakness deserved protective labor laws.

By 1912, the NWTUL shifted its priorities from organization to legislation, and in that year Massachusetts passed the first minimum-wage law to protect women and children. Predictably, labor unions demonstrated little enthusiasm for protective legislation, for they continued to believe that organization and strikes were the only way to protect workers, male and female. A few women's groups also resisted "women-only" legislation, fearing that, as one leader stated, "welfare legislation will protect women to the vanishing point." These groups recognized that protective legislation not only identified women workers as a distinct group, but also emphasized their physical weakness and child-bearing abilities. They preferred that women continue to stand and fight on equal grounds with male workers.

Opening the Professions to Women

Women not only showed their mettle in the labor movement, but pried open cracks in the professions as well, especially midwifery, nursing, teaching, and library and social work. In 1890, women comprised approximately 35 percent of professional people but only 15 percent of the employed. During the 1890s and early 1900s, women continued to constitute a higher proportion of the professions than of the general work force.

Generally, women found it easier to enter certain professions deemed more suitable to their gender. People tended to accept women in professions that appeared related to domesticity; they also responded more to women who offered services that expanded on domestic duties, such as health care and teaching. Women, the perennial caregivers, could also successfully combine families and medical careers. As a case in point, female midwives prevailed among immigrants, in rural areas, and in the South. In 1910, midwives, who earned credentials in European or American schools or by apprenticeship, attended approximately 50 percent of all births.

In addition, by 1900 nursing was a well-established profession and a wide array of training programs were available to women, including those of color. After Mary E. Mahoney, the first black trained nurse, graduated from the New England Hospital for Women and Children in 1879, hundreds of other black women followed her lead. When denied jobs in white hospitals, the Army Nurse Corps, and the Red Cross, newly trained black female nurses adapted by taking jobs within the black community and working as private nurses. And, when the American Nurses' Association denied them membership, in 1908 they formed the National Association of Colored Graduate Nurses to improve their situation.

Also in 1900, nearly 9,000 women held physicians' licenses. A decade later, women comprised 6 percent of medical practitioners. Among these were a significant number of black women. In 1890, 155 black female physicians lived and worked in the United States; this number grew to 160 by 1900. Matilda A. Evans, for example, graduated in 1897 from the Woman's Medical College of Pennsylvania. Evans established a practice in Columbia, South Carolina, where she also founded a hospital for black Americans and a black nurses' training school. In 1901, however, Dr. Eliza Anna Grier, a physician in Greenville, South Carolina, drew attention to the odds against which such women worked. Grier lamented that "there are a great many forces operating against the success of the Negro. These, however, I hope someday will be overcome."

After 1900, more women also decided to enter scientific fields. Between 1900 and 1910, twenty-three women described themselves as being involved in a new scientific field that offered women untold opportunities—home economics. The career of Ellen Swallow Richards illustrates the effective fusing of domesticity and a home economics career. A holder of a chemistry degree from Massachusetts Institute of Technology, Richards became a professor of "sanitary chemistry" and a leader in the new field of home economics. Richards also promoted conservation and ecology, arguing in 1910 that "to secure and maintain a safe environment there must be inculcated *habits* of using the material things in daily life in such a way as to promote and not to diminish health." She solved the confusion between domesticity and career by merging the two, much to the acclaim of her male colleagues. Richards claimed that her hesitancy to "scorn womanly duties" and to regard it "a privilege to clean up" won her strong allies.

Given the obstacles confronting women scientists during the early twentieth century, it is remarkable that so many not only persevered but produced significant work. Among these, anatomist Florence Sabin, a researcher and professor at Johns Hopkins, became the first woman member of the National Academy of Sciences. Geologist Florence Bascom, a researcher and professor at Bryn Mawr College, was the first woman member of the Geological Society of America. In 1896, Bascom also joined the U.S. Geological Survey as its first woman member. Subsequently, Bascom spent her summers combing mountains on horseback or in a buggy, and her winters teaching and writing scientific reports.

Other science-minded women, including those of color, worked outside the academy. By 1900, the U.S. Patent Office patented 370 inventions by black women and men. In 1905, Sarah Breedlove (Madam C. J.) Walker invented a chemical method for hair-grooming; she patented the Walker method as well as other products. Soon a millionaire and philanthropist, Walker refuted the accusation that she had designed a product to "straighten" black women's hair. Rather, Walker explained to an Indianapolis reporter, she intended to help "the great masses of my people to take a greater pride in their personal appearance and to give their hair proper attention."

Because Americans continued to associate art and literature with women's supposed cultural sensibilities, a growing number of women entered these fields as well. Around the turn of the twentieth century, Lilla Cabot Perry proved herself as a portrait painter and an adept Impressionist. Cecilia Beaux, a leading portraitist in New York during the early 1900s, gained acclaim for her portraits of famous women. And Mary Cassatt, the most distinguished woman artist of the age, achieved wide renown for her impressionist paintings and her printmaking.

By 1910, women accounted for 45.2 percent of artists and art teachers. The acclaimed career of modern artist Sonia Delaunay, who adapted the abstract style of Orphism, began with a patchwork blanket made for her son in 1912. The following year, the Armory Show in New York included a piece of crazy quilt, introducing viewers to what show organizers termed "modern art."

Women also drew cartoons, comic strips, and illustrated journals and novels. After attending the Philadelphia School of Design for Women and becoming self-supporting at age fifteen, Alice Barber Stephens achieved popularity as an illustrator. Stephens's work appeared in such magazines as the *Ladies Home Journal* and in books published by Houghton Mifflin and Thomas Y. Crowell. The work of Frances Johnston, probably the most renowned woman photographer of the era, also appeared in such magazines as *Ladies Home Journal* and *Frank Leslie's*. In addition, Johnson actively worked to open photography to women; by 1900 over thirty-five hundred women held employment as professional photographers.

In the field of literature, women also exhibited energy and creativity. In 1892, for example, Frances Ellen Watkins Harper published *Iola Leroy,*

Shadows Uplifted, generally recognized as the first novel by a black woman. Yet other women contributed to an emerging writing style known as regionalism. Marietta Holley of upstate New York used local color and satirical humor to support reform causes, especially feminism. Holley's primary character, Samantha Smith Allen, was an eloquent feminist who romped her way "episodin' and allegorin'" through twenty novels and a number of short stories. Not so well-known at the time but better-known today, was Kate Chopin, who combined feminist ideas with Creole local color in *The Awakening* (1899) and other novels.

Maine author Sarah Orne Jewett also wrote about rural people living in her own area. A strong disciple of regionalism, Jewett attracted notice for works concentrating on Maine's rich history, including *The Country of the Pointed Firs* (1896) and *The Tory Lover* (1901). Willa Cather, another regionalist, presented farm and prairie life devoid of the usual romantic gloss. She is best remembered for her stories of Nebraska life, *O Pioneers* (1913) and *My Antonia* (1918). Similarly, Mary Hallock Foote wrote of western mining camps and towns, both in serials published in *Scribner's Monthly* and in books. Among Foote's best-known novels were *The Chosen Valley* (1892) and *Edith Bonham* (1917).

In addition, a number of women succeeded in the field of journalism. Ida M. Tarbell established herself as a muckraker with her harsh exposé, *The History of The Standard Oil Company* (1904). Elizabeth Seaman worked until 1895 as a famous New York *World* reporter known as Nellie Bly. And Sophie Loeb publicized the cause of mothers' pensions through her feature articles in the New York *Evening World*.

As the theater generated growing enthusiasm in the United States, women also achieved prominence on the stage. Because women composed the majority of theater audiences and large numbers of them attended matinee performances unescorted, many actresses played to their female audiences by addressing women's issues. On and off the stage, Mary Shaw supported women's clubs, suffrage, and feminism. The embodiment of the "American Beauty," Lillian Russell, lent her glamour to women's physical exercise programs and to woman suffrage. The "American Girl," Ethel Barrymore, used her status as a cult figure to advocate assistance for working women and emancipation for women. In the play, *The Twelve Pound Look*, Barrymore zealously portrayed a woman who chose economic independence over marriage.

Clearly, women had capitalized on the changing economic situation and changes in attitudes toward women to expand their professional opportunities. Still, difficulties remained. For whatever profession they chose, women usually received lower wages than men employed in the same areas. The discrepancy in teachers' pay illustrates this point. In 1890, men teachers averaged $33.00 a week and women $13.00. In 1900, men earned $34.00 and women $14.00. And in 1910, men received $36.00

and women $17.00. In the area of medicine, despite women's gains as physicians, they failed to dominate any one specialty, including gynecology and pediatrics. And, even though *American Men [sic] of Science* listed 149 women in 1906 and 204 women in 1910, such women often held inferior positions and were denied membership in professional scientific societies.

Also, despite women's efforts, a number of areas stayed essentially closed to them. The ministry, for example, remained a male-dominated field. One of the few women to succeed in it was Mary Baker Eddy, who founded the Christian Science Church during the 1870s. Eddy achieved overwhelming success because she capitalized on what were considered womanly attributes—her spirituality and intuition—to build a religious sect. When she died in 1910, Eddy left a huge, permanent, and wealthy religious institution behind her. Not quite so effective was Sarah Jane Farmer, who in 1901 tried to establish the Baha'i faith in the United States. Although Farmer suffered a nervous breakdown in 1910, Baha'i's count her among the critical early leaders of their movement.

Law also continued to dampen women's resolve. Although a small number of women graduated from law schools around the turn of the century, they found themselves excluded from courtroom practice. Some, like Sophonisba Breckinridge, admitted to the bar in Kentucky during the 1880s, left the law for academic life. By 1910, there were only fifteen hundred women attorneys in the United States, most of whom were forced to find work with governmental agencies, legal journals, and women's organizations.

Despite women's desire for advancement and willingness to work hard, it was obvious that the American economic and social system could only stretch so far at one time. Consequently, professional women also gradually came around to the support of woman suffrage, in hopes that political power would bring about further changes.

THE NEW SOUTH DURING THE PROGRESSIVE ERA

Reform also bubbled and fermented in the increasingly industrialized South. Despite the emergence of renewed racial prejudice, the development of the "Mammy" image, and the restrictions imposed by Jim Crowism, southern black women, especially of the middle and upper classes, asserted themselves in a variety of ways. The emergence of black women's clubs during the late 1890s and early 1900s was especially vigorous in southern communities. In such cities as Savannah and New Orleans, where welfare institutions excluded African Americans, black women's clubs established kindergartens, daycare centers, orphanages, schools, healthcare programs, and myriad other social services.

Gradually, local clubs throughout the South multiplied and joined together in statewide federations. In Mississippi in 1901, for example, native Mississippian Margaret Murray Washington urged women to elevate themselves through women's clubs. In 1903, local clubs created the Mississippi State Federation of Colored Women's Clubs to coordinate the efforts of clubwomen throughout the state. Largely college-educated and upwardly mobile, these women provided homes for black working women, established libraries, funded scholarships, operated camps and recreation centers for young people, and assisted the hearing- and sight-impaired, the physically and mentally challenged, and the tubercular.

Among these southern black "new women" were a number of exceptional reformers and leaders. Janie Porter Barret of Virginia taught at Hampton Institute and in 1890 founded the South's first settlement house for blacks. Mary McLeod Bethune, a daughter of former slaves, attended Scotia Seminary in North Carolina and the Moody Bible Institute in Chicago, Illinois. After teaching in various southern schools during the 1890s, Bethune decided to establish in Florida a school for girls similar to Scotia in North Carolina. With only $1.50 in cash, Bethune collected wooden boxes to serve as benches, begged for other necessities, and sold ice cream and sweet-potato pies to construction workers. When she opened her school of six students in 1904, Bethune lacked the $5.00 she had promised as payment for her schoolhouse, but she said that she retained "faith in a living God, faith in myself, and a desire to serve." Bethune's little school soon grew into the widely respected Daytona Normal and Industrial Institute, which later became Bethune-Cookman College.

Similarly, although ideas of chivalry and woman's place hung on well after the Civil War, a number of middle- and upper-class white southern women began to create a southern "woman movement." In growing numbers, these women joined all manner of clubs, including missionary societies of various churches, chapters of the WCTU, school reform associations, and eventually woman suffrage organizations. In the 1890s, women also joined such patriotic societies as Colonial Dames, Daughters of the American Revolution, and United Daughters of the Confederacy.

Umbrella associations soon appeared to draw individual groups together and coordinate their efforts. For instance, in 1888 southern Baptist women consolidated individual missionary groups into the Woman's Missionary Society. In North Carolina in 1901 the North Carolina Federation of Women's Clubs organized under the leadership of Sallie Sims Southall Cotten, and in 1902 the Woman's Association for the Betterment of Public School Houses formed.

One especially articulate Southern "new woman" was Belle Kearney, a WCTU organizer and later the first woman senator in the Mississippi legislature. Other examples were Jean Gordon of Louisiana, who battled for a child-labor law during the early 1900s, and Mary Partridge, who in 1910 began organizing woman suffrage societies in Alabama. By 1910, Anglo women throughout the South asked for their rights and willingly contributed their energies to reform activities.

Southern white women also continued to enter agriculture and take jobs in offices, stores, and factories. As early as 1890, slightly more than two out of five textile workers in the South were female. Southern women also invaded many of the professions that had so long barred them. In North Carolina, Cornelia Ann Phillips Spencer became a noted journalist and educational crusader who in 1891 helped found the Normal and Industrial School for Women (now the University of North Carolina at Greensboro).

THE NEW WEST DURING THE PROGRESSIVE ERA

In the West, a majority of women continued to engage in domestic production and agriculture. Others, such as Elinore Pruitt Stewart, who wrote *Letters of a Woman Homesteader* (1913–1914) and other books, took up government homestead lands on their own. In addition, a growing number of women, especially Anglos living in western cities, took jobs in manufacturing, office work, and sales. Many also took advantage of the relative scarcity of women and worked as prostitutes. By 1890, 13 percent of western women worked outside of their homes, as compared to 17 percent nationally.

Western women were highly represented in the professions, however, with 14 percent employed in professional areas as opposed to 8 percent nationally. Ella L. Knowles, for example, passed the Montana bar examination in 1889 with distinction, thus becoming the state's first female attorney. Knowles practiced law in Helena, played an active role in the People's (Populist) Party, and after 1890 campaigned for woman suffrage.

Western women also committed themselves to agrarian reform. Mary Elizabeth Lease, a controversial speaker for the Farmers' Alliance and the Populist Party during the 1890s, shocked Kansans, Missourians, and far Westerners with blunt speeches supporting the free coinage of silver and other Populist proposals. In 1894 another western reformer, Luna Kellie, first came to public attention when the National Farmers' Alliance elected her Nebraska state secretary. Kellie not only kept Alliance records and lectured on behalf of Alliance causes, but in 1895 bought a used printing press and began to publish an Alliance newspaper on her dining-room table. In 1900, Kellie and her husband attended as delegates the National Populist Convention in Cincinnati. Soon after that, however, Kellie, disappointed by lack of economic reform, sold her press and resigned from the Alliance.

Western women also campaigned for suffrage. The efforts of Oregonian Abigail Scott Duniway and her suffrage newspaper, *The New Northwest*, played an important role in Washington Territory passing a woman suffrage measure in 1883 and Idaho in 1896. Duniway, an Oregon pioneer, developed an incredible sense of regional pride and a realistic recognition that woman suffrage could be attained only through the affirmative votes of men. Duniway often told eastern and southern women that women must convince men "that we are inspired by the same patriotic motives that induce them to prize" the vote.

Women gained the right of suffrage initially in western states and territories, yet there is little evidence that a revolution in sex roles or women's rights was under way. Nor were western women ready to confront fully racial issues. Although reformers and missionaries had finally recognized that American Indians needed help, those who worked with Indians, such as agents and field matrons (dorm mothers or superintendents), usually preached the necessity of assimilation and the full abandonment of native ways. The Bureau of Indian Affairs (BIA) initiated an active program of educating native girls at nonreservation boarding schools, such as the Carlisle Indian School in Pennsylvania, arguing that the girls could help their families and future mates assimilate. In such schools, in order to discourage the retention of cultural traits, no two children of the same tribe were put in the same dormitory or classroom. Rather than returning home to their families at vacation times, most Indian students spent them with Anglo families. Even missionaries sympathetic to Indians, like Elaine Goodale Eastman, teacher on the Sioux reservation in the Dakota territory until 1891 and writer on Indian causes until her death in 1953, ultimately agreed that an absorption process must be applied to Native Americans.

Government policies designed to hasten the acculturation of American Indians had far-reaching effects on native women. The Dawes Severalty Act of 1887 initiated the dissolution of Indian tribes and the division of tribal lands among individual members. Later, one major plan implemented around 1900 was intended to transform Sioux Indians in the Dakotas into self-sufficient farmers. Indian men received plots of land, tools, stock, and annuities from the government, an ownership pattern that usurped women's agricultural functions and subsequently helped erode women's political and economic power within their tribal groups.

Indian women marshaled their own resources to deal with the changed situation. Sioux women adapted by producing textiles and other commodities for sale in the off-reservation marketplace. They combined traditional techniques of quillwork and beading with newer skills, including quilting, crocheting, and lacemaking. Consequently, at least they earned small incomes over which they exercised full control. They also continued to utilize their right to leave unsatisfactory marriages at will, a practice that appalled and upset white missionaries and teachers. Other Indian women solved the problem of their diminishing power by following the adage "if you can't beat them, join them," and married soldiers, agents, traders, and other non-Indian men.

For Latinos, especially those who had dark rather than light skins and thus experienced racial discrimination, federal and state agencies created similar assimilationist policies. They especially hoped to assimilate Mexicans whose numbers were increasing due to a wave of immigration from Mexico during the 1880s and another beginning in 1900. When New Mexico gained statehood in 1912 and constitutionally insured bilingualism, Anglo officials of New Mexico discouraged traditional Mexican celebrations, while declaring the Fourth of July an official holiday. Also, Spanish-speakers often had to use only English in New Mexico schools. Gregorita Rodriquez, a *curandera* from Cerro Gordo, recalled that "most of us [children] knew only Spanish and we had no way to understand."

In the face of such difficulties, Chicanas turned for assistance to the Catholic church, agencies of the Protestant church, reform groups, or settlement houses. In El Paso, the Women's Charity Association, founded in 1903, especially tried to improve public health and sanitary facilities. In such cities as El Paso, Houston, and San Antonio, Chicanas often volunteered their services but seldom held administrative positions.

Latinas also derived strength and support from extended kin networks. Even in urban areas, such traditional kinship structures had not dissolved entirely. In fact, in many cases Latino kin systems revived and expanded in urban *barrios*. Thus, Latinas turned to other women among relatives, god-mothers, *compadres,* and marginal kin to help them learn English, as well as to provide them with medical care, childcare, food and other supplies, and assistance during floods, fires, and epidemics.

Latinas also developed their own brand of feminism. During the early 1900s, Mexico's *Partido Liberal Mexicano* (PLM), a political party that called for the advancement of women, influenced women on both sides of the border. In the United States, such women as Andrea and Teresa Villareal in Texas and María Talvera and Francisca Mendoz in Los Angeles staunchly supported the PLM and its programs. These included opposition to lynching of Latinos and Latinas, promoting better jobs and educational opportunities, and equal pay for male and female workers.

The Mexican Revolution of 1910, in which thousands of women fought, further spurred the feminist movement among Chicanas in the United States. In 1911, representatives from *mutualistias* (mutual aid societies) from all over Texas met in Laredo to attend the *Congreso Mutualista*. Here they discussed such issues as civil rights, better education, and combatting violence against Tejanos. Led by Jovita Idar and Soledad Peña, women formed the *Liga Femenil Mexicanista* to address gender- and family-related issues.

Other western women of color also drew upon their own resources and became similarly strong and adaptable. In Kansas, for example, black women began organizing clubs as early as the 1880s and 1890s. In 1900, these Kansas clubs combined into a statewide federation. For women interested in achieving Victorian ideals of womanhood, club meetings and annual conventions emphasized art, needlework, and domestic science, but the Kansas federation also actively pursued social and relief programs, including providing homes for the elderly, orphans, and homeless; establishing scholarship funds; and assisting unwed mothers. The federation motto proclaimed that its members are "rowing, not drifting."

In the meantime, Asian women faced searing prejudice and exclusion laws that continued to inhibit the establishment of Asian families in the United States. Chinese Exclusion Acts, renewed in 1882, 1892, and 1902 and written permanently into law in 1917, severely limited numbers of Chinese immigrants and often resulted in split families. Beginning in 1910, immigration officials routinely detained at San Francisco's Angel Island Immigrant Station those Chinese women who did obtain permission to immigrate. Here, women spent a few weeks to a few years enduring physical examinations, answering questions about their family backgrounds, and waiting for officials to cross-check the information. Once released, most joined their husbands in such rural areas as Monterey County, California, where they provided much-needed labor in the fields. Chinese women also settled in San Francisco and Los Angeles, while some went to Chicago, Detroit, Philadelphia, and New York.

Journalist Edith Maud Eaton, the daughter of a Chinese mother and English father, who wrote under the name Sui Sin Far, first disclosed the reality of Chinese women's lives in the United States. Twenty-three of her stories appeared in popular journals and the anthology *Mrs. Spring Fragrance* (1912). Besides frequently living in neglected, segregated housing where they maintained their families with hand labor—cooking on wood-burning stoves, laboring by kerosene lamps, and carrying their own water—these women struggled daily with anti-Chinese prejudice. Even women of the middle and upper classes, who often lived isolated lives as wives of merchants and entrepreneurs in Chinatowns, could not avoid bigotry.

The Protestant church, especially the Lutheran church, proved an essential element in the lives of Asian women. Besides converting Asian women to Christianity, Protestant women's and missionary groups provided schools for Asian women and children, established shelters for homeless women and orphans, and discouraged such practices as footbinding and concubinage. In addition, women coped by relying upon themselves. After the turn of the twentieth century, Chinese women took paid employment, founded women's organizations, participated in public affairs, and educated their daughters. They also turned to Chinese clan and district associations, which located jobs, extended credit, assisted the aged and infirm, and maintained Chinese cemeteries.

Japanese and Korean women also migrated to the United States, especially after 1900. Both Japanese and Korean men returned home to marry, sent for women they had known before immigration, or agreed to marry a "picture bride," meaning a wife selected through the custom of arranged marriage. Over forty-one thousand Japanese and Korean women entered the United States as picture brides, but many discovered to their dismay that their husbands were older and poorer than they had represented themselves.

Filipinos also immigrated during these years. Although the United States had obtained the Philippines as a result of the Spanish-American War in 1898, it was not until around 1907 that Filipino women began to come to the United States. Largely farmworkers, they especially settled in California's Imperial Valley, Hawaii, and Washington State. Although they were Catholic and educated, most Filipino women suffered the same prejudice directed at other Asian women. Like them, they turned to their communities, churches, and to women's clubs to learn English, improve their environments, and obtain further education.

But western women were not always segregated by race and ethnicity. They worked in each others' homes, copied each others' clothing styles, and traded childcare tips and recipes. Anglo women adopted bits of sartorial elegance from clothing worn by women of color, and Anglo women regularly visited urban areas known as Old Mexico, Chinatown, and Little Tokyo. In turn, women of color often imitated Anglo women's fashions, foods, and beliefs. Still, although western women shared a gender, as well as its travails and rewards, in most cases women perceived their differences more often than they identified their similarities. As a result, reform that reached across cultural boundaries would have to develop in a period other than the Progressive era.

For all its limitations, the Progressive era proved momentous in the history of both the nation and its women. Despite disagreements regarding both substance and style, women's culture grew strong and supple, while millions of women proved themselves determined and effective. Victorianism and the concept of separate spheres showed signs of decay. Also, some women were now well educated and achievement oriented; the 1914 edition of *Who's Who* listed nine thousand women.

At the same time, however, the argument for expanded women's roles continued to derive its strength from the belief that women played a special part in society because of their female morality and ability to "keep house" at home or in the community. Also, reform was far from finished and divisions among women far from overcome; women remained largely divided along class, racial, and other lines. Still, any regrets or reservations women might have felt toward the Progressive revolution faded in light of their growing conviction that political power was the answer and woman suffrage the panacea. Typically, they savored their gains, fully expecting to achieve even more in the immediate future.

Suggestions for Further Reading

Abelson, Elaine. *When Ladies Go A-Thieving: Middle-Class Shoplifters in the Victorian Department Store.* New York: Oxford University Press, 1989.

Albers, Patricia. "Sioux Women in Transition: A Study of Their Changing Status in a Domestic and Capitalist Sector of Production," 175–234, in *The Hidden Half: Studies of Plains Indian Women,* edited by Patricia Albers and Beatrice Medicine. Washington, DC: University Press of America, 1983.

Alexander, Adele Logan. *Ambiguous Lives, Free Women of Color in Rural Georgia, 1789–1879.* Fayetteville: University of Arkansas Press, 1991.

Alexander, Ruth Ann. "Finding Oneself through a Cause: Elaine Goodale Eastman and Indian Reform in the 1880s," *South Dakota History* 22 (Spring 1992): 1–37.

Antler, Joyce. "Feminism as Life-Process: The Life and Career of Lucy Sprague Mitchell," *Feminist Studies* 71 (Spring 1981): 134–57.

———. *Lucy Sprague Mitchell: The Making of a Modern Woman.* New Haven, CT: Yale University Press, 1987.

Aron, Cindy S. *Ladies and Gentlemen of the Civil Service: Middle Class Workers in Victorian America.* New York: Oxford University Press, 1987.

Baker, Paula. "The Domestication of Politics: Women and American Political Society, 1780–1920," *American Historical Review* 89 (June 1984): 620–47.

Banner, Lois W. *Women in Modern America: A Brief History.* San Diego: Harcourt Brace Jovanovich, Publishers, 1984.

Banta, Martha. *Imaging American Women: Idea and Ideals in Cultural History.* New York: Columbia University Press, 1987.

Bargo, Michael. "Women's Occupations in the West in 1870," *Journal of the West* 32 (January 1993): 30–45.

Barker-Benfield, G. J. *The Horrors of the Half-Known Life: Male Attitudes Toward Women and Sexuality in Nineteenth-Century America.* New York: Harper and Row, 1976.

Basen, Neil K. "Kate Richards O'Hare: The 'First Lady' of American Socialism, 1901–1917," *Labor History* 21 (Spring 1980): 165–99.

Beesley, David. "From Chinese to Chinese American: Chinese Women and Families in a Sierra Nevada Town," *California History* 67 (September 1988): 168–79.

Berch, Bettina. *The Endless Day: The Political Economy of Women and Work.* New York: Harcourt Brace Jovanovich, Inc., 1982.

Berkin, Carol Ruth, and Mary Beth Norton, eds. *Women of America: A History.* Boston: Houghton Mifflin Company, 1979. Part III.

Berrol, Selma. "When Uptown Met Downtown: Julia Richman's Work in the Jewish Community of New York, 1880–1912," *American Jewish History* 70 (September 1980): 35–51.

Blair, Karen J. *The Clubwoman as Feminist: True Womanhood Redefined, 1868–1914.* New York: Holmes & Meier Publishers, Inc., 1980.

Blocker, Jack S., Jr. "Separate Paths: Suffragists and the Women's Temperance Crusade," *Signs* 10 (Spring 1985): 460–76.

Boime, Albert. *The Art of Exclusion: Representing Blacks in the Nineteenth Century.* Washington, DC: Smithsonian Institution Press, 1989.

Bordin, Ruth. *Women and Temperance: The Quest for Power and Liberty, 1873–1900.* Philadelphia: Temple University Press, 1981.

———. *Frances Willard: A Biography.* Chapel Hill: University of North Carolina Press, 1986.

———. *Alice Freeman Palmer: The Evolution of a New Woman.* Ann Arbor: University of Michigan Press, 1993.

Brady, Marilyn Dell. "Kansas Federation of Colored Women's Clubs, 1900–1930," *Kansas History* 9 (Spring 1986): 19–31.

Brownlee, W. Elliot. "Household Values, Women's Work, and Economic Growth, 1800–1930," *Journal of Economic History* 39 (March 1979): 199–209.

Buhle, Mari Jo. *Women and American Socialism, 1870–1920.* Urbana: University of Illinois Press, 1983.

Campbell, Barbara Kuhn. *The 'Liberated' Woman of 1914: Prominent Women in the Progressive Era.* Ann Arbor: UMI Research Press, 1979.

Canfield, Gae Whitney. *Sarah Winnemucca of the North Paiutes.* Norman: University of Oklahoma Press, 1983.

Chan, Sucheng. "Chinese Livelihood in Rural California: The Impact of Economic Change, 1860–1880," *Pacific Historical Review* 53 (Aug. 1984): 273–307.

Collier-Thomas, Bettye. "The Impact of Black Women in Education: An Historical Overview," *Journal of Negro Education* 51 (Summer 1982): 173–80.

Connolly, Mark Thomas. *The Response to Prostitution in the Progressive Era.* Chapel Hill: University of North Carolina Press, 1980.

Cookingham, Mary E. "Combining Marriage, Motherhood, and Jobs before World War II: Women College Graduates, Classes of 1905–1935," *Journal of Family History* 9 (Summer 1984): 178–95.

Cooper, Patricia A. *Once a Cigar Maker: Men, Women, and Work Culture in American Cigar Factories, 1900–1919.* Urbana: University of Illinois Press, 1987.

Davies, Margery W. *Woman's Place Is at the Typewriter: Office Work and Office Workers, 1870–1930.* Philadelphia: Temple University Press, 1982.

Declerq, Eugene R. "The Nature and Style of Practice of Immigrant Midwives in Early Twentieth Century Massachusetts," *Journal of Social History* 19 (Fall 1985): 113–30.

Degler, Carl N. "What Ought To Be and What Was: Women's Sexuality in the Nineteenth Century," *American Historical Review* 79 (December 1974): 1467–90.

D'Emilio, John, and Estelle B. Freedman. *Intimate Matters: A History of Sexuality in America.* New York: Harper and Row, 1988.

Deutsch, Sarah. "Women and Intercultural Relations: The Case of Hispanic New Mexico and Colorado," *Signs* 12 (Summer 1987): 719–39.

———. *No Separate Refuge: Culture, Class, and Gender on an Anglo-Hispanic Frontier in the American Southwest, 1880–1940.* New York: Oxford University Press, 1989.

Dewhurst, C. Kurt., Betty McDowell, and Marsha MacDowell. *Artists in Aprons: Folk Art by American Women.* New York: E. P. Dutton, 1979.

Drachman, Virginia G. "Female Solidarity and Professional Success: The Dilemma of Women Doctors in Late Nineteenth-Century America," *Journal of Social History* 15 (Summer 1982): 607–19.

DuBois, Ellen Carol. "Working Women, Class Relations, and Suffrage Militance: Harriot Stanton Blatch and the New York Woman Suffrage Movement, 1894–1909," *Journal of American History* 74 (June 1987): 34–58.

Dye, Nancy Schrom. "Creating a Feminist Alliance: Sisterhood and Class Conflict in the New York Women's Trade Union League, 1903–1914," *Feminist Studies* 2 (1975): 24–38.

———. "Feminism or Unionism? The New York Women's Trade Union League and the Labor Movement," *Feminist Studies* 3 (1976): 111–25.

Eisenstein, Sarah. *Give Us Bread but Give Us Roses: Working Women's Consciousness in the United States, 1890 to the First World War.* London: Routledge, 1983.

Emmerich, Lisa E. "'Right in the Midst of My Own People': American Women and the Field Matron Program," *American Indian Quarterly* 15 (Spring 1991): 201–16.

———. "Marguerite LaFlesche Diddock: Office of Indian Affairs Field Matron," *Journal of the Great Plains Quarterly* 13 (Summer 1993): 162–71.

Epstein, Barbara Leslie. *The Politics of Domesticity: Women, Evangelism, and Temperance in Nineteenth-Century America.* Middletown, CT: Wesleyan University Press, 1981.

Evans, Sara M. *Born for Liberty: A History of Women in America.* New York: Free Press, 1989. Chapters 6–7.

Ewen, Elizabeth. "City Lights: Immigrant Women and the Rise of the Movies," *Signs* 5 (Spring 1980): 545–65.

Fish, Virginia Kemp. "'More than Love': Marion Talbot and Her Role in the Founding Years of the University of Chicago," *International Journal of Women's Studies* 8 (May/June 1985): 228–49.

Fitzpatrick, Ellen. *Endless Crusade: Women Social Scientists and Progressive Reform.* New York: Oxford University Press, 1990.

Folbre, Nancy. "The Unproductive Housewife: Her Evolution in Nineteenth-Century Economic Thought," *Signs* 16 (Spring 1991): 463–84.

Frankel, Noralee, and Nancy S. Dye, eds. *Gender, Class, Race and Reform in the Progressive Era.* Lexington: University Press of Kentucky, 1992.

Friedman, Jean E., William G. Shade, and Mary Jane Capozzoli, eds. *Our American Sisters: Women in American Life and Thought.* Lexington, MA: D. C. Heath and Company, 1987. 4th ed. Chapters 12–19.

Gamber, Wendy. "A Precarious Independence: Milliners and Dressmakers in Boston, 1860–1890," *Journal of Women's History* 4 (Spring 1992): 60–88.

García, Mario T. "The Chicana in American History: The Mexican Women of El Paso, 1880–1920: A Case Study," *Pacific Historical Review* 49 (May 1980): 315–38.

———. *Desert Immigrants: The Mexicans of El Paso, 1880–1920.* New Haven: Yale University Press, 1981.

Giddings, Paula. *When and Where I Enter . . . The Impact of Black Women on Race and Sex in America.* New York: William Morrow & Co., 1984.

Gilfoyle, Timothy J. *City of Eros: New York City, Prostitution, and the Commercialization of Sex, 1790–1920.* New York: W. W. Norton & Co., 1992.

Gilmore, Glenda. *Gender and Jim Crow: Women and the Politics of White Supremacy in North Carolina, 1896–1920.* Washington, DC: Smithsonian Institution Press, 1993.

Golden, Claudia. "The Work and Wages of Single Women, 1870 to 1920," *Journal of Economic History* 40 (March 1980): 81–88.

Gordon, Linda. "Family Violence, Feminism, and Social Control," *Feminist Studies* 12 (Fall 1986): 453–78.

———. *Heroes of Their Own Lives: The Politics and History of Family Violence, Boston, 1880–1960.* New York: Viking Press, 1988.

———. *Gender and Higher Education in the Progressive Era.* New Haven, CT: Yale University Press, 1990.

Gordon, Lynn D. "The Gibson Girl Goes to College: Popular Culture and Women's Higher Education in the Progressive Era, 1890–1920," *American Quarterly* 39 (Summer 1987): 211–30.

———. *Gender and Higher Education in the Progressive Era.* New Haven, CT: Yale University Press, 1990.

Griswold, Robert L. *Family and Divorce in California 1850–1890: Victorian Illusions and Everyday Realities.* Albany: State University of New York Press, 1982.

———. "Law, Sex, Cruelty, and Divorce in Victorian America, 1840–1900," *American Quarterly* 38 (Winter 1986): 721–45.

Grossberg, Michael. *Governing the Hearth: Law and Family in Nineteenth-Century America.* Chapel Hill: University of North Carolina Press, 1985.

Guy-Sheftall, Beverly. *Daughters of Sorrow: Attitudes Toward Black Women, 1880–1920.* Brooklyn: Carlson Publishing, 1990.

Haller, Jr., John S. "From Maidenhood to Menopause: Sex Education for Women in Victorian America," 71–85, in *Procreation or Pleasure? Sexual Attitudes in American History,* edited by Thomas L. Altherr. Malabar, FL: Robert J. Krieger Publishing Company, 1983.

Harley, Sharon. "Anna J. Cooper: A Voice for Black Women," 87–96, in *The Afro-American Woman: Struggles and Images,* edited by Sharon Harley and Rosalynn Terborg-Penn. Port Washington, NY: Kennikat Press, 1978.

Harris, Ann Sutherland, and Linda Nochlin. *Women Artists, 1550–1950.* New York: Alfred A. Knopf, 1979.

Harris, Katherine. "Homesteading in Northeastern Colorado, 1873–1920: Sex Roles and Women's Experience," *Frontiers* 7 (1984): 43–49.

Hayden, Dolores. "Charlotte Perkins Gilman and the Kitchenless House," *Radical History Review* 21 (Fall 1979): 225–47.

Hewitt, Nancy A., ed. *Women, Families, and Communities: Readings in American History.* Part II. Glenview, IL: Scott, Foresman, 1990. Part 6.

Hewitt, Nancy A., and Suzanne Lebsock, eds. *Visible Women: New Essays on American Activism.* Urbana: University of Illinois Press, 1993.

Higginbotham, Evelyn Brooks. *Righteous Discontent: The Women's Movement in the Black Baptist Church, 1880–1920.* Cambridge: Harvard University Press, 1993.

Hine, Darlene Clark. *When the Truth is Told: A History of Black Women's Culture and Community in Indiana, 1875–1950.* Indianapolis: National Council of Negro Women, 1981.

———. "From Hospital to College: Black Nurse Leaders and the Rise of Collegiate Nursing Schools," *Journal of Negro Education* 51 (Summer 1982): 222–37.

Hyman, Paula E. "Immigrant Women and Consumer Protest: The New York City Kosher Meat Boycott of 1902," *American Jewish History* 70 (September 1980): 91–105.

Ichioka, Yuji. "Amerika Nadeshiko: Japanese Immigrant Women in the United States, 1900–1924," *Pacific Historical Review* 49 (May 1980): 339–57.

Jacoby, Robin Miller. "The Women's Trade Union League and American Feminism," *Feminist Studies* 3 (1976): 126–40.

Jameson, Elizabeth. "Women as Workers, Women as Civilizers: True Womanhood in the American West," *Frontiers* 7 (1984): 1–8.

Jeffrey, Julie Roy. "'There is Some Splendid Scenery': Women's Responses to the Great Plains Landscape," *Great Plains Quarterly* 8 (Spring 1988): 69–78.

Jones, Beverly W. "Mary Church Terrell and the National Association of Colored Women, 1896 to 1901," *Journal of Negro History* 67 (Spring 1982): 20–33.

Jordan, Teresa. *Cowgirls: Women of the American West.* New York: Anchor Press, 1982.

Kasper, Shirl. *Annie Oakley.* Norman: University of Oklahoma Press, 1992.

Katzman, David M. *Seven Days a Week: Women and Domestic Service in Industrializing America.* Urbana: University of Illinois Press, 1981.

Kenneally, James J. "Women and Trade Unions, 1870–1920: The Quandary of the Reformer," *Labor History* 14 (Winter 1973): 42–55.

Kennedy, Susan Estabrook. *If All We Did Was to Weep at Home: A History of White Working Class Women in America.* Bloomington: Indiana University Press, 1979.

Kerber, Linda, and Jane DeHart-Mathews, eds. *Women's America: Refocusing the Past.* New York: Oxford University Press, 1987, 2d edition. Part IIB.

Kessler-Harris, Alice. *Out to Work: A History of Wage-Earning Women in the United States.* New York: Oxford University Press, 1982.

Kirby, Diane. "Class, Gender, and the Perils of Philanthropy: The Story of Life and Labor and Labor Reform in the Women's Trade Union League," *Journal of Women's History* 4 (Fall 1992): 36–51.

Kleinberg, Susan J. "Technology and Women's Work: The Lives of Working Class Women in Pittsburgh, 1870–1900," *Labor History* 17 (Winter 1976): 58–72.

Lane, Ann J. *To Herland and Beyond: The Life and Work of Charlotte Perkins Gilman.* New York: Pantheon, 1990.

Lang, William L. "The Nearly Forgotten Blacks on Last Chance Gulch, 1900–1912," *Pacific Northwest Quarterly* 70 (April 1979): 50–57.

Leach, William R. "Transformation in a Culture of Consumption: Women and Department Stores, 1890–1925," *Journal of American History* 71 (September 1984): 319–42.

Leavitt, Judith Walzer. *Brought to Bed: Childbearing in America, 1750 to 1960.* New York: Oxford University Press, 1986.

LeCompte, Mary Lou. *Cowgirls of the Rodeo: Pioneer Professional Athletes.* Urbana: University of Illinois Press, 1994.

Lerner, Gerda. *The Majority Finds Its Past: Placing Women in History. New York.* Oxford University Press, 1979. Chapter 6.

———, ed. *Black Women in White America: A Documentary History.* New York: Vintage Books, 1973.

Letoudis, II, James L. "School Reform in the New South: The Woman's Association for the Betterment of Public School Houses in North Carolina, 1902–1919," *Journal of American History* 69 (March 1983): 886–909.

Levine, Susan. *Labor's True Woman: Carpet Weavers, Industrialization.* Philadelphia: Temple University Press, 1984.

Lindgren, H. Elaine. *Land in Her Own Name: Women as Homesteaders in North Dakota.* Fargo: North Dakota Institute for Regional Studies, 1991.

Litoff, Judy Barrett. *American Midwives: 1860 to the Present.* Westport, CT: Greenwood Press, 1978.

Lomawaima, K. Tsianina. "Domesticity in the Federal Indian Schools: The Power of Authority over Mind and Body," *American Ethnologist* 20 (May 1993): 227–40.

Lystra, Karen. *Searching the Heart: Women, Men, and Romantic Love in Nineteenth-Century America.* New York: Oxford University Press, 1989.

Marilley, Suzanne M. "Frances Willard and the Feminism of Fear," *Feminist Studies* 19 (Spring 1993): 123–46.

Marín, Christine N. *The Chicano Experience in Arizona.* Tempe: University Libraries, Arizona State University, 1991.

Mathes, Valerie Sherer. *Helen Hunt Jackson and Her Indian Reform Legacy.* Austin: University of Texas Press, 1990.

Matthews, Glenna. *Just a Housewife: The Rise and Fall of Domesticity in the United States.* New York: Oxford University Press, 1987.

May, Elaine Tyler. "The Pressure to Provide: Class, Consumerism, and Divorce in Urban America, 1880–1920," 154–68, in *The American Family in Social-Historical Perspective,* edited by Michael Gordon. New York: St. Martin's Press, 1983.

McCarthy, Kathleen D. *Women's Culture: American Philanthropy and Art, 1830–1930.* Chicago: University of Chicago Press, 1993.

Melosh, Barbara. *"The Physician's Hand": Nurses and Nursing in the Twentieth Century.* Philadelphia: Temple University Press, 1982.

Miller, Sally M. *From Prairie to Prison: The Life of Social Activist Kate Richards O'Hare.* Columbia: University of Missouri Press, 1993.

Mintz, Steven. *A Prison of Expectations: The Family in Victorian Culture.* New York: New York University Press, 1983.

Mintz, Steven, and Susan Kellogg. *Domestic Revolutions: A Social History of American Family Life.* New York: Free Press, 1988.

Mohr, James C. *Abortion in America: The Origins and Evolution of National Policy, 1800–1900.* New York: Oxford University Press, 1978.

Monoson, S. Sara. "The Lady and the Tiger: Women's Electoral Activism in New York City Before Suffrage," *Journal of Women's History* 2 (Fall 1990): 100–35.

Morton, Marian J. *Emma Goldman and the American Left: "Nowhere at Home".* New York: Twayne, 1992.

Moynihan, Ruth B., Susan Armitage, and Christiane Fischer Dichamp, eds., *So Much to be Done: Women Settlers on the Mining and Ranching Frontier.* Lincoln: University of Nebraska Press, 1990.

Murphy, Mary. "The Private Lives of Public Women: Prostitution in Butte, Montana, 1878–1917," *Frontiers* 7 (1984): 30–35.

Murphy, Maureen. "Charlotte Grace O'Brien and the Mission of Our Lady of the Rosary for the Protection of Irish Immigrant Girls," *Mid-America* 74 (October 1992): 253–70.

Neverdon-Morton, Cynthia. "The Black Woman's Struggle for Equality in the South, 1895–1940," 43–57, in *The Afro-American Woman: Struggles and Images,* edited by Sharon Harley and Rosalyn Terborg-Penn. Port Washington, NY: Kennikat Press, 1978.

O'Donnell, Margaret G. "Charlotte Perkins Gilman's Economic Interpretation of the Role of Women at the Turn of the Century," *Social Science Quarterly* 69 (March 1988): 177–92.

Pascoe, Peggy. "Gender Systems in Conflict: The Marriages of Mission-Educated Chinese American Women, 1847–1939," *Journal of Social History* 2 (June 1989): 631–52.

———. *Relations of Rescue: The Search for Female Moral Authority in the American West, 1874–1939.* New York: Oxford University Press, 1990.

Patton, Phil. "Mammy: Her Life and Times," *American Heritage* 44 (September 1993): 78–87.

Peiss, Kathy. *Cheap Amusements: Working Women and Leisure in Turn-of-the-Century New York.* Philadelphia: Temple University Press, 1986.

Peterson, Susan, and Courtney Vaughn-Roberson. *Women with Vision: The Presentation Sisters of South Dakota, 1880–1985.* Urbana: University of Illinois Press, 1988.

Petrik, Paula. *"No Step Backward": Women and Family on the Rocky Mountain Mining Frontier, Helena, Montana, 1865–1900.* Helena: Montana Historical Society Press, 1987.

———. "'If She Be Content': The Development of Montana Divorce Law, 1876–1907," *Western Historical Quarterly* 23 (July 1987): 261–92.

Pleck, Elizabeth H. *Domestic Tyranny: The Making of Social Policy Against Family Violence from Colonial Times to the Present.* New York: Oxford University Press, 1987.

Pratt, Norma Fain. "Culture and Radical Politics: Yiddish Women Writers in America, 1890–1940," 131–52, in *Decades of Discontent: The Women's Movement, 1920–1940,* edited by Joan M. Jensen and Lois Scharf. Westport, CT: Greenwood Press, 1983.

Reitano, Joanne. "Working Girls Unite," *American Quarterly* 36 (Spring 1984): 112–34.

Riley, Glenda. *The Female Frontier: A Comparative View of Women on the Prairie and the Plains.* Lawrence: University Press of Kansas, 1988.

———. *The Life and Legacy of Annie Oakley.* Norman: University of Oklahoma Press, 1994.

Roeder, Richard B. "Crossing the Gender Line: Ella L. Knowles, Montana's First Woman Lawyer," *Montana the Magazine of Western History* 32 (Summer 1982): 64–75.

Rosen, Ruth. *The Lost Sisterhood: Prostitution in America, 1900–1918.* Baltimore: Johns Hopkins University Press, 1982.

Rosenberg, Rosalind. *Beyond Separate Spheres: Intellectual Roots of Modern Feminism.* New Haven, CT: Yale University Press, 1982.

Rossiter, Margaret W. "Women Scientists in America before 1920," *American Scientist* 62 (May/June 1974): 312–23.

Rothman, David J., and Sheila M. Rothman, eds. *On Their Own: The Poor in Modern America.* Reading, MA: Addison-Wesley Publishing Company, 1972.

Rothman, Ellen K. *Hands and Hearts: A History of Courtship in America.* New York: Basic Books, 1987.

Rouse, Jacqueline. *Lugenia Burns Hope, Black Southern Reformer.* Athens, University of Georgia Press, 1989.

Ruray, John L. *Education and Women's Work: Female Schooling and the Division of Labor in Urban America, 1870–1930.* Albany: State University of New York Press, 1991.

Scharnhorst, Gary. *Charlotte Perkins Gilman: A Biography.* Metuchen, NJ: Scarecrow Press, 1985.

Schlissel, Lillian, Byrd Gibbens, and Elizabeth Hampsten, eds. *Far From Home: Families of the Westward Journey.* New York: Schocken Books, 1989.

Schwantes, Carlos A. "Western Women in Coxey's Army in 1894," *Arizona and the West* 26 (Spring 1984): 5–20.

Scott, Anne Firor. *Making the Invisible Woman Visible.* Urbana: University of Illinois Press, 1984.

———. "On Seeing and Not Seeing: A Case of Historical Invisibility," *Journal of American History* 71 (June 1984): 7–21.

———. *Natural Allies: Women's Associations in American History.* Urbana: University of Illinois Press, 1991.

Seller, Maxine Schwartz, ed. *Immigrant Women.* Philadelphia: Temple University Press, 1981.

Seraile, William. "Susan McKinney Steward: New York State's First African-American Woman Physician," *Afro-Americans in New York Life and History* 9 (July 1985): 27–44.

Shaw, Stephanie J. "Black Club Women and the Creation of the National Association of Colored Women," *Journal of Women's History* 3 (Fall 1991):

Sheppard, Alice. "There Were Ladies Present: American Women Cartoonists and Comic Artists in the Early Twentieth Century," *Journal of American Culture* 7 (Fall 1984): 38–48.

Sicherman, Barbara. "Reading and Ambition: M. Carey Thomas and Female Heroism," *American Quarterly* 45 (March 1993): 73–103.

Sklar, Kathryn Kish. "Hull House in the 1890s: A Community of Women Reformers," *Signs* 10 (Summer 1985): 658–77.

Sklar, Kathryn Kish, and Thomas Dublin, eds. *Women and Power in American History: A Reader.* Vol. II. Englewood Cliffs, NJ: Prentice Hall, 1991. Parts 1–5.

Sluby, Patricia Carter. "Black Women and Inventions," *Sage* 6 (Fall 1989): 33–35.

Smith-Rosenberg, Carroll. "The Female World of Love and Ritual: Relations between Women in Nineteenth Century America," *Signs* 1 (August 1975): 1–29.

Solomon, Barbara Miller. *In the Company of Educated Women: A History of Women and Higher Education in America.* New Haven, CT: Yale University Press, 1985.

Stefanco, Carolyn. "Networking on the Frontier: The Colorado Women's Suffrage Movement," *Frontiers* 7 (1984): 43–49.

Sterling, Dorothy, ed. *We Are Your Sisters: Black Women in the Nineteenth-Century.* New York: W. W. Norton & Company, 1984.

Strong, Bryan. "Ideas of the Early Sex Education Movement in America, 1890–1920," 127–44, in *Procreation or Pleasure? Sexual Attitudes in American History,* edited by Thomas L. Altherr. Malabar, FL: Robert J. Krieger Publishing Company, 1983.

Sunoo, Sonia S. "Korean Women Pioneers of the Pacific Northwest," *Oregon Historical Quarterly* 79 (March 1978): 50–63.

Tamura, Eileen H. *Americanization, Acculturation, and Ethnic Identity.* Urbana: University of Illinois Press, 1994.

Tentler, Leslie Woodcock. *Wage-Earning Women: Industrial Work and Family Life in the United States, 1900–1930.* New York: Oxford University Press, 1979.

Terborg-Penn, Rosalyn. "Nineteenth Century Black Women and Woman Suffrage," *Potomac Review* 7 (Spring/Summer 1977): 13–24.

Thurber, Cheryl. "The Development of the Mammy Image and Mythology," 87–108, in *Southern Women: Histories and Identities,* edited by Virginia Bernhard, Betty Brandon, Elizabeth Fox-Genovese, and Theda Perdue. Columbia: University of Missouri Press, 1992.

Thurner, Manuela. "'Better Citizens Without the Ballot': American Antisuffrage Women and Their Rationale During the Progressive Era," *Journal of Women's History* 5 (Spring 1993): 33–60.

Toll, William. "A Quiet Revolution: Jewish Women's Clubs and the Widening Female Sphere, 1870–1920," *American Jewish Archives* 41 (Spring/Summer 1989): 7–26.

Towne, Marion K. "Charlotte Gilman in California," *Pacific Historian* 28 (Spring 1984): 5–17.

Trennert, Robert A. "Educating Indian Girls and Women at Nonreservation Boarding Schools, 1878–1920," *Western Historical Quarterly* 13 (July 1982): 271–90.

Turbin, Carole. *Working Women of Collar City: Gender, Class, and Community in Troy, New York, 1864–86.* Urbana: University of Illinois Press, 1992.

Underwood, Kathleen. *Town Building on the Colorado Frontier.* Albuquerque: University of New Mexico Press, 1987.

Waldstreicher, David. "Radicalism, Religion, Jewishness: The Case of Emma Goldman," *American Jewish History* 80 (Autumn 1990): 74–92.

Walsh, Mary Roth. *"Doctors Wanted—No Women Need Apply: Sexual Barriers in the Medical Profession, 1835–1975.* New Haven, CT: Yale University Press, 1977.

Wegars, Priscilla. "'Inmates of Body Houses': Prostitution in Moscow, Idaho, 1885–1910," *Idaho Yesterdays* 33 (Spring 1989): 25–38.

Wein, Roberta. "Women's Colleges and Domesticity, 1875–1918," *History of Education Quarterly* 15 (Spring 1974): 31–47.

Wertheimer, Barbara Mayer. *We Were There: The Story of Working Women in America.* New York: Pantheon Books, 1977.

Wilson, Elizabeth. *The Sphinx in the City: Urban Life, the Control of Disorder, and Women.* Berkeley: University of California Press, 1992.

Wilson, Margaret Gibbons. *The American Woman in Transition: The Urban Influence, 1870–1920.* Westport, CT: Greenwood Press, 1979.

Winter, Kate H. *Marietta Holley: Life With "Josiah Allen's Wife."* Syracuse: Syracuse University Press, 1984.

Woloch, Nancy. *Women and the American Experience.* New York: Alfred A. Knopf, 1984. Chapters 11–12.

Yost, Nellie Snyder. "Nebraska's Scholarly Athlete: Louise Pound, 1872–1958," *Nebraska History* 64 (Winter 1983): 476–90.

Yung, Judy. "The Social Awakening of Chinese American Women as Reported in *Chung Sai Yat Po,* 1900–1911," 195–207, in *Unequal Sisters: A Multicultural Reader in U.S. Women's History,* edited by Vicki L. Ruiz and Ellen Carol DuBois. 2d ed. New York: Routledge, 1994.

The New Woman
World War I and After, 1914 to 1929

7

In response to the outbreak of World War I in Europe in 1914, President Woodrow Wilson declared U.S. neutrality. Despite Wilson's attempt to keep the United States out of combat, however, in April 1917 the U.S. Congress declared war against Germany. For women, the World War I years and after seemed to offer unparalleled opportunities. The conflict drew women out of their homes in unprecedented numbers; Progressive spirit survived and helped underwrite the final push for woman suffrage; and the mood of the 1920s encouraged women to express themselves as independent, sexual, and political individuals.

Still, even though this era, which came to an abrupt end with the disastrous stock-market crash of 1929, appeared to extend tremendous liberation to women, many of the changes would prove more superficial than substantial.

WOMEN DURING WORLD WAR I, 1914–1918

Persistence of Progressivism

Progressivism was far from dead among women. In 1915, for example, the Women's City Club of New York organized to improve housing, education, and health, and to educate women for what they believed would be the imminent granting of suffrage.

Women activists focused on war-related issues as well. Because they believed in their moral responsibility to bring order to a chaotic world, they enthusiastically supported peace by organizing such groups as the Woman's Peace Party (WPP). Founded in 1915 and led by Jane Addams and other well-known reformers, the WPP dedicated itself to promoting pacifism and feminism. Its leaders denounced the "man-made" war raging in Europe and called for neutral mediation and limitation of armaments. The WPP leaders also maintained that woman suffrage and women's participation in government would help stop war. To them, World War I represented the failure of male leaders; the "mother half of humanity" should govern instead.

Civil liberties also emerged as a major issue in the United States. Women leaders of the peace movement especially helped found such groups as the National Civil Liberties Bureau, Non-Conscription League, League for the Amnesty of Political Prisoners, and American Liberty Defense Union. Meanwhile, such individual civil libertarians as Jessie Wallace Hughan, a Socialist and pacifist, organized yet other associations. In 1915, Hughan established the Anti-Enlistment League and later the War Resisters League, both to support women and men who opposed war and refused to support it in any way. Hughan also wrote numerous pamphlets, books, and poems promoting socialism, pacifism, and the idea of a worldwide government.

Similarly, Lugenia Burns Hope, a black Atlantan, worked for civil rights, not only in her own city but nationwide. Hope believed that the participation of black Americans in the war should lead to a broadening of their rights. Gradually, Hope's own Neighborhood Union, first founded in 1908, became a model for urban reform and later part of the Community Chest.

Women's War Relief Work

When the United States entered the war in 1917, the situation changed somewhat. The WPP decreased it criticism of male leaders who had chosen to join the conflict. But WPP leaders continued to support pacifism, claiming this would be the last war in human history. They also instituted educational programs to inform the American public about the "causes and cures" of war and continued to demand the "further humanizing of governments by the extension of the franchise to women."

At the same time, woman-suffrage leaders encouraged women to support the war. Maintaining that women must appear as patriotic as possible, suffragists advised women to undertake whatever war work seemed necessary, including heavy factory labor. At first, however, it appeared that women's war efforts would not include industrial work. In June of 1917, *World's Work* predicted that women would not put on "trousers or an unbecoming uniform and try to do something that a man can do better." Throughout the summer of 1917, the Department of Labor repeatedly announced that no additional female laborers would be needed, that plenty of male workers existed to fill the jobs created by war industries.

The Department of Labor, as well as labor leaders, advised women to bolster the war effort in other ways. Thus, as homemakers, women conserved food and other resources needed for the war effort. They created meatless, wheatless, and butterless meals, while they knitted their own socks and sweaters and cut their skirts short to save material. And, as in previous wars, they maintained alone their homes, farms, and families.

Women also volunteered their services for war relief, joining by the thousands war-bond drives and even selling bonds in club meetings, in shops, and on the streets. Others helped the Red Cross provide medical supplies and services to the military. Yet others worked with governmental agencies or with one of the many women's wartime voluntary associations.

Still other women enlisted. As members of the Women's Motor Corps, many of them drove trucks and ambulances. Others entered the United States Army Nurse Corps. Since its founding in 1901, such factors as high requirements, low pay, and few enlistments had hampered the ANC's development. When the ANC reorganized in 1917 pay increased, but benefits remained nonexistent. In addition, a nurse's rank roughly equaled that of a cadet. Despite the drawbacks, female nurses supplied critical services and performed an onerous job. War nurse Vera Brittain wrote that she often cared for "gassed men on stretchers, a writhing travesty of manhood, reeking of mud and green bandages, their yellowed faces gasping for air."

The ANC not only comprised the first group of women to achieve official recognition as a corps, but fielded 8,538 nurses to assist the American Expeditionary Forces in Europe. The Navy Nurse Corps (NNC), founded in 1908, supplied another 11,275 nurses.

In line with the racial attitudes of the era, most of these organizations excluded black women. As a result, black women often worked in their own organizations, which they formed to conserve resources, sponsor and hold bond drives, and provide war supplies. The Atlanta Colored Women's War Council, for example, established Patriotic Leagues for young black women, initiated food conservation programs, launched a "suppression of liquor campaign," and organized community and camp entertainment.

Throughout the South, the Committee on Women's Defense Work of the Council of National Defense exerted steady pressure on local groups and governments to integrate black women into the war efforts. Although many white Southerners resisted the idea, in 1918 black field representative Anna Dunbar Nelson traveled through the South organizing black women. Discouraged to learn that "government employment bureaus here recognize in every colored girl who applies for work only a potential scrub woman, no matter how educated and refined the girl may be," Nelson nevertheless pursued her mission. After visiting with black women, Nelson discovered that they preferred semi-independent, statewide organizations of their own which would parallel white women's groups. This structure eventually emerged in Florida, but, due to prejudice against blacks, not throughout the South.

Despite problems of organization, the work of Nelson and the Women's Committee opened new opportunities to black women, while quietly attacking the caste system of the South. The white state chairperson of Mississippi recognized the potential implications of black women's war work: "I am vitally interested in this, and can see its far reaching effect—not alone now—but after the war, when we will need trained hands and brains, for the great work awaiting."

Women in War Industries

As early as 1917, one observer pointed out that the United States could not possibly supply enough men for the front and for home industry as well. Every man at the front, he noted, required twenty workers at home producing war supplies. The first draft, held on 20 July 1917, alone called 1,347,000 men away from home.

Employers attempted to fill the resulting job vacancies with experienced female workers. Employers quickly exhausted this source and mobilized unemployed women. During the fall of 1917, the United States Employment Service attacked the problem by launching a governmental campaign to recruit women workers for war-industry jobs. As they always had in times of war and national emergency, women now came out of their homes to do the jobs and provide the services the country needed.

A survey of more than five-hundred factories revealed the 14,402 women employed before the first draft became a total of 19,783 after the first draft and 23,190 after the second draft. By the winter of 1917–1918, the YWCA noted that "avenues of work heretofore unthought of" for women had multiplied greatly. Journals and magazines reported women working in dirigible factories, machine shops, steel mills, oil refineries, railway yards, chemical plants, automobile factories, and iron and steel mills.

In addition, newspaper headlines announcing "Steel Mills Want Women" and "Women Print Liberty Bonds in U.S. Bureau of Engraving" became commonplace. A report from Idaho observed that "women are being employed in considerable numbers in the lumber mills. . . . They wear overalls, do a man's work and receive a man's wages." By early 1918, women unloaded heavy freight, carried huge shells and steel parts, painted steel tanks, and operated welding equipment, all with great proficiency.

Over the course of World War I, four hundred thousand women joined the labor force for the first time, while eight million already employed women switched to better paying industrial jobs. In addition, earning ratios between women and men closed somewhat, while bars against married women began to disappear in certain occupations. In 1900, only 5.6 percent of married women had worked outside their homes, but by 1910 this figure had reached 10.7 percent and continued to rise slowly to 11.7 percent in 1930.

Mothers with small children also entered the labor force in growing numbers, but they could choose instead to stay home and receive a mother's pension. In 1911, Kansas City, Missouri, enacted the first mothers' pension law, and by 1919 thirty-nine states had followed. This forerunner of today's Aid to Dependent Children program offered assistance to widowed mothers, and occasionally to divorced and deserted women as well.

Naturally, women's expectations for employment opportunities and wages rose during the war years. Women workers often sought better-paying positions, joined trade unions to protect their jobs and engaged in widespread militancy when they did not receive what they thought just treatment. Middle-class reformers, referred to as "allies," helped working women by lobbying federal and state legislatures for equal pay provisions, laws regulating working conditions, and the right of women to join or organize unions. The National Women's Trade Union League proved especially supportive of working women's causes, while in turn drawing female wage earners' attention to feminist issues.

Women in War Agriculture

In 1917, although women had long participated in farming as wives and daughters and as migratory workers, most Americans believed that heavy, physical farm labor was beyond women. As in industry, however, a shortage of agricultural workers soon occurred. To interest women in agricultural labor and convince farm employers that women were capable of the work, such private women's groups as the New York Woman's Suffrage Party and the New York City Mayor's Committee of Women on National Defense organized agricultural training camps for women. Trained recruits were then bussed to nearby farms in work squads.

In February 1918, a larger organization formed. Joining together, the Women's National Farm and Garden Association, the Garden Clubs of America, the Women's Committee of the Council of National Defense, and a number of women's colleges created the American Woman's Land Army (WLA). The WLA guaranteed to recruits basic training and a minimum wage in return for at least two months of service.

WLA women soon worked in squads in dairying, livestock, and poultry care, fruit picking, planting, weeding, hoeing, mowing, and operating such equipment as harvesters. By late summer of 1918, the WLA had placed fifteen thousand women in 127 units in twenty states, many through the *Farmerette*, which described various farm jobs, hours, wages, and training camps. In addition, thirty-four women's colleges offered training and numerous women's clubs offered scholarships to potential recruits.

By 1918, farmers who had once refused to hire women willingly paid them substantial wages, and by 1919, the WLA had not only overcome the skepticism of farmers, but had opened new employment opportunities and demonstrated women's capacity for demanding physical labor. The women themselves seemed pleased with the experiment. In 1919, a woman who shocked wheat and cultivated corn wrote: "Some life! Its great, don't think I shall come back to Omaha until after corn-picking is over."

Prejudice Against Women War Workers

Anglo women working in industry and agriculture early confronted gender prejudice, for men generally proved unreceptive to female co-workers. The traditional idea of women as wives and mothers persisted; many men believed that women who had to work should be limited to certain "female" occupations and that women who did not have to work should stay home. Moreover, union leaders worried that widespread female labor would lower wages and dilute craft skills.

Because of their apprehensions, men frequently staged protests and strikes to resist the hiring of women. They also used protective legislation to block women from a variety of jobs. And they either barred, or very grudgingly admitted, women to their unions. Afraid of losing their jobs to women, union men cooperated with women workers only in gender-segregated situations. For instance, male laundry drivers in Kansas City encouraged female laundresses to strike for better wages and working conditions, while male telephone installers and repairers urged the unionization of female telephone operators.

Discriminatory attitudes and practices permeated nearly every industry and business. Even the federal government failed to free itself from gender prejudice. In 1917, the U.S. Civil Service Commission released its usual employment announcement for male stenographers in federal agencies. When a women's committee filed a complaint, departmental officials trivialized the matter or flatly denied the existence of discriminatory practices. One official explained that "certain positions in the public service cannot be filled by women" who could not tolerate the "strain" involved.

Gradually, however, the situation changed. Some businesses came to grips with the problem of reconciling traditional attitudes toward women with the reality of wartime America. The Wells Fargo Express Company, for example, initially welcomed women largely in gender-specific jobs, including agents, cashiers, stenographers, telephone operators, accountants, and auditors. In March, 1918, however, a special edition of the *Wells Fargo Messenger* devoted to the topic "Women in the Express" revealed a changing situation.

One author described a female "Wells Fargo man" who efficiently ran a Montana office, and two women investigators who were "shattering the theory" that investigation was a male-only task. Some pages later, the same edition of the *Messenger* proclaimed that women performed men's jobs so effectively that "man is fairly certain to have to make a good showing to get the job back again."

In that same year, suffrage leader Harriot Stanton Blatch similarly declared in *Mobilizing Woman-Power* that, despite resistance, "American women have begun to go over the top." Blatch waxed enthusiastic over women's "quick wits and deft fingers," and their "muscles," which they used "vigorously at three dollars a day." According to her, women had "opened up every line of service" and were found in every type of job. "When men go a-warring," Blatch wrote, "women go to work."

For women of color, however, the situation proved more complicated. They experienced double-jeopardy, that is, gender *and* race prejudice. Consequently, wartime demands for labor opened only a limited number of industrial jobs, an opportunity women of color seized whenever it appeared. Also, Mary Church Terrell's experiences as a clerk in segregated "colored" sections of the War Risk Insurance Bureau and the Census Bureau suggest that a number of black women filled government jobs. Still, despite wartime opportunities, the majority of women of color continued to work primarily in agriculture and domestic service.

Even those women of color who migrated northward in hopes of locating better jobs were usually disappointed. Because many southern black women believed cities might offer them more opportunities, a significant number migrated. One Florida woman assured a Chicago employment agency that she could perform "any kind of housework laundress nurse good cook who has cooked for northern people," while a Mississippi women described herself as a "willen workin woman" who could serve as a cook or domestic. To their dismay, they discovered that even in domestic service, urban areas were unable, and often unwilling, to absorb them.

National War Labor Board

Recognizing the many difficulties that mobilization created, in April 1918 President Wilson organized the National War Labor Board (NWLB). He charged the NWLB to pay special attention to issues concerning female laborers, especially that of equitable pay, for in 1918 women workers received only one-half to two-thirds the wages earned by men. The claim that women worked for supplemental funds or for "pin money" rationalized this disparity. Yet the introduction of one and a half million women into war industries contradicted this argument; many women now worked because they provided the primary or sole support of their families.

The NWLB therefore adopted the principle of equal pay for equal work. In practice, however, the NWLB, confronted with a rapidly changing work world on the one hand and numerous people who still viewed women primarily as "mothers of the race" on the other, often set women's wages at three-fourths of the standard (male) rate.

By the time hostilities ended on 11 November 1918, the NWLB had gained shorter workdays and established women's right to join unions, but it had failed to devise any consistent policy on working women or to establish the basic equality of women in industry and business. The board also failed to prepare for demobilization and attendant difficulties of replacing women in the labor force with returning veterans.

Return to a Peacetime Economy

Believing that the traditional image of the American woman as passive, docile, and homebound still had the same relevance as in the postwar United States, most Americans failed to anticipate the problems of demobilization. Employers, government officials, and policymakers invoked gender expectations and social constructs regarding women to soften the blow. They assured women that they were needed far more in their homes than in their jobs, and that they must return home to repopulate the United States and help democracy remain strong in the world.

Despite this rhetoric, working women opposed the surrendering of their high-paying jobs to veterans. More than half of working women voiced their preference to continue working and indicated that they expected to earn equitable wages. Women of color especially resisted leaving industrial jobs to return to domestic and other menial employment. And women who held governmental and relief-agency positions were often just as disinclined to return to full-time wife- and motherhood.

In spite of the protests and strikes by women, beginning in late 1918 heavy industries phased out women workers. According to census data, several trends developed as women left their wartime jobs. Women lost their wartime jobs at a rapid rate in such areas as steel, chemicals, electrical goods, and airplanes and automobiles. At the same time, female employment not only remained relatively high in such women-employing sectors as tobacco, leather, and food processing, clerical work, and sales, but absorbed additional women laid off by wartime industry. Women in the clerical sector, including telephone and telegraph operators, clerks, bookkeepers, stenographers, secretaries, and sales personnel, experienced significant gains during this period. Thus, the labor force looked more like its prewar profile than its wartime one.

WOMAN SUFFRAGE TRIUMPHANT

Carrie Chapman Catt and the Winning Plan

Unlike previous times of war and emergency, during World War I most women reformers refused to abandon women's rights. Rather, they hoped to initiate the final push that would make woman suffrage a reality in every state of the nation.

Women's determination to enter fully the political realm was a logical outcome of the Progressive era, in which political power seemed to offer solutions to all problems. Women now believed that their admission to the public sphere would allow them to reform the workplace, schools and colleges, and the family structure that so severely restricted their lives. Thus, they intensified their argument that it was "expedient" to give women the vote so they could clean up society more effectively than in the past. They also argued that their war efforts deserved the granting of suffrage.

At the same time, NAWSA underwent an organizational fervor, which resulted in the proliferation of state and local suffrage associations. In Missouri in 1914, for example, Emily Newell Blair began to edit a suffrage magazine called *Missouri Woman*. Blair used the paper to establish links between the Missouri Equal Suffrage Association and such other women's groups as the Missouri Parent-Teacher Association and the Federation of Women's Clubs.

NAWSA also experimented with such tactics as open-air meetings, silent pickets, leaflet campaigns, and suffrage parades. In addition, it acquired such aggressive new leaders as Inez Milholand, an attorney and Socialist who paraded and picketed on behalf of woman suffrage and women workers. In 1915, NAWSA persuaded educator and suffrage organizer Carrie Chapman Catt, originally from Iowa, to resume its presidency.

Catt planned to capitalize on women's and men's growing interest in woman suffrage. The issue seemed to permeate the very air: women could now vote in eleven states; newspapers continually discussed the suffrage issue; and public opinion appeared increasingly positive. Thus, Catt combined her years of experience working with the Woman Suffrage Party of New York City, a two million dollar anonymous bequest, and her own political savvy to devise her "Winning Plan," which would coordinate concentrated lobbying on the federal level with state campaigns. Catt's goal was to gain a suffrage amendment to the U.S. Constitution by December 1920.

This intense campaign on behalf of woman suffrage intensified even more when President Wilson declared the war one "to save democracy." Women contended that the United States had not yet achieved democracy itself. Where is our democracy at home, they cried, when we, American citizens, cannot even vote or hold office in our own country?

NAWSA soon hired such women organizers as Maud Wood Park to travel from state to state forming suffrage associations. Park later recalled that when she joined the NAWSA Congressional Committee she first learned about file cases that held "531 portfolios, 96 for the Senate and 435 for the House." These provided "all the known data about a senator or representative." From sketches of a legislator's life to "facts supplied by our members in the state about his personal, political, business and religious affiliations" to "his stand on woman suffrage," Park could find it in the files.

From these and other files, NAWSA headquarters in Washington directed to its workers a steady, massive flow of information and suffrage literature to help them increase pressure on state senators and representatives. Soon, these state suffrage groups became highly sophisticated in their organization. Using dynamic and politically savvy techniques, Massachusetts suffragists attempted to push their decidedly antisuffrage state into the prosuffrage column. Working in concert, the Massachusetts Woman Suffrage Association, the College Equal Suffrage League, and the Boston Equal Suffrage Association for Good Government utilized a string of open-air meetings, touring speakers, leaflets, petitions, and "Votes for Women" buttons in its campaign.

Many western states also developed highly effective suffrage clubs. The West had long proved more receptive to woman suffrage than other regions. In California, suffrage groups persuaded voters to adopt woman suffrage as early as 1911 and to later strongly endorse the federal amendment. But in some parts of the West opposition existed. For instance, in South Dakota, suffragists battled a strong antisuffrage component of conservative German immigrants and liquor interests who, like national liquor representatives, feared that enfranchised women would vote for prohibition. Beginning in 1910, suffrage leader Mary Shields Pyle pushed the South Dakota Universal Franchise League to copy NAWSA in style and tactics, a move that resulted in the enfranchisement of South Dakota women in November 1918 and subsequent support of the federal amendment.

In the South, progress came more slowly. Such women as Madelina McDowell Breckinridge, the central figure in the Kentucky Equal Rights Association, worked long and hard to bring woman suffrage to fruition, but many southern men heartily disliked the idea of voting alongside women, especially black women. As a result, although NAWSA groups in the South worked on behalf of the Nineteenth Amendment, at the same time they often undercut their own efforts by making the compromise statement that suffrage should come from states rather than from the federal government.

Opponents of suffrage raised other complaints as well. Antisuffragists especially maintained that women should influence the home rather than politics. After its founding in 1911, the National Association Opposed to Women Suffrage (NAOWS) operated in New York. In 1917, its members, generally Protestant, middle-class, middle-aged women, established a national headquarters in Washington, D.C. In its newspaper, called the *Woman's Patriot*, NAOWS repeated its belief that women could best effect reform through their influence on male family members. It also tried to invalidate woman suffrage by linking it with socialism and treason. In addition, such male antisuffrage groups as the National American Constitutional League, state-level Man-Suffrage Associations, ethnic and religious groups, business interests who feared that voting women would oppose child labor, and liquor interests who worried women would prohibit alcohol also fought suffrage. In addition, even though the Democratic Party had supported woman suffrage "on the same basis as men," conservative southern Democrats—or Dixiecrats—adamantly opposed this.

Despite such opposition, NAWSA soon became the nation's largest voluntary organization. Through it, two million women across the country voiced their support of state and federal suffrage legislation. In Washington, the central office exerted a steady pressure on President Wilson to endorse woman suffrage, especially by lobbying, educating, and cajoling Wilson to change his conservative view of women in favor of a prosuffrage stance.

Black Women Suffragists

Black women sometimes joined or even led Anglo suffrage groups. In New York City in 1917, the largely white New York Woman Suffrage Party elected black suffragist Annie K. Lewis as vice-chair. Generally, however, woman suffrage leaders tried to avoided estranging white southern members and voters by involving black women in their efforts. Also in 1917, the *Crisis*, the official newspaper of the National Association for the Advancement of Colored People, warned against woman suffrage because of such antiblack attitudes on the part of white females who would be casting ballots. Other black leaders feared the introduction of a "grandmother" clause after suffrage that would deny most black women the right to vote.

Such predictions were not far wrong. In hopes of gaining the support of southern white suffragists and white supremacist Democrats, Catt and other white suffrage leaders even decided to refuse to support the enfranchisement of black women. In some southern states, this policy translated into the outright prevention of black female suffrage in order to gain white backers.

By 1919, NAWSA spurned efforts of black women to join them, including an especially energetic, hardworking group of black women suffragists in New Bedford, Massachusetts. This attitude further alienated many black Americans from the suffrage cause, but large numbers of black women refused to desert. Apparently, black women recognized the potential influence they could wield and the good they might achieve through the vote, especially in southern states. Thus, black suffragists organized suffrage clubs, participated in rallies and demonstrations, spoke and lectured on suffrage, and wrote articles. Such black women's groups as the National Federation of Afro-American Women, the National Association of Colored Women, and the Northeastern Federation of Colored Women's Clubs worked enthusiastically for women's right to vote.

The Woman's Party

First organized as the Congressional Union in 1913, suffragist Alice Paul's Woman's Party had years of experience with suffrage campaigning. Although a Quaker, Paul believed in the high-pressure techniques she had observed in England. Thus, beginning in 1917, the Woman's Party initiated twenty-four-hour pickets of the White House. When troops arrested, jailed, and force-fed these women to avert hunger strikes, dramatic headlines resulted. In addition, female picketers persisted in carrying banners reading "Democracy Should Begin at Home," "How Long Must Women Wait For Liberty!" and "Kaiser Wilson" outside the White House. The resulting riots, arrests, and additional hunger strikes by imprisoned women attracted even more publicity and placed greater pressure on President Wilson.

Polish-born Rose Winslow (Ruuza Wenclawska), a member of the Woman's Party, was arrested during White House demonstrations. While in prison, she smuggled her thoughts out on small scraps of paper directed to her husband and to suffragists. "If this thing is necessary we will naturally go through with it," she wrote early in her prison stay, but, she added, "force is so stupid a weapon." In later notes, Winslow described fainting spells and vomiting caused by the tube used to force-feed her. One of the most poignant missives read: "Alice Paul is in the psychopathic ward." Winslow added that Paul had dreaded the forced feeding, an emotion she well understood. "I had a nervous time of it," she continued, "gasping a long time afterward, and my stomach rejecting during the process. The poor soul who fed me got liberally besprinkled during the process. I heard myself making the most hideous sounds."

These hunger strikes and other actions of Woman's Party members embarrassed NAWSA, who often branded them irrational and unproductive. But the Woman's Party maintained that it was its militant tactics that finally forced the hands of the President and members of Congress. It is more likely that the combined efforts of both groups finally persuaded President Wilson to advise a group of Democrats, on 9 January 1918, to vote for the suffrage amendment "as an act of right and justice to the women of the country and of the world."

Jeannette Rankin and the "Anthony" Amendment

The day after Wilson's announcement a stirring drama occurred in the House of Representatives. The galleries overflowed with women who wanted to watch as Representative Jeannette Rankin introduced the "Anthony" amendment, as the suffrage measure was called. Simple in its language, the amendment said "the right of citizens of the United States to vote shall not be denied or abridged by the United States or by any State on account of sex."

To support the amendment, one very ill representative was carried in on a stretcher to cast his vote, while another came from the deathbed of his suffragist wife. When the tally came in it stood at 274 votes for and 136 against, one vote more than the necessary two-thirds majority. As women of NAWSA and the Woman's Party streamed into the hallways, they sang "Praise God from whom all blessings flow."

The suffrage amendment moved next to the Senate where it remained mired for a year and a half. NAWSA worked against the reelection of four antisuffrage senators, while the Woman's Party again took to the streets in protest. President Wilson took the unprecedented step of personally addressing the Senate on behalf of suffrage. Finally, after several negative votes, on 4 June 1919 the Senate finally approved woman suffrage by a vote of sixty-three to thirty.

Next, the suffrage provision went to the states for ratification; it needed the support of three-fourths (thirty-six) of the states. Eleven ratifications poured in during the first month, and eleven more states approved the amendment during the next five months. But the opposition proved tough and well organized, and needed to hold back only thirteen states. Both NAWSA and the Woman's Party worked hard to combat the "antis," as the antisuffrage forces were called.

The tension peaked in August 1920. Thirty-five states had ratified woman suffrage. Only one was needed and only one possibility existed—Tennessee. Suffragists poured into Nashville to campaign and to lobby. On 13 August, the Tennessee Senate ratified the measure. When the issue went to the House, the vote tied. It now rested in the hands of Representative Harry Burns, at twenty-four years of age the youngest member of the Tennessee House of Representatives. When he cast his decision for suffrage, the amendment carried. Reportedly, Burns had just received a message from his mother instructing him to "vote for suffrage and don't keep them in doubt. . . . Don't forget to be a good boy and help Mrs. Catt put 'Rat' in Ratification."

The Nineteenth Amendment

On 26 August 1920, the Secretary of State proclaimed the ratification of the Nineteenth Amendment. Seventy-two years had passed since the convention at Seneca Falls, where women had first asked for the right of franchise. Many suffragists were elated, while those who supported prohibition believed the panacea was at hand.

Because they had invested so much emotional energy and hope for the future in the vote, activist women were crushed when they learned it was not "the" answer after all. Within a few years, it became evident that women did not vote in blocs or react uniformly to women's issues. Like men, individual women voted in terms of such factors as their social class, educational level, race, religious affiliation, geographical location, and similar influences.

Another complication developed when NAWSA, the Woman's Party, and other women's groups drastically disagreed on how further reforms for women might be activated, or if they were necessary at all. Most American women seemed to feel that women now had all necessary rights, and that the unending discussion concerning women could finally cease. Women's efforts after 1920 were thus fragmented. Anna Howard Shaw foresaw this development when she stated that "I am sorry for you young women who have to carry on the work for the next ten years, for suffrage was a symbol, and now you have lost your symbol."

Just as Shaw prophesied, the suffrage movement soon broke into factions, including social feminists (dedicated to the reform of society), feminists (advocates of enlarged roles for women), pacifists, and women interested in changing the worlds of labor and the professions. "We all went back to a hundred different causes and tasks that we'd been putting off all those years," one former suffragist explained. "We just demobilized."

WOMEN'S CONCERNS DURING THE 1920s

League of Women Voters

Because some women leaders believed that further progress would result only from women's political education and action, in 1919 NAWSA president Carrie Chapman Catt announced to the NAWSA convention in St. Louis: "Let us then raise up a league of women voters . . . that shall be nonpartisan and nonsectarian in nature." In 1920, NAWSA officially became the League of Women Voters.

League members hoped to demonstrate that women could become effective, involved citizens. Thus, the League advocated political education for women, social reform, and the elimination of discriminatory laws against women, all within the framework of a nonpartisan and moderate position. As an ancillary achievement, the League provided a solid training ground for women. For instance, Lavinia Engle, Director of the Maryland League in 1920, subsequently won election to the Maryland state legislature, and in 1936 achieved appointment as an officer of the U.S. Social Security Administration.

Unfortunately, because League members believed in "the aloof detachment of the scientific method" and in "wooing our legislators in a dignified and league-like manner," they frequently produced more speeches and literature than action. The League enhanced its influence, however, by initiating, also in 1920, the Women's Joint Congressional Committee (WJCC). Led by League president and former suffragist Maud Wood Park, this umbrella organization brought together ten women's groups, including the League of Women Voters, the National Women's Trade Union

League, the General Federation of Women's Clubs, the Women's Christian Temperance Union, and the National Consumer League.

The Congressional Committee engaged largely in joint lobbying. Recognizing that 250,000 children died—many of diseases and neglect—in the United States each year, the WJCC supported the Sheppard-Towner Act of 1921, which established public health centers and prenatal clinics. The following year, the WJCC campaigned for the Cable Act, which granted individual citizenship to married women and would prevent American women engaged to foreign nationals from losing citizenship upon marriage. By 1924, the WJCC encompassed twenty-one women's groups.

As with the earlier club movement, few black women found membership in any of the predominantly white women's political groups attractive. Instead, most chose to join the Colored Women's Political Group and other similar clubs. By 1920, "Colored Women's Voter's Leagues" were common throughout the South. Then, in 1922, one black female Socialist exhorted black women to "explain the correct use of the ballot . . . then make a demand and see to it that it is carried out by those whom you have elected into office."

Equal Rights Amendment

A handful of other women believed that suffrage and women's political action was inadequate and that further constitutional gains were needed. Alice Paul and her followers maintained that an equal rights amendment to the Constitution was an absolute necessity to protect women from discriminatory laws and practices at the national and state levels. These women formed the National Woman's Party (NWP) which proposed a simply stated provision that "men and women shall have equal rights throughout the United States and every place subject to its jurisdiction." The NWP initiated its campaign for a single cause, the Equal Rights Amendment (ERA). In 1923, Paul introduced the ERA to Congress but found both members of Congress and the American public generally laconic regarding any further "women's" amendments.

The NWP's commitment to the ERA kept the spirit of feminism alive during the 1920s, but its clear-cut stance made cooperation among women activists difficult. Feminists, such as those in the NWP, supported both the ERA and equality in all areas of life. They also hoped to eradicate protective labor legislation for women because they viewed it as unfair and restrictive of women's work rights. Social feminists, however, believed the ERA too extreme and desired equality primarily in social and economic areas. They also strongly supported protective labor legislation. As a result of their many differences, feminists and social feminists formed two separate, and often warring, factions, which ultimately hurt the effectiveness of both groups.

On-going Reforms

The spirit of Progressivism retained some of its vitality during the 1920s. If anything, World War I and its aftermath demonstrated a greater need than ever for improvement in American society. Consequently, on-going reforms such as those of the Women's Trade Union League, the Consumers' League, and the YMCA continued to require women's attention.

In addition, because the United States had achieved the position of world leader, it had to confront such issues as peace more fully than before. In hopes of helping lead the world to peace, in 1921 two new groups organized: the Women's Peace Union of the Western Hemisphere and the Women's Committee for World Disarmament. In that year, the PTA also lent its support to the cause of peace, arguing that schools must educate the next generation of Americans to avoid war. Then, in 1925, Carrie Chapman Catt organized the National Conference on the Cause and Cure of War, while Jane Addams began to play an active role in the Women's International League for Peace and Freedom.

Other women assisted the nation's accelerating search for solutions to worsening industrial problems. Alice Hamilton, the country's leading industrial toxicologist, had begun her career well before World War I. She had combined her interest in reform and medicine by taking in 1897 the position of Professor of Pathology at the Chicago's Woman's Medical School of Northwestern University and by living at Hull House. Given the industrial reform interests of Hull House leaders, it was probably inevitable that Hamilton develop an interest in the contamination of factory workers and the pureness of products. Soon, Hamilton began to work with the National Consumers' League, and in 1925 published *Industrial Poisons in the United States*, which established her reputation worldwide.

Educated and skilled women also voiced concerns about their place in postwar America. In 1919, a group of teachers and clerical workers formed the National Federation of Business and Professional Women's Clubs to achieve equal rights for professional women. Also, for the first time college-educated women formed their own national association. In 1921, the Association of Collegiate Alumnae (1882) merged with the Western Association of Collegiate Alumnae (1883) and the Southern Association of College Women (1903) to form the American Association of University Women (AAUW). Like its forerunners, the AAUW awarded scholarships for women, funded women's dormitories, helped improve women faculties' salaries, and promoted the admission of women students and the hiring of women faculty.

Women also expressed a growing interest in the future of the American environment. Clubs formed to study science, nature, photography, and conservation, while others devoted themselves to hiking and nature travel. Other women flocked to the burgeoning field of nature study, begun in the early twentieth century. During the 1920s, approximately 60 percent of the members of the Nature Study Association were women, while 90 percent of nature study teachers were female. The latter introduced into science classrooms such techniques as nature walks, school museums, weather data collection stations, aquariums, and terrariums.

The dominant reform issue of the 1920s, however, was the prohibition of alcoholic beverages in the United States. Women's long-term fight for temperance culminated in prohibition instead. With the passage of the Eighteenth Amendment, ratified in 1918, and the Volstead Act, passed in 1919, the United States prohibited liquor and established harsh penalties for those who produced and sold it.

Rather than bringing salvation from a long-standing problem, national prohibition drove liquor consumption underground. During the 1920s, alcohol production turned into a corrupt industry, which led to bootleggers, gang wars, and a general disrespect for law and order. Women, who were no longer arrested for merely smoking in public, now smoked *and* drank openly. Prostitution thrived as well. In Silverton, Colorado, for example, "boardinghouses" with such colorful names as the "Diamond Bell" and the "Mikado" lined Blair Street. According to a long-time resident, during the 1920s Silverton was "like a little Las Vegas, the gambling houses and bordellos were open 24 hours a day, seven days a week. You could buy bootleg booze in any saloon or whorehouse."

Calls for the repeal of prohibition accelerated by the end of the 1920s. The depression strengthened arguments against prohibition, and Congress finally repealed the disillusioning experiment in 1933.

Racial Issues

Women also expanded their interest in racial issues, which increasingly included attention to the plight of Native Americans. A Dakota Sioux named Gertrude Simmons Bonnin, also known as Zitkala-Sa or Redbird, was especially active, working for Native American causes through the Society of American Indians, founded in 1911. Bonnin campaigned especially for Indian citizenship, finally granted in 1924; the equitable settlement of land claims; and investigations of the federal government's relations with individual tribes. In 1926, Bonnin founded the National Congress of American Indians, which she led for years.

Moreover, during the 1920s Bonnin convinced the General Federation of Women's Clubs to join the Indian Rights Association and support further exploration of Indian grievances. Through her writings in such journals as *Atlantic Monthly, Harper's Monthly,* and *The American Indian Magazine,* Bonnin brought native dilemmas to the notice of the American public.

The situation of Latinos also garnered growing attention. Beginning in 1924, a young civil rights leader from Mexico, María Hernández, spoke and wrote in Texas on behalf of increased liberty. Hernández advocated cooperation between women and men in fighting against racial and ethnic segregation; for improved education in *barrios*; and for enhanced activism by Latinos in both politics and the workplace. In 1929, Hernández helped her husband organize a male civil rights group known as the *Orden Caballeros de America* and later helped develop the *Raza Unida* party in Texas.

Still, for most women the term "racial issues" meant African American difficulties. Black women took the lead in distributing information and implementing change. In 1924, for example, clubwoman Nannie Burroughs helped establish the National League of Republican Colored Women and accepted appointment as its first president. Burroughs used her spellbinding oratorical powers not only in support of Republican candidates but on behalf of domestic servants, black wageworkers, equal justice, and black pride. Rather than wait for "deliverance" at the hands of Anglos, Burroughs urged black Americans to "arise and go over Jordan" themselves.

Unlike Burroughs and her colleagues, many black women seemed more interested in social than political action. In 1927, for example, Selena Sloan Butler founded the National Congress of Colored Parents and Teachers, a child-advocacy group especially intent upon improving segregated schools in the South. Thousands of others joined church groups, community improvement organizations, and women's clubs of various types. In 1921, eight Montana clubs met in Butte to organize a state-wide federation. The resulting Montana State Federation of Negro Women's clubs dedicated itself to unifying black women, providing college scholarships, fighting for civil rights and against discrimination in athletics and school events, and forming interracial clubs to help intergroup relations.

A divisive point of disagreement for black women activists was the wisdom of working with Anglo women. Some black women opposed such action. Jamaican-born black-nationalist Amy Jacques Garvey spoke and wrote on behalf of the most successful Pan-African movement ever. As supporter and spouse of Marcus Garvey and his Universal Negro Improvement Association (UNIA), Amy Garvey contributed a strong voice for cultural unity as a vehicle for racial uplift.

Others believed that interracial cooperation had to underwrite change. Instances of black-white interaction occurred in the Commission on InterRacial Cooperation of the Women's Council of the Methodist Episcopal Church, which in 1920 sponsored a major conference on race relations. Also in 1920, a group of black women appealed to the predominantly white YWCA for black-oriented programs, eventual integration of black women into the organization, and black representation on the national board. The first black woman on the staff of the YWCA, social worker Eva Bowies, supported this appeal by emphasizing that "white women do not properly appreciate the strength of our colored women throughout the country." The YWCA responded to the request, and in 1924 even elected the first black woman, social worker Elizabeth Ross Haynes, to its national board.

The most pressing issue to black women during the 1920s, and one that frequently led to collaboration between black and white women, was lynching. The antilynching movement dated back to 1895, to the one-person crusade of Ida Wells-Barnett. In 1922, black reformer Mary B. Talbert organized a movement called the Anti-Lynching Crusade with hopes of bringing together "a million women," both white and black, "to stop lynching" in the United States. Talbert's group released studies disclosing that not only black men fell victim to lynching: eighty-three women had been lynched since 1892 as well. Exact numbers of total lynchings, however, were unknown because white authorities sometimes regarded black lives with such disdain that they neglected to report the lynching of a black man or woman. Members, including women, of the Ku Klux Klan, which reached its peak membership during the 1920s, and other racist groups usually conducted the lynchings.

Also in 1922, the National Council of Women, which represented thirteen million women, voted to "endorse the AntiLynching Crusade recently launched by colored women of this country." The following year, Talbert reported that over seven hundred women leaders in twenty-five states had joined the antilynching crusade, and that her executive committee recommended such action as pressuring Congress and state legislatures for antilynching legislation, pursuing suits against lynchers, and widely publicizing episodes of lynching.

Then, in 1924, the League of Women Voters established a Committee on Negro Problems. Southern white women especially supported this program and called for an end to lynching. The persistence of the image of the Southern Lady may have hampered their effectiveness, however. Crusty with age and heavy with the weight of tradition, old-fashioned notions of the southern female continued to plague women activists throughout the postwar decade.

Labor Reform

Labor problems also continued to attract women's attention. By 1920, one out of every five workers was female. Of women workers, 25.6 percent of women worked in business-related jobs, 23.8 percent in manufacturing, especially the automobile industry, which, according to *Motor Magazine* in 1927 had "almost over night become a feminine business with a feminine market." Another 18.2 percent worked in domestic service and 12.9 percent in agriculture.

For women of color the statistics were more dismal. Fully 75 percent of all employed women of color labored in three fields: domestic service, laundry work, and agricultural employment. In a number of large cities, the proportion of black women and other women of color in domestic service rose to 85 percent. In addition, restrictive policies generally barred them from factories and offices; if hired in factories and shops, women of color usually worked in separate rooms and lacked such amenities as lunchrooms and clean bathrooms.

In 1920, the U.S. government responded to the needs of working women by creating a special division within the Department of Labor. Led by former labor organizer Mary Anderson, the new Women's Bureau collected data, studied women workers, and lobbied for protective legislation. In a 1920 report, the Women's Bureau observed that World War I had "forced the experiment of woman labor in the craftsmanly occupations." The bureau also reported the surprise of employers when observing the skills and abilities of women workers. According to one manufacturer, "there is hardly a line of work in which a woman cannot adapt herself."

The Women's Bureau especially supported the passage of protective laws for women. Between the peak years of 1912 to 1919, fourteen states, mainly in the Midwest and on the West Coast, enacted legislation limiting the number of hours women worked; prohibiting night work; and banning women from selling liquor, carrying mail, running elevators, and working in foundries and mines. Women's employers also had to provide seats, rest periods, ventilation, and good light.

In addition to the Bureau's efforts, Florence Kelley and the National Consumers' League led a wide-based coalition in lobbying for minimum-wage laws. Employers and male unionists generally opposed such laws and in 1923 the U.S. Supreme Court agreed; it ruled gender-specific wage laws unconstitutional because they privileged one gender over the other.

Other women took a far different tack. Because they believed that women's equality and working-class suffrage would provide solutions, numerous Socialist women joined the Communist Party after its organization in the United States in 1919. Among others, Mary "Mother" Jones, Lucy González Parsons, and Elizabeth Gurley Flynn served as Communist leaders and activists. During the 1920s, these women pushed the Communist Party in the direction of championing not only women but people of color as well.

Despite such innovations as the Women's Bureau and the Communist Party, some labor reformers remained convinced that only strikes, protests, and even violence would force employers to institute reforms. Unfortunately, such demonstrations often resulted in tragic outcomes. In a 1919 strike in West Natrona, Pennsylvania, Allegheny Coal and Coke Company deputy sheriffs shot and killed labor organizer and Socialist Fannie Mooney Sellins. Sellins had first organized garment workers, then beginning in 1913 had helped miners' wives and children and recruited miners for union membership. Sellins also recruited black workers, explaining to them that companies had brought them north as strikebreakers rather than legitimate workers. Because coal company executives feared Sellins, it is likely that she was the intentional target of violence in the 1919 strike.

Ten years later, a 1929 strike in Elizabethton, Tennessee, had a slightly better outcome. When workers in a rayon textile plant left machines to protest low wages, work quotas, and "hard rules," laborers in a nearby plant joined them and organized a local of the United Textile Workers of the American Federation of Labor (UTW-AFL). The strike soon spread over the entire area, causing chaos and defiance. Strikers ignored injunctions against picketing, while a local business owner kidnapped a union organizer. Women, who constituted 37 percent of rayon workers in Elizabethton, wrapped themselves in American flags and walked through the streets, blocked roads with their bodies, and, with fists and picket signs, assaulted members of the National Guard sent to control them. Although many women were jailed and the strike ended after six weeks with minimal gains, the workers felt empowered, especially when their strike set off a wave of protests in other southern textile factories.

WOMEN'S LIVES AND ACHIEVEMENTS DURING THE 1920S

Marriage and Family

During the 1920s, some women appeared content with such personal pursuits as bridge, home decoration, gardening, and current fashions, but others found such domesticity old-fashioned. To them, personal autonomy was the order of the day.

As a result, concepts of marriage and family shifted into a "modern" mode. Consumerism and advertising further raised women's expectations of standards of living in marriage to unrealistic levels. Soon, novelist F. Scott Fitzgerald and his wife Zelda captured the popular imagination as the "ideal" couple. The Fitzgeralds reflected the 1920s flapper mode, acting thoroughly spoiled, selfish, and hedonistic. Clearly, the Fitzgeralds modeled an impractical marriage, yet thousands of Americans found it romantic and admirable.

At the same time, media images of romance and everlasting happiness proved untenable to both women and men on a daily basis. Women's attempts to act like "flappers," which the *Ladies Home Journal* described as morbid women who smoked, wore short skirts, performed obscene dances, favored one-piece bathing suits, listened to jazz, entered psychoanalysis, practiced birth control, and leaned toward Bolshevism, also did little to contribute to satisfaction in traditional marriages. In addition, women who could now vote and hold paid employment were less willing to suffer abuse at the hands of spouses than were their mothers and grandmothers. Little wonder, then, that marriages failed at a rising rate during the 1920s. By the end of the decade slightly more than one in six marriages ended in divorce.

Still, the American woman's dream continued to focus largely on romance, a blissful marriage, and a model family. During the 1920s, motherhood now required "psychological" knowledge. Advice literature counseled mothers to refrain from controlling their children, for "how can tied hands ever learn to be useful." In addition, the "new family" bound its members by affection rather than rules. Companionate marriage, or one based more on partnership than patriarchy, constituted the ideal, while lesbian love fell into disrepute. People of the 1920s increasingly viewed lesbian relationships as a threat to marriage.

Moreover, the happy and prosperous family was increasingly a smaller family. A public health nurse in New York named Margaret Sanger had long been concerned about women's desire to control family size. In 1914, Sanger had coined the term "birth control" and had begun to distribute her monthly publication, the *Woman Rebel,* on the streets and through the mails. Aimed primarily at working-class women, the *Rebel* advocated women's right to sexual freedom and control of their own bodies. When faced with arrest under the Comstock Law because she distributed the journal through the U.S. mail, in 1914 Sanger fled to Europe where she studied family planning clinics.

When Sanger returned to the United States, she reportedly smuggled in a number of diaphragms in her girdle. In 1916, Sanger and her sister established the first birth-control clinic, but they were arrested and sentenced to the workhouse where Sanger's sister went on a dramatic hunger strike that almost caused her death. Although the resulting publicity brought the issue of birth control before the public and created great interest, it also alienated suffrage leaders and feminists who had hoped for a more dignified reform and one over which they could hold sway. Instead, the court case and discussions that ensued put treatment in the hands of physicians, allowing them to dispense a restricted amount of birth-control information.

Sanger turned increasingly to middle-class women and medical doctors for reinforcement and financial subsidies. In 1919, the Voluntary Parenthood League formed to lobby Congress for modifications in the Comstock law. Using the term "voluntary parenthood" rather than "birth control," the League declared that American citizens should have the right to make individual, reasoned decisions regarding family size.

Then, in 1921, the year of the first American Birth Control Conference, Sanger founded the American Birth Control League (ABCL) to promote the dissemination of birth-control information; dispense spring-type diaphragms and lactic-acid jelly; and distribute the names of New York physicians willing to help women with birth control. Although her efforts drew fire and the threat of imminent riots from opponents who feared "race suicide" and increased promiscuity, Sanger persevered. She responded that "we want children to be conceived in love, born of parents' conscious desire and born into the world with healthy and sound bodies and sound minds."

Rising expectations of marriage and the increasing ability to control family size affected primarily native-born Anglo women. Many immigrant women had to deal with the realities of urban and ghetto life, including stressful marriages and large families. A 1930 study of Polish families in Chicago showed that wife-beating was acceptable and that the patriarchal family structure remained strong.

By the second generation, however, these women gradually developed expectations similar to native-born women's. Those who held paid employment outside their homes quickly learned American ways, while the most popular women's journal, *Good Housekeeping*, helped women do things the "American" way. Moving picture films indoctrinated thousands more into the values and beliefs of American women. One of the most popular film series during the 1920s, *Perils of Pauline*, must have stunned its women viewers. For twenty episodes, Pauline challenged tradition, including flying an airplane, racing an automobile, and refusing a suitor in favor of a career. American women seemed to have indeed entered a new era.

Women Actors

Certainly, women appeared everywhere. On stage, black singer and dancer Josephine Baker traveled during the 1910s with the Dixie Steppers. In 1921, Baker captured a part in Eubie Blake's and Noble Sissle's musical, *Shuffle Along*, which catapulted her to stardom. After captivating American audiences, Baker repeated her triumph in Paris; on one occasion, she appeared at the Folies-Bergere wearing a costume of rhinestone-studded bananas, an outfit which she then adopted as her trademark.

A few years later, an unnamed dancer invented the striptease at Minsky's Burlesque House in New York City. During a 1925 police raid, she broke her shoulder strap and the audience went wild; she obligingly repeated the performance in subsequent shows. Most of her many imitators developed routines based on the gradual removal of long gloves, evening gowns, and undergarments. Of all the striptease dancers, however, Mae Dix developed the most interesting act. Dix wrapped herself in newspapers and read the headlines to music, while allowing people who held box seats to tear sheets off and slowly expose her body.

Women Artists

In the art world, one of the 1920s better-known works was Florine Stettheimer's 1924 painting "Beauty Contest." Other women artists, however, preferred more modern formats, especially cubism and fauvism.

In 1920, a modernist-cubist painter, Katherine Dreier, helped establish the Société Anonyme in New York City, the first gallery dedicated to modern art. Gertrude Vanderbilt Whitney, herself a sculptor as well as a patron of art, also displayed an interest in avant-garde work. She first organized the Whitney Studio Club in New York as a place for artists to meet and display their work, and in 1931 founded the Whitney Museum of Modern Art.

Painter Georgia O'Keefe, who was just beginning her career during the 1920s, also produced unusual work. O'Keefe's New York skylines, abstract landscapes, skulls and horns against a New Mexico background, and huge, erotic flowers that filled an entire canvas mystified her critics, who often dismissed her work as an expression of extreme female "sensibility" and emotionalism.

At the same time, Malvina Cornell Hoffman, who studied in France with famous sculptor Auguste Rodin, proved herself in the American art world. In harmony with the era's interest in primitivism and portrait busts, Hoffman sculpted heads of famous people, including her friend and renowned ballet star Anna Pavlova. Hoffman also achieved renown for a series of 110 bronzes titled "The Races of Man," specially commissioned by the Field Museum of Natural History in Chicago.

Women Athletes

Women also participated in the so-called Golden Age of Sports. In 1922, Floretta McCutcheon defeated the reigning bowling champion, Jimmy Smith. In 1926, Gertrude Ederle became the first woman to swim the English Channel, with a time that improved on the existing male record by two hours. During the same period, Glenna Collett was the first woman to break eighty for eighteen holes of golf, while Helen Wills dominated women's tennis.

In rodeo, such stars as Tad Lucas and Mabel Strickland wowed audiences with their roping, trick riding, and bronc-busting. Like other women of the time, they hoped to have both men's work and femininity too. As Strickland said, "I love dresses and everything that goes with them. I can't tolerate the mannish woman any more than I can stand the womanish man."

Women Aviators

Barnstorming and stunt flying enthralled Americans during the 1920s, and women were among the dauntless pilots who swooped and dived over everything from air fields to corn fields. Daredevil pilot Mabel Cody even traveled with her own "flying circus."

Their share of tragedies occurred also. Bessie Coleman crashed and died while practicing for an air show in Orlando, Florida. Coleman, who in 1921 became the first black woman to earn a pilot's license, was well remembered, however. After her death, her friends and fans took up her dream of establishing a flying school for black Americans, naming it the Bessie Coleman School.

By the end of the decade, women pilots vied against each other in formal competition. In 1929, the first national aviation competition—the Women's Air Derby—offered monetary awards as well as the opportunity for women to prove themselves as pilots. Soon after, Clara Trenchmann of the Curtiss Flying Service on Long Island, New York, asked four women pilots to write to the 126 licensed women pilots in the United States to explore the possibility of organizing a female pilots' organization. Ninety-nine women responded positively. Thus, on 2 November 1929 twenty-six women gathered in a Curtiss hangar and established the Ninety-Nines, so-named for its charter members.

Of course, the one woman pilot who gained the most celebrity during the 1920s and soon became a national symbol of "new" womanhood was Amelia Earhart. She set her first world record in 1922; flying her own Kinner Canary, she achieved the highest altitude flown by a woman. Soon, Earhart began experimenting with distance flights. She went on in the early 1930s to fly alone over the Atlantic Ocean and from the Atlantic to the Pacific and back again, but she tragically disappeared in 1937 while attempting to fly around the world.

Female Religious Leaders

Women attained prominence in the realm of religion as well. Although Aimee Semple McPherson, evangelist and founder of the International Church of the Foursquare Gospel, was not the only female religious leader in the United States, she was certainly the most famous. When seventeen years old, Aimee had experienced conversion at a Pentecostal revival. Within the year, she married Robert James Semple, the evangelist who converted her. After Semple's death in China, Aimee and her daughter worked for the New York City Salvation Army. Then, in 1912, Aimee married Harold McPherson and had a son. After a long illness, Aimee returned to preaching; she was to work her way across the country and back eight times between 1918 and 1923.

In 1921, Aimee also began building her dream, the Angelus Temple near Los Angeles, which became the center for her conservative "Church of the Foursquare Gospel." There she preached every evening and three times on Sunday to crowds of five thousand people or more—crowds that included women and men, young and old, Anglos and people of color. By the late 1920s, Sister Aimee, as she was called, had toured the United States, the British Isles, and even preached in Paris, carrying her message of redemption to thousands anxious to listen.

Women Writers

During the 1920s, women also published more books, essays, and poetry than ever before. Realistic novelist Ellen Glasgow brought southern women into vivid perspective, while Willa Cather depicted assertive western women, especially in *My Antonia* (1918). At the same time, Edith Wharton wrote about women in New York "society." Noted for her attention to detail and sensitive portrayals, Wharton became in 1920 the first woman to receive the Pulitzer Prize. Besides her prize-winning *Age of Innocence*, Wharton wrote several other novels and eighty-five short stories.

Yet others who wrote for and about women included Fannie Hurst, Edna Ferber, and Gertrude Atherton. Atherton alone contributed forty novels, numerous short stories and essays, and an engaging autobiography. Atherton preferred a combination of romantic and realistic styles. Her plots hinged upon a melding of heredity and environment to create dramatic events in her characters' lives. She was also fond of characters, especially women, who could overcome and conquer.

In poetry, Edna St. Vincent Millay prevailed. Living in New York City's Greenwich Village during the 1920s, Millay reflected post–World War I thinking regarding women. Like their creator, Millay's always-witty female characters in her dramatic poems were independent and sexually free. They not only promoted reform, especially the cause of world peace, but spoke against such ideas of the period as Fascism.

Mabel Dodge Luhan, who presided over the most illustrious salon in Greenwich Village, remembered the 1920s as exciting times indeed. Luhan recalled that her parties attracted "Socialists, Trade-Unionists, Suffragists, Poets, Relations, Lawyers, Murderers, Old Friends, Psychoanalysts, I.W.W.'s, Single Taxers, Birth Controlists, Newspapermen, Artists, Modern-Artists, Clubwomen, Woman's-place-is-in-the-home Women, clergymen, and just plain men" who all met in her home to exchange "a variousness in vocabulary called, in euphemistic optimism, Opinions."

Luhan failed to mention women of color, but they contributed to the literary ferment of the 1920s as well. An American Indian woman, Humishu-ma (Chrystal Quintasket) gained renown for her novel, *Co-go-wea, the Half-Blood* (1927); while African American writers experimented with female images important to their people, writing of mothers, entertainers, and black women of great beauty and sensuality.

Such magazines as *Crisis* and the Urban League's *Opportunity* encouraged black writers and poets to deal with themes important to them as black women. The emerging Harlem Renaissance, which demonstrated black Americans' literary talents and creative imagination to the nation, further inspired the work of black writers. In *Quicksand*, Nella Larsen presented the first black heroine in American fiction. Both Larsen's *Quicksand* (1928) and *Passing* (1929), reprinted several times, revealed the inner turmoil of a woman of a mixed racial background who never fully resolved her identity.

Others, notably Jessie Redmon Fauset, also contributed to the Harlem Renaissance. In looking back at her novels *There is Confusion* (1924) and

Plum Bun (1929), Fauset explained that she chose black Americans as her subjects "partly because of all the other separate groups which constitute the American cosmogony none of them, to me, seems to be naturally endowed with the stuff of which chronicles may be made."

Women Singers

Black female blues singers, at the heart of the Harlem Renaissance, embraced traditional ways of singing but also developed new ones. During what is now referred to as the "classic" blues era of the 1920s, such singers as Gertrude Pridgett "Ma" Rainey, Bessie Smith, Rosa Hill, Ida Cox, Sippie Wallace, and Georgia White created a unique form of artistic expression. Their lyrics reflected the anxieties of black women, especially fear of poverty and abandonment by men. Another dominant theme was migration, both South to North and rural to urban, in which men often left women behind. Called the "railroad blues," this genre featured "Freight Train Blues" and "Chicago Bound Blues."

Among blues aficionados, Ma Rainey earned the title "Mother of the Blues." Rainey began appearing in tent shows and on the black vaudeville circuit in the early 1900s, but not until 1923 did she achieve national stardom by recording with Paramount Records. Rainey's renditions of such blues standards as "See, See Rider" brought phenomenal record sales and standing-room-only performances. Unlike other blues singers of the time, Rainey composed more than a third of the songs she recorded.

Bessie Smith, however, captured the appellations the "empress of the blues" and the "world's greatest blues singer." Smith began her career in 1912 touring with the acclaimed Rabbit Foot Minstrels on the black vaudeville circuit. She not only worked with Ma Rainey but developed a friendship with Rainey that lasted the rest of their lives. In 1913, Smith located in Atlanta, and in the early 1920s moved to Philadelphia. Smith drew audiences in both cities, but to many her voice sounded rough and coarse by the usual standards. Finally, in 1923 Smith had the opportunity to record with Columbia Records, and soon after with Okah and Paramount. Smith's powerful, husky voice soon reached millions via radio and established what is now known as the classic blues style.

ASSESSING THE CHANGES OF THE 1920s

Charlotte Perkins Gilman and Carrie Chapman Catt

Overall, American feminists seemed pleased with their progress. In 1923, only three years after American women obtained the right to vote, Charlotte Perkins Gilman proclaimed that the "breath of woman's new freedom" blew strongly through the land. She cited women's mental and physical development, advances in education, and success in the professions, politics, and independent lifestyles as evidence of "rapid and serious change." In spite of the "new status of women," Gilman reassured worried Americans that "women are first, last and always mothers." Besides, she added, "in our dread of the 'new woman' we should not lose sight of the fact that we never were satisfied with the old kind."

Just four years later, in 1927 a special issue of *Current History* devoted to the topic, "The New Woman," asked former suffragists to comment on changes they had witnessed. Charlotte Perkins Gilman again emphasized the progress of women in politics, reform, jobs and professions, and the development of autonomy, while Carrie Chapman Catt reminded readers that suffrage had been the result of a long and difficult struggle dating back to 1848. Catt added that women wanted the vote to enhance their reform efforts, an ideal that had been partially achieved.

Lingering Barriers

But Gilman and Catt failed to mention lingering barriers. In education, women received one-third of graduate degrees but accounted for only 4 percent of full professors. Quotas determined the number of female students admitted to law and medical schools.

In the work force, women neither caught up with men in wages nor increased significantly in numbers (23 percent of American women held jobs in 1920; 24 percent in 1930). Women workers dominated offices but had to accept low pay and lack of opportunity for advancement. They seldom filled executive, managerial or other high-level positions. In business, women most often succeeded by designing and marketing products for other women.

Even areas that seemed to have undergone drastic revision were often not, upon closer examination, experiencing truly significant change. Most of the women who became members of Congress were widows who had been nominated to take their deceased husbands' congressional places. Women ministers existed, especially in western areas, but remained an exception. And women pilots often gained their jobs because the airline industry hoped to convince passengers they would be as safe in the air as at home with "mother." By the end of the decade, women were more often hired as "hostesses," a job requiring a nursing degree at the time.

Antifeminism

Americans typically believed that women had achieved all their rights. In her autobiography, playwright Lillian Hellman recalled: "By the time I grew up the fight for the emancipation of women, their rights under the law, in the office, in bed, was stale stuff. . . . My generation were not conscious that the designs we saw around us had so recently been formed or that we were still part of that formation." At the same time, Sigmund Freud told women that they would continue to be incomplete and ridden by "penis envy" until they had fulfilled themselves through childbearing.

Other writers and commentators argued that consumerism, fashion, beauty, and sex constituted valid female activities. One even warned women that "the return to the home is going to be almost as long and hard a struggle as the struggle for women's rights." In a 1927 issue of *Harper's Magazine*, journalist Dorothy Dunbar Bromley summed up the situation: "Feminism has become a term of opprobrium to the modern young woman" who "freely admits that American women have so far achieved but little in the arts, sciences, and professions as compared with men." According to Bromley, a "Feminist–New Style" had more interest in individual expression than in "women's" issues and preferred to combine career, marriage, and family.

Modern Femininity: White and Black

During the 1920s, an immense—and also antifeminist—interest developed in beauty, youth, and thinness for women. Advertisements depicted young, slim women doing their housework with the vast array of home appliances now available to them. Such advertisements clearly sent the message that women were most feminine at home, pursuing domestic tasks and consuming commercial goods.

This early version of what would later be termed the feminine mystique also emphasized that artificial means, especially cosmetics, were crucial to a woman's attractiveness. Moreover, an undergarment known as the brassiere was increasingly critical in molding one's figure into an appealing shape. Ida Rosenthal's Maidenform, Inc., first produced the brassiere, reportedly derived from flappers' habit of binding their breasts to look boyish.

In 1921, businesspeople in Atlantic City capitalized on these trends by staging the first Miss America pageant. Although they attempted to emphasize the athletic prowess and wholesome aspects of contestants, the pageant soon took on a coarse side, including a festival atmosphere and charges of bribed judges. The Miss America contest halted in 1927 not to return until 1933, but the idea had taken hold: across the nation Miss New Yorks, Miss American Rodeos, and Miss Cherry Blossoms abounded.

Silent films also reinforced such "feminine" behaviors and values. The 1920s became the age of giant studios, such powerful movie moguls as Louis B. Mayer, and the "star" system. The first female movie heroines emerged during the war years when movie vamp Theda Bara popularized the eye makeup Helena Rubenstein developed for her and Lillian Gish portrayed the girl-next-door. A similar contradiction in female images continued during the 1920s when Clara Bow, the "It Girl," personified the kittenish and sexy flapper and Mary Pickford, "America's Sweetheart," characterized the eternally youthful, innocent, and forever feminine woman.

Two movie stars who especially provided role models for young women, Gloria Swanson and Joan Crawford, played characters exhibiting women's new sexual freedom. According to a 1929 study concerning the impact of films on American youth, Swanson and Crawford established a standard of behavior and appearance for female moviegoers. One sixteen-year-old girl commented that "these modern pictures give me a feeling to imitate their ways. I believe that nothing will happen to the carefree girl like Joan Crawford but it is the quiet girl who is always getting into trouble and making trouble."

Entrepreneurs and advertisers quickly jumped on the bandwagon of invented femininity. Charles Revson and Elizabeth Arden created new cosmetic products that underwrote business empires. Advertisements counseled women watching their weight to "Reach for a Lucky [Strike cigarette] Instead of a Sweet." At the same time, producers of mass media cranked out novels, magazines, radio shows, and films giving Americans the type of women they seemed to want.

Of course, the essence of such ideas of beauty and femininity were Anglo coloring, complexion, and hair. No place existed for women of color in early beauty pageants. This led to many women of color imitating white women. As a case in point, while working for entrepreneur Madam C. J. Walker, Annie Turnbo Malone developed a scalp treatment that straightened hair and a line of other beauty products copyrighted under the business name Poro. The business based on making black women's hair more like that of white women soon became the largest black business in St. Louis, but Malone did use her wealth to promote the status and acceptance of black women. During the 1920s, Malone actively participated in organizations ranging from the Colored Women's Federated Clubs of St. Louis to the Commission on Inter-Racial Cooperation. By the time Malone moved to Chicago in 1930, she had achieved a reputation as a philanthropist, a model for young black women, and one of the world's wealthiest women.

Other Women of Color

In 1929, sociologists Helen Lynd and Robert Lynd studied Muncie, Indiana, for eighteen months. In their report, *Middletown: A Study in American Culture*, the Lynds stated that social class supplied the single most significant determinant of how Americans lived their daily lives. But Muncie was a largely white community. Had the Lynds looked elsewhere they might have viewed race as the most important factor.

American Indian women, for example, now clustered on government reservations and in urban ghettoes. In addition, some scattered rural Indian women worked as domestics and agricultural workers. Everywhere they experienced poverty. In 1915, Kate Luckie deplored the "soreness" of the land that Anglos seemed to create: "the white people plow up the ground, pull up the trees, kill everything." A few years later, a Pima woman rose daily at 3:00 P.M. to prepare beans and stacks of tortillas for the men to eat before working their small forty-acre farm with a horse-drawn plow.

Native American women also fought to retain their status in the face of governmental policies that imposed capitalistic means of production on their societies, both by clinging to old ways and adopting new ones. For example, when the U.S. Agricultural Extension Service established a program to teach New Mexico women canning techniques, Indian women refused to purchase or use jams, jellies, and canned goods. Along with their Chicana neighbors, Native American women preferred the more efficient technique of drying foodstuffs.

At the same time, Native American women formed women's clubs, much like those that Anglo women organized. Among the Ojibway of Minnesota, women founded the First Daughters of America, which met twice monthly to do beading, to knit, to quilt, to study methods of gardening and canning, and to sponsor community projects. It also drew upon the resources offered by Catholic and Episcopal churches, meeting there for family dinners, First Daughters' events, and holiday celebrations.

In Alaska, Indian women also stood together. In 1920, Tlingit women formed the Alaska Native Sisterhood, which brought together local women's clubs. Although the Sisterhood initially supported the programs of the Alaska Native Brotherhood, they soon developed their own agenda, including lobbying the Alaska Territorial government and U.S. Congress to preserve native cultural identity, protect native fishing grounds, and settle land claims.

Similarly, Spanish-speaking women and their descendants struggled to preserve their language and culture, which now included diverse Latin American heritages. In New York City, for example, a growing number of Puerto Rican men migrated to seek work as cigarmakers, shoemakers, and industrial workers, while women migrated primarily as domestic servants and cooks. Puerto Ricans usually formed *colonias,* especially in Harlem and Brooklyn. Here, a small Puerto Rican professional class served the communities and provided leadership, and women of the *colonias* attempted to conserve the Puerto Rican legacy. As a case in point, Pura Belpré, the first Puerto Rican librarian in the New York Public Library system, initiated Puerto Rican cultural projects, including storytelling sessions.

In addition, during the war years and after, continuing turmoil in Mexico, combined with the demand for unskilled labor in North America, prompted massive immigration to the United States. Migrants lived primarily in Arizona, California, New Mexico, and Texas, but during the 1920s, they also fanned out over the Midwest, working as industrial and agricultural laborers, especially for railroads, in steel mills and automobile plants, and in sugar beet fields. Women and children of the migrant families often worked as well, especially in canneries and the fields, where they endured inadequate nutrition, poor sanitary conditions, and the continued scattering of their extended families.

Meanwhile, American hostility to Asians continued to flower. In 1920, 40 percent of the Chinese population lived in San Francisco and New York, usually segregated in urban businesses and industry. Although gender still largely determined women's role, such customs as foot-binding and total seclusion had nearly disappeared. Because so few Chinese women obtained permission to immigrate by 1930, 80 percent of the Chinese population were men, who typically took refuge in Chinatowns, now residential communities and tourist centers.

Unlike Chinese immigrants, the majority of Japanese often worked as migratory laborers in agriculture, canneries, and for railroads. Others established themselves as small farmers. In urban areas, both Issei (first generation Japanese) and Nisei (second generation) grouped in sections referred to as Little Tokyos. Women usually divided their time between domestic duties and work, often helping in family businesses, or holding wage jobs in domestic service or factories. Women of the upper classes, usually wives of merchants, spent a greater proportion of their time on domestic activities.

Smaller groups of Asians, including Filipinos, Asian Indians, and Koreans, also migrated to the United States. In 1920, the 5,603 Filipinos who lived in the mainland United States could claim American citizenship as a result of the transfer of the Phillipines to U.S. ownership due to the Spanish-American War. In that same year, 6,400 Asian Indians and 1,677 Koreans lived in the United States. Of the Koreans, 75 percent were male. Women migrated primarily as "picture brides," that is, through the custom of arranged marriage. Among Asian agricultural workers, women ran kitchens and laundries, or worked in the fields alongside men. Like other women, they also attempted to maintain their own language and culture.

When the catastrophic stock-market crash of 1929 ended the era of World War I and the 1920s, the national scene had clearly altered. Such factors as widespread disillusionment with the outcome of World War I, fear of Bolshevism, women's entry into the political arena, and prohibition had reshaped American ideas, values and society.

But were American laws, policies, and expectations regarding women significantly different? Probably not. Too many of the changes originated in wartime emergency and could be easily rescinded. Others were only anticipated—what suffrage *could* bring and what women officeholders *might* achieve. And, even though the 1920s appeared radical in many ways, people could not transform themselves or their society overnight.

Still, even though changes might be more apparent than real, they *were* in place. Anticlimactic as they might in some ways seem, such innovations as woman suffrage, the antilynching movement, and birth control provided not only giant steps forward but building blocks for the future.

Suggestions for Further Reading

Allen, Michael. "The Rise and Decline of the Early Rodeo Cowgirl: the Career of Mabel Strickland, 1916–1941," *Pacific Northwest Quarterly* 83 (October 1992): 122–27.

Alonso, Harriet Hyman. "Jeannette Rankin and the Women's Peace Union," *Montana the Magazine of Western History* 29 (Spring 1989): 34–49.

Alpern, Sara, and Dale Baum. "Female Ballots: The Impact of the Nineteenth Amendment," *Journal of Interdisciplinary History*, 16 (Summer 1985): 43–67.

Banner, Lois. *American Beauty*. New York: Alfred A. Knopf, 1983.

Barnet, Evelyn Brooks. "Nannie Burroughs and the Education of Black Women," 97–108, in *The Afro-American Woman: Struggles and Images*, edited by Sharon Harley and Rosalyn Terborg-Penn. Port Washington, New York: Kennikat Press, 1978.

Baxandall, Rosalyn, Linda Gordon, and Susan Reverby, eds. *America's Working Women*. New York: Random House, 1976.

Becker, Susan D. *The Origins of the Equal Rights Amendment: American Feminism Between the Wars*. Westport, CT: Greenwood Press, 1981.

Benson, Susan Porter. *Counter Cultures: Saleswomen, Managers, and Customers in American Department Stores, 1890–1940*. Urbana: University of Illinois Press, 1988.

Berkin, Carol Ruth, and Mary Beth Norton, eds. *Women of America: A History*. Boston: Houghton Mifflin Company, 1979. Chapters 11–12, 14.

Blee, Kathleen M. *Women of the Klan: Racism and Gender in the 1920s*. Berkeley: University of California Press, 1991.

Blewett, Mary H. *The Last Generation: Work and Life in the Textile Mills of Lowell, Massachusetts, 1910–1960*. Amherst: University of Massachusetts Press, 1990.

Brady, Marilyn Dell. "Kansas Federation of Colored Women's Clubs, 1900–1930," *Kansas History* 9 (Spring 1986): 19–31.

Breen, William J. "Black Women and the Great War: Mobilization and Reform in the South," *Journal of Southern History* 44 (August 1978): 421–40.

Broker, Ignatia. *Night Flying Woman: An Ojibway Narrative*. St. Paul: Minnesota Historical Society Press, 1983.

Brown, Dorothy M. *Setting a Course: American Women in the 1920s*. Boston: Twayne, 1987.

Buhle, Mari Jo, and Paul Buhle, eds. *The Concise History of Woman Suffrage: Selections from the Classic Work of Stanton, Anthony, Gage, and Harper*. Urbana: University of Illinois Press, 1979.

Carby, Hazel V. "It Jus Be's Dat Way Sometime: The Sexual Politics of Women's Blues," *Radical America* 20 (1986): 9–24.

Chalfen, Richard. *Turning Leaves: The Photograph Collections of Two Japanese American Families*. Albuquerque: University of New Mexico Press, 1991.

Chan, Sucheng. *Entry Denied: Exclusion and the Chinese Community in America, 1882–1943*. Philadelphia: Temple University Press, 1991.

Chesler, Ellen. *Woman of Valor: Margaret Sanger and the Birth Control Movement in America*. New York: Simon & Schuster, 1992.

Coburn, Carol K. "Learning to Serve: Education and Change in the Lives of Rural Domestics in the Twentieth Century," *Journal of Social History* 25 (Fall 1991): 109–22.

———. *Life at Four Corners: Religion, Gender, and Education in a German-Lutheran Community, 1868–1945*. Lawrence, University Press of Kansas, 1992.

Conner, Valerie J. "'The Mothers of the Race' in World War I: The National War Labor Board and Women in Industry," *Labor History* 21 (Winter 1979–80): 31–54.

Conway, Jill. "Women Reformers and American Culture, 1870–1930," *Journal of Social History* 5 (Winter 1971–72): 164–77.

Corn, Joseph J. "Making Flying 'Thinkable': Women Pilots and the Selling of Aviation, 1827–1940," *American Quarterly* 31 (Fall 1979): 556–71.

Cott, Nancy F. "Feminist Politics in the 1920s: The National Woman's Party," *Journal of American History* 71 (June 1984): 43–68.

Davis, Ronald L. *Hollywood Beauty: Linda Darnell and the American Dream*. Norman: University of Oklahoma Press, 1991.

Davis, Thadious M. *Nella Larsen, Novelist of the Harlem Renaissance: A Woman's Life Unveiled*. Baton Rouge: Louisiana State University Press, 1993.

Downey, Betsy. "Battered Pioneers: Jules Sandoz and the Physical Abuse of Wives on the American Frontier," *Great Plains Quarterly* 12 (Winter 1992): 31–49.

DuBois, Ellen Carol. "The Radicalism of the Woman Suffrage Movement: Notes Toward the Reconstruction of Nineteenth-Century Feminism," *Feminist Studies* 3 (Fall 1975): 63–71.

Easton, Patricia O'Keefe. "Woman Suffrage in South Dakota: The Final Decade, 1911–1920," *South Dakota History* 13 (Fall 1983): 206–26.

Evans, Sara M. *Born for Liberty: A History of Women in America*. New York: Free Press, 1989. Chapter 8.

Ewen, Elizabeth. *Immigrant Women in the Land of Dollars: Life and Culture on the Lower East Side, 1890–1925*. New York: Monthly Review Press, 1985.

Fine, Lisa M. "Between Two Worlds: Business Women in a Chicago Boarding House, 1900–1930," *Journal of Social History* 19 (Spring 1986): 511–20.

———. *The Souls of the Skyscraper: Female Clerical Workers in Chicago, 1870–1930*. Philadelphia: Temple University Press, 1990.

Finn, Barbara R. "Anna Howard Shaw and Women's Work," *Frontiers* 4 (Fall 1979): 21–25.

Foner, Philip S. *Women and the American Labor Movement: From World War I to the Present*. New York: The Free Press, 1980.

Friedman, Jean E., William G. Shade, and Mary Jane Capozzoli, eds. *Our American Sisters: Women in American Life and Thought*. 4th ed. Lexington, MA: D.C. Heath and Company, 1987. Chapter 20.

Geidel, Peter. "The National Woman's Party and the Origins of the Equal Rights Amendment, 1920–1923," *The Historian* 42 (August 1980): 557–82.

Gertzog, Irwin N. "The Matrimonial Connection: The Nomination of Congressmen's Widows for the House of Representatives," *Journal of Politics* 42 (August 1980): 820–33.

Glazer, Penina M., and Miriam Slater. *Unequal Colleagues: The Entrance of Women into the Professions, 1890–1940*. New Brunswick, NJ: Rutgers University Press, 1987.

Glenn, Evelyn Nakano. "The Dialectics of Wage Work: Japanese-American Women and Domestic Service, 1905–1940,". *Feminist Studies* 6 (September 1980): 432–71.

———. "Occupational Ghettoization: Japanese Women and Domestic Service, 1905–1970," *Ethnicity* 8 (December 1981): 352–86.

Golden, Claudia. *Understanding the Gender Gap: An Economic History of American Women*. New York: Oxford University Press, 1990.

Gordon, Linda. *Woman's Body, Woman's Right: A Social History of Birth Control in America*. New York: Grossman Publishers, 1976.

Graebner, William. "'Uncle Sam Just Loves the Ladies': Sex Discrimination in the Federal Government, 1917," *Labor History* 21 (Winter 1979–80): 75–85.

Graham, Sally Hunter. "Woodrow Wilson, Alice Paul, and the Woman Suffrage Movement," *Political Science Quarterly* 98 (Winter 1983–84): 665–80.

Greenwald, Maurine Weiner. *Women, War, and Work: The Impact of World War I on Women Workers in the United States*. Westport, CT: Greenwood Press, 1980.

———. "Working Class Feminism and the Family Wage Ideal: The Seattle Debate on Married Women's Right to Work, 1914–1920," *Journal of American History* 76 (June 1989): 118–50.

Hall, Jacquelyn Dowd. "Disorderly Women: Gender and Labor Militancy in the Appalachian South," *Journal of American History* 73 (September 1986): 354–82.

———. "Private Eyes, Public Women: Images of Class and Sex in the Urban South, Atlanta, Georgia, 1913–1915," *Atlanta History* 36 (Winter 1993): 24–39.

Hamilton, Michael S. "Women, Public Ministry, and American Fundamentalism, 1920–1950," *Religion and American Culture* 3 (Summer 1993): 283–303.

Harrison, Daphne Duval. "Black Women in the Blues Tradition," 58–73, in *The Afro-American Woman: Struggles and Images*, edited by Sharon Harley and Rosalyn Terborg-Penn. Port Washington: Kennikat Press, 1978.

———. *Black Pearls: Blues Queens of the 1920s*. New Brunswick, NJ: Rutgers University Press, 1988.

Hewitt, Nancy A., ed. *Women, Families, and Communities: Readings in American History*. Part II. Glenview, IL: Scott, Foresman, 1990. Part 4.

Higonnet, Margaret R., Jane Jenson, Sonya Michel, and Margaret C. Weitz, eds. *Behind the Lines: Gender and the Two World Wars*. New Haven, CT: Yale University Press, 1987.

Hinckley, Ted C. "Glimpses of Societal Change Among Nineteenth-Century Tlingit Women," *Journal of the West* 33 (July 1993): 12–24.

Hine, Darlene Clark. *Black Women in White: Racial Conflict and Cooperation in the Nursing Profession, 1890–1950*. Bloomington: Indiana University Press, 1989.

Horowitz, Daniel. *The Morality of Spending: Attitudes Toward the Consumer Society in America, 1875–1940*. Chicago: Ivan R. Dee, Inc., 1993.

Ichioka, Yuji. "*Amerika Nadeshiko*: Japanese Immigrant Women in the United States, 1900–1924," *Pacific Historical Review* 49 (May 1980): 339–58.

Jaros, Dean. *Heroes Without Legacy: American Airwomen, 1912–1944*. Niwot: University Press of Colorado, 1993.

Jensen, Billie Barnes. "'In the Weird and Wooly West': Anti-Suffrage Women, Gender Issues, and Woman Suffrage in the West," *Journal of the West* 32 (July 1993): 41–51.

Jensen, Joan M. "The Evolution of Margaret Sanger's Family Limitation Pamphlet, 1914–1921," *Signs* 6 (Spring 1981): 548–55.

———. "Canning Comes to New Mexico: Women and the Agricultural Extension Service, 1914–1919," *New Mexico Historical Review* 57 (October 1982): 361–86.

Jensen, Joan M., and Lois Scharf, eds. *Decades of Discontent: The Women's Movement, 1920–1940*. Westport, CT: Greenwood Press, 1983.

Johnson, David L., and Raymond Wilson. "Gertrude Simmons Bonnin, 1876–1938: 'Americanize the First Americans,'" *American Indian Quarterly* 12 (Winter 1988): 130–43.

Jones, Beverly Washington. *Quest for Equality: The Life and Writings of Mary Eliza Church Terrell, 1863–1954*. Brooklyn: Carlson Publishing, 1990.

Kerber, Linda K., and Jane DeHart Mathews, eds. *Women's America: Refocusing the Past*. New York: Oxford University Press, 1982. Part IIB.

Kessler-Harris, Alice. *Out to Work: A History of Wage-earning Women in the United States*. New York: Oxford University Press, 1982.

Koester, Susan H. "'By the Words of the Mouth Let Thee Be Judged': The Alaska Native Sisterhood Speaks," *Journal of the West* 27 (April 1988): 35–44.

Krause, Corinne Azen. "Urbanization Without Breakdown: Italian, Jewish, and Slavic Immigrant Women in Pittsburgh, 1900–1945," *Journal of Urban History* 4 (May 1978): 291–305.

Ladd-Taylor, Molly. *Mother-Work: Women, Child Welfare, and the State, 1890–1930*. Champaign, University of Illinois Press, 1994.

Landsman, Gail H. "The 'Other' as Political Symbol: Images of Indians in the Woman Suffrage Movement," *Ethnohistory* 39 (Summer 1992): 247–84.

LeCompte, Mary Lou. *Cowgirls of the Rodeo: Pioneer Professional Athletes*. Champaign: University of Illinois Press, 1993.

Lemons, J. Stanley. *The Woman Citizen: Social Feminism in the 1920s*. Charlottesville: University Press of Virginia, 1990.

Levine, Susan. "Workers' Wives: Gender, Class, and Consumerism in the 1920s United States," *Gender and History* 3 (Spring 1991): 45–64.

Lieb, Sandra R. *Mother of the Blues: A Study of Ma Rainey*. Amherst: University of Massachusetts Press, 1984.

Lunardini, Christine A., and Thomas J. Knock. "Woodrow Wilson and Woman Suffrage: A New Look," *Political Science Quarterly* 95 (Winter 1980–81): 655–71.

———. *From Equal Suffrage to Equal Rights: Alice Paul and the National Woman's Party, 1910–1928*. New York: New York University Press, 1986.

Martelet, Penny. "The Woman's Land Army, World War I," 136–46, in *Clio Was a Woman: Studies in the History of American Women*, edited by Mabel E. Deutrich and Virginia C. Purdy. Washington, DC: Howard University Press, 1980.

Martin, Patricia Precíado, ed. *Images and Conversations: Mexican Americans Recall a Southwestern Past*. Tucson: University of Arizona Press, 1983.

May, Elaine Tyler. *Great Expectations: Marriage and Divorce in Post-Victorian America*. Chicago: University of Chicago Press, 1981.

McDonagh, Eileen L., and H. Douglas Price. "Woman Suffrage in the Progressive Era: Patterns of Opposition and Support in Referenda Voting, 1910–1918," *American Political Science Review* 79 (June 1985): 415–35.

Meyerowitz, Joanne J. *Women Adrift: Independent Wage Earners in Chicago, 1880–1930*. Chicago: University of Chicago Press, 1988.

Muncy, Robyn. *Creating a Female Dominion in American Reform*. New York: Oxford University Press, 1991.

Norwood, Stephen H. *Labor's Flaming Youth: Telephone Operators and Worker Militancy, 1878–1923*. Urbana: University of Illinois Press, 1990.

Perry, Elisabeth Israels. *Belle Moskowitz: Feminine Politics and the Exercise of Power in the Age of Alfred E. Smith*. New York: Oxford University Press, 1987.

———. "Women's Political Choices After Suffrage: The Women's City Club of New York, 1915–1990," *New York History* 71 (October 1990): 417–34.

Pleck, Elizabeth H. "Challenges to Traditional Authority in Immigrant Families," 482–503, in *The American Family in Social-historical Perspective*, edited by Michael Gordon. New York: St. Martin's Press, 1983.

Rakow, Lana F. *Gender on the Line: Women, the Telephone, and Community Life*. Urbana: University of Illinois Press, 1992.

Rodríguez, Clara E. *Puerto Ricans: Born in the U.S.A.*. Boston: Unwin Hyman, 1989.

Rosen, Marjorie. *Popcorn Venus: Women, Movies and the American Dream*. New York: Avon Books, 1973.

Rossiter, Margaret W. *Women Scientists in America: Struggles and Strategies to 1940*. Baltimore: Johns Hopkins University Press, 1982.

Rushing, Andrea Benton. "Images of Black Women in Afro-American Poetry," 74–86, in *The Afro-American Woman: Struggles and Images*, edited by Sharon Harley and Rosalyn Terborg-Penn. Port Washington: Kennikat Press, 1978.

Sánchez, George J. "'Go After the Women': Americanization and the Mexican Immigrant Woman, 1915–1929," 284–97, in *Unequal Sisters: A Multicultural Reader in U.S. Women's History*, edited by Vicki L. Ruiz and Ellen Carol DuBois. 2d ed. New York: Routledge, 1994.

Scharff, Virginia. *Taking the Wheel: Women and the Coming of the Motor Age*. New York: Free Press, 1991.

Scott, Anne Firor. *Making the Invisible Woman Visible*. Urbana: University of Illinois Press, 1984.

Seller, Maxine Schwartz, ed. *Immigrant Women*. Philadelphia: Temple University Press, 1981.

Shaw, Stephanie J. "Black Club Women and the Creation of the National Association of Colored Women," *Journal of Women's History* 3 (Fall 1991): 1290–91.

Sklar, Kathryn Kish, and Thomas Dublin, eds. *Women and Power in American History: A Reader*. Vol. II. Englewood Cliffs, NJ: Prentice Hall, 1991. Parts 6–13.

Steinson, Barbara J. "'The Mother Half of Humanity': American Women in the Peace and Preparedness Movements in World War I," 259–84, in *Women, War, and Revolution*, edited by Carol R. Berkin and Clara M. Lovett. New York: Holmes and Meier, Inc., 1980.

Stephens, Sandra L. "The Women of the Amador Family, 1860–1940," 257–78, in *New Mexico Women: Intercultural Perspectives*, edited by Joan M. Jensen and Darlis A. Miller. Albuquerque: University of New Mexico Press, 1986.

Strom, Sharon Hartman. "Leadership and Tactics in the American Woman Suffrage Movement: A New Perspective from Massachusetts." *Journal of American History* 12 (September 1975): 296–315.

———. *Beyond the Typewriter: Gender, Class, and the Origins of Modern American Office Work, 1900–1930*. Champaign: University of Illinois Press, 1992.

Takaki, Ronald. *Strangers from a Different Shore: A History of Asian Americans*. New York: Little, Brown, 1989.

Tentler, Leslie Woodcock. *Wage-Earning Women: Industrial Work and Family Life in the United States, 1900–1930*. New York: Oxford University Press, 1979.

Terborg-Penn, Rosalynn. "Discontented Black Feminists: Prelude and Postscript to the Passage of the Nineteenth Amendment," 262–78, in *Decades of Discontent: The Women's Movement, 1920–1940*, edited by Joan M. Jensen and Lois Scharf. Westport, CT: Greenwood Press, 1983.

Thomas, Mary Martha. *The New Woman in Alabama: Social Reforms and Suffrage, 1890–1920*. Tuscaloosa: University of Alabama Press, 1992.

———. "The Ideology of the Alabama Woman Suffrage Movement, 1890–1920," 109–28, in *Southern Women: Histories and Identities*, edited by Virginia Bernhard, Betty Brandon, Elizabeth Fox-Genovese, and Theda Perdue. Columbia: University of Missouri Press, 1992.

Todd, Ellen Wiley. *The "New Woman" Revised: Painting and Gender Politics on Fourteenth Street*. Berkeley: University of California Press, 1993.

Tucker, Cynthia Grant. *Prophetic Sisterhood: Liberal Women Ministers of the Frontier, 1880–1930*. Boston: Beacon Press, 1990.

Turner, Elizabeth Hayes. "'White-Gloved Ladies' and 'New Women' in the Texas Woman Suffrage Movement," 129–56, in *Southern Women: Histories and Identities*, edited by Virginia Bernhard, Betty Brandon, Elizabeth Fox-Genovese, and Theda Perdue. Columbia: University of Missouri Press, 1992.

Van Rapphorst, Donna L. *Union Maid Not Wanted: Organizing Domestic Workers, 1870–1940*. New York: Praeger, 1988.

Vargas, Zaragosa. "Armies in the Fields and Factories: The Mexican Working Classes in the Midwest in the 1920s," *Mexican Studies/Estudios Mexicanos* 7 (Winter 1991): 47–71.

Ware, Susan. *Still Missing: Amelia Earhart and the Search for Modern Feminism*. New York: W. W. Norton & Co., 1993.

Wheeler, Marjorie Spruill. *The New Women of the New South: The Leaders of the Woman Suffrage Movement in the Southern States*. New York: Oxford University Press, 1993.

Wilson, Joan Hoff. "Jeanette Rankin and American Foreign Policy: Her Life Work as a Pacifist," *Montana the Magazine of Western History* 30 (Spring 1980): 38–53.

Wolf, Beverly Hungry. *The Ways of My Grandmothers*. New York: William Morrow and Co., Inc., 1980.

Woloch, Nancy. *Women and the American Experience.* New York: Alfred A. Knopf, 1984. Chapters 13–16.

Yang, Eun Sik. "Korean Women of America: From Subordination to Partnership, 1903–1930," *Amerasia* 2 (Fall/Winter 1984): 1–28.

Young, Louise M. *In the Public Image: The League of Women Voters, 1920–1970.* Westport, CT: Greenwood Press, 1989.

Making Do and Pitching In
The Depression and World War II

8

After the stock market collapsed during the fall of 1929, the American economy crumbled. The controversial New Deal soon emerged; then, barely on its feet again, the reconstructed nation became embroiled in the largest and most destructive war in history. The years between the beginning of the Great Depression in 1929 and the end of World War II in 1945 were indeed trying ones. Most people felt unnerved and uncertain. Did economic forces drive their lives? How much could political action achieve? What was the role of human agency? Was democracy any longer viable?

Because former certainties regarding these questions now seemed meaningless, people set out to reconstruct their lives and beliefs. In the process, women contributed their skills and energies in the home, workplace, and military to help the nation endure. As a result, traditional gender expectations and the forces that underlay them also wavered and modified, at least temporarily.

THE GREAT DEPRESSION OF THE 1930s

The Stock Market Crash of 1929

When the stock market plunged to the depths in October and November of 1929, the crash brought fads, fashions, American prosperity, and even individual lives to an end. One former flapper discovered her father hanging from the end of a rope, one of many apparent suicides to escape economic ruin.

The situation rapidly worsened. Between 1930 to 1933, 5,504 banks closed their doors, while the national banking system teetered on the

brink of collapse. Meanwhile, in 1932, American voters desperate for relief from economic distress carried Franklin Delano Roosevelt into the
presidency. Having lost faith in President Herbert Hoover's policies, they
felt willing to take a chance on Roosevelt's ideas. After the 1932 election,
journalist Anne O'Hare McCormick wrote, "Now the question is: Where
are we? What's the government going to do?"

McCormick concluded that this may be "our last chance to prove that
there is initiative enough left in democracy to make it worth saving." But
Roosevelt faced a panoply of intricate, seemingly unsolvable problems,
many involving the nation's women.

Unemployed Women

For women of color, a majority of whom held the lowest-paid jobs in
the United States, the depression hit fast and hard. In 1929, nearly 40 percent of black women and girls were in the workforce, almost two-thirds
in domestic service and agriculture. By 1931, more than one-quarter of
these black wage-earning women had lost their jobs. Because employers
fired women of color first, this figure represented a far higher rate of job
loss than that suffered by Anglo women. As the depression worsened,
over half of black women lost their jobs, while three out of ten white
women did so.

Throughout the 1930s, black women had to tolerate higher rates of
unemployment than did white women. Black women could not even
turn to the old standby of domestic service because the number of these
jobs had declined rapidly, while unemployed Anglo women had taken
some of the remaining jobs in domestic service. Barred from clerical, sales,
and factory jobs because of their race, many black women found themselves with no employment opportunities at all. To make matters worse,
relief and welfare programs designed to aid males whom society expected
to be "breadwinners" often excluded black women workers.

Women of color coped by using a strategy of downward mobility—
that is, they took whatever jobs they could get. Rural black women often
left their homes, migrating in larger numbers than black men to urban
areas in search of employment. Urban black women also became small-
scale entrepreneurs, peddling such goods as home-baked bread or home-
raised vegetables on the streets or door to door. Urban black women also
responded to economic hard times by gathering into so-called slave markets on street corners each morning, where they offered their labor to the
highest bidder on an hourly basis, often for as little as ten cents an hour.
In New York City, an observer noted that hundreds of "forlorn and half-
starved" girls were lucky to find a few hours' work one or two days each
week.

Throughout the 1930s, such poverty-stricken and desperate black
women frequently had to call upon various governmental agencies for as-

sistance. Their stories often revolved around racial discrimination in hiring. In 1941, a Chicago woman wrote directly to President Franklin D. Roosevelt: "We are citizens just as much or more than the majority of this country." She continued, "this is supposed to be a free country regardless of color, creed or race but still we are slaves. . . . Won't you help us?" The objective of these women was a simple one—to get the President to create jobs that would be available to blacks, just as he had done for whites.

By 1933, the year Roosevelt was inaugurated as President of the United States, over 25 percent of American workers were unemployed, a phenomenon that affected not just working-class families, but middle-class families as well. One college-educated, middle-class woman described the terrors confronting those whose "normal" lives the depression had interrupted. She and her husband both lost their jobs in 1933 shortly before their first child was due. They spent their last twelve dollars on a rat-infested, leaky, cold apartment.

This couple turned to the Emergency Home Relief Bureau for help. After numerous investigations and delays, they received woefully small checks. Their baby was born in a public ward, and the mother returned home weak from inadequate care and poor food. She and her husband devoted all their time to searching for work, begging for relief, and carrying home coal and other necessities, all on one meal a day so that their sickly baby could have milk. "We feel ourselves always on the edge of a precipice," she wrote, "with nothing to save us, sooner or later, from the abyss."

Employed Women

In 1930, 22 percent of American workers were female. Pushed now by economic necessity, women took whatever jobs they could find, thus driving this figure up to over 25 percent by 1940. During the 1930s, approximately three out of every ten female workers held clerical and sales positions, two were factory operatives, two were in domestic service, one was a professional (usually a teacher or a nurse), and one worked in a service job.

For such labor, women continued to receive low wages. During the early 1930s, a woman could earn an average of $525 yearly, while men could collect $1,027. The typical domestic worker earned only $312.60 per year. In addition, because such employment often stood between them and starvation, female workers often tolerated long hours, poor working conditions, and abusive treatment from employers and supervisors.

The Right-to-Work Issue

Married women who were employed especially encountered antipathy toward them. Public opinion, as well as leaders of such male-dominated unions as the American Federation of Labor, favored all available positions going to men rather than to married women. Union leaders argued that because men had to support families while women, it was supposed, did not, jobs should naturally go to men. People still believed that women worked only for "pin-money" rather than to support themselves or their families. Moreover, some people feared the role reversals that occurred in families in which men held only marginal employment or none at all while women worked and provided the family's primary support. Others pointed out that wife- and child-abuse had increased because of the strain on such families.

Public hostility resulted in laws effectively barring married female workers from certain jobs. For instance, under the Economy Act of 1933 two members of the same family could no longer hold positions in federal governmental service. Although such groups as the League of Women Voters and the National Women's Party protested, these policies forced a significant number of workers, three-fourths of whom were female, to resign.

State and local governments also refused to employ married women. In 1931, three out of four school boards prohibited the hiring of married female teachers. In that year, one New York official branded the employment of married women "reprehensible" and called upon "our federal, state and local governments" to cooperate in removing "these undeserving parasites." Soon, even women's colleges urged their graduates to forego paid employment.

Despite such opposition, the number of wage-earning married women increased during the 1930s. In 1930, 11.7 percent of married women held jobs; by 1940, 15.3 percent did so. Married women worked for myriad reasons. Some held paid jobs because their husbands earned inadequate wages or were unemployed. Others held jobs to supplement their family's income, but some worked because they preferred to do so. Because necessity was virtually the only socially acceptable reason for women to work, even women who worked for other reasons tended to use necessity as a rationale.

The Women's Bureau pointed out that denying a woman the right to work posed a potential threat to all citizens who also might be refused employment. Similarly, the Business and Professional Women's Clubs declared in its newspaper, *Independent Woman*, that it was important to fight for "the freedom to seek self-realization," a freedom "that men and women should guard jealously." In addition, the League of Women Voters actively opposed nepotism rules in the federal civil service, and other legislation that barred married women from jobs.

Despite these efforts, little public sympathy developed for married women workers, except those who worked out of dire want. On more than one occasion, the *Ladies' Home Journal* reflected the widespread sentiment that women should hold paid employment only when absolutely necessary. As one *Journal* editorial observed, women who deserved to hold paid jobs had "no selfish desire for a career . . . simply the pressure of financial need."

Women in the Professions

Another major issue concerning employed women during the depression years revolved around their continued participation in the professions. As job opportunities tightened, many men expressed interest in entering such fields as teaching where women were in the majority of available positions. These male teachers initially displaced married women teachers, then blocked young single women from teaching jobs as well. As a consequence, men, who at the beginning of the 1930s accounted for 19 percent of all teachers, comprised 24.3 percent of teachers at the end of the decade. At the same time, the number of men enrolled in teacher-training programs rose from 31 to 40 percent of total enrollments.

Because similar developments occurred in the other professions, the proportion of women in them fell from 14.2 percent in 1930 to 12.3 percent by the end of the decade. Women lost ground in medicine, law, science, and university teaching. In nursing, social work, and librarianship, the trend toward feminization halted. The decline of women in these fields created a multiplier effect; that is, once female role models decreased, fewer women aspired to these positions. Concomitantly, the proportion of women in the nation's college enrollment dropped from 43.7 percent in 1930 to 40.2 percent by 1940. Instead of pursuing professions and careers, women moved into clerical, sales, and similar jobs lower on the economic and status scale.

The Women's New Deal

After Roosevelt assumed the presidency in 1933, his "New Deal" created such new agencies as the National Industrial Recovery Act (NIRA), the Agricultural Adjustment Act, the Works Progress Administration (WPA), and the Civilian Conservation Corps (CCC). Although no evidence exists that he intended specifically to do so, Roosevelt also devised a New Deal for women.

In 1933, for example, Congress established the Federal Emergency Relief Administration (FERA), which gave federal funds to states for distribution to individual recipients, of whom 12 percent were women. In that same year, Congress also approved the Civil Works Administration (CWA) to pursue large-scale construction projects. Before its termination in March 1934, the CWA hired approximately 300,000 women in lighter jobs and clerical positions. In 1935, the Works Progress Administration (WPA) also began a number of building projects, and hired women in research, health and nutrition, clerical, and library positions. The WPA also funded the Federal Art Project, which hired artists to paint murals in public buildings. The Music, Theater, and Writers Projects also employed women. Some 400,000 women benefited from WPA programs at its peak.

Also in 1933, the NIRA established maximum hour and minimum wage guidelines for both men and women workers. In addition, it limited and regulated industrial piecework done in the home. When in 1935 the Supreme Court declared this legislation unconstitutional, Congress replaced it with the Fair Labor Standards Act of 1938, which reaffirmed maximum-hour and minimum-wage standards.

The program aimed most directly at women, however, was the Social Security Act of 1935, which included the Aid to Dependent Children (ADC) program. Among other provisions, ADC furnished maternity care for expectant women who were poor and pediatric treatment for babies and other children.

Women of color fared less well with New Deal programs. The various WPA projects hired women of color, but in far smaller numbers than they hired Anglo women. Moreover, although they were eligible for ADC, many women of color felt degraded by what they thought of as "charity."

Besides fostering New Deal legislation beneficial to women, President Roosevelt helped women challenge customary gender expectations in three additional ways. The most basic of these was his favorable attitude toward women in public service, gained during his years in New York state government. He willingly trusted women with important policy-making positions and appointed significant numbers of women to high-level jobs. Some of the better known of these were Frances Perkins as secretary of labor, Ellen Sullivan Woodward as head of women's and professional projects for the WPA, Josephine Roche as assistant secretary of the treasury, Nellie Tayloe Ross as director of the mint, Marion Glass Banister as assistant treasurer of the United States, and Lucille Foster McMillin as civil service commissioner. In the diplomatic field, Ruth Bryan Owen served as minister to Denmark between 1933 and 1936, while Florence Jaffray Harriman was ambassador to Norway between 1937 and 1941. Moreover, many of Roosevelt's appointments of women were "firsts": first woman cabinet member, first woman director of the mint, and first woman ambassador.

A second technique Roosevelt used that shaped the women's New Deal was expanding governmental services and initiating a wide variety of social welfare programs that demanded trained social workers to administer them. From the Consumer's League, the Women's Trade Union League, and a wide variety of other reform organizations came trained women eager to tackle governmental assignments. Women had decades of experience in being the "moral housekeepers" of society; now the New Deal offered them the chance to apply their expertise on a national scope.

A third way that Roosevelt built a women's New Deal was by introducing his wife, Eleanor—an important presence in her own right—to the Washington scene. Already a crusader for women's issues, black Americans, and the poor, Eleanor Roosevelt soon became the social conscience of America. In addition, she provided access to the president for scores of women. As one of Eleanor Roosevelt's colleagues said, "When I wanted help on some definite point, Mrs. Roosevelt gave me the opportunity to sit by the President at dinner and the matter was settled before we finished our soup."

Eleanor Roosevelt

Eleanor Roosevelt, clearly the most active First Lady to date, came to this position by a circuitous route. Born to a wealthy and prestigious New York couple in 1884, she had lost both her parents by the time she was ten years old. Raised by her maternal grandmother, she lived a lonely life. When she was eighteen years of age, Eleanor initiated her lifelong commitment to social reform by joining Florence Kelley's National Consumers' League. As she visited workplaces, Roosevelt observed firsthand the hardships endured by working women. At the same time, she participated in the Junior League and the Rivington Street Settlement House in New York.

In 1905, Eleanor Roosevelt married a distant cousin, Franklin Roosevelt. Because Franklin's mother Sara dominated the household, Eleanor's feelings of inadequacy as a wife and mother duplicated those she had felt as an ungainly young girl. When Franklin gained election as Democratic assemblyperson from Dutchess County, New York, in 1910, Eleanor sought fulfillment in contributing to her husband's political career. Later, after Franklin's appointment as assistant secretary of the navy in 1913, Eleanor developed expertise in orchestrating social and political gatherings. But once World War I began, Eleanor Roosevelt resumed with a passion her interest in welfare work and social reform.

After World War I, Eleanor Roosevelt became active in the League of Women Voters and the Women's Trade Union League. When polio struck Franklin in 1921, Eleanor acted as his political representative. At the Democratic National Convention of 1924, she worked for platform planks supporting equal pay, child-labor legislation, and other women's reform issues. By 1928, Eleanor Roosevelt had built a wide reputation as a reformer and politician.

When Franklin ran for the presidency in 1932, Eleanor coordinated the activities of the Women's Division of the Democratic National Committee. Along with her friend and Democratic colleague, Molly (Mary) Dewson, she mobilized huge numbers of women activists as potential administration members. Once she became First Lady, Eleanor toured the country observing the condition of workers, visiting relief projects, and speaking on behalf of human rights. Beginning in 1936, Roosevelt also wrote a syndicated newspaper column called "My Day," and she reached millions of other Americans through radio programs.

Despite the fact that the marriage between Franklin and Eleanor had collapsed in 1918 because of his involvement with Lucy Mercer, the two were able to work together as a political team. Although she offered to divorce him, the Roosevelts had decided to stay together. Personally, Eleanor Roosevelt's emotional energies poured into close relationships with women. Publicly, Roosevelt devoted her vigor and growing influence to reform causes.

Eleanor Roosevelt was a conservative feminist who had not believed in suffrage at the time of her marriage, but she now did much to advance the cause of women. Roosevelt, for example, initiated press conferences for women only. This gave a tremendous boost to female journalists. Bess Furman, who covered Eleanor Roosevelt for the Associated Press, commented that "no newspaperwoman could have asked for better luck." Many reporters became Roosevelt's closest friends, particularly Lorena Hickok, who some scholars now believe was Eleanor's long-term companion and lover.

Eleanor Roosevelt also supported the appointment of hundreds of women to official positions, acted as clearing agent of women's project proposals to the WPA, and emphasized the need for numerical guidelines regarding women's employment in New Deal programs. She helped to organize the White House Conference on the Emergency Needs of Women, pushed for the inclusion of women in the WPA and CCC, and worked for the establishment of minimum wages and maximum hours for female workers.

Roosevelt also emerged as an outstanding advocate for blacks during the New Deal. She acted as a lobbyist for civil rights and championed the causes of the National Association for the Advancement of Colored People, especially the passage of legislation defining lynching as a federal crime. Roosevelt argued vigorously for the inclusion of black men and women in the WPA and the CCC, while she encouraged the work of black writers, artists, and performers.

In 1940, Eleanor Roosevelt wrote that women deserved credit for "the government's attitude of concern for the welfare of human beings." She added that "there has been a tremendous change in the outlook of government, which can be attributed to the fact that women have the ballot." Roosevelt modestly failed to include her own numerous contributions.

Other New Deal Women

A huge number of women assisted Eleanor Roosevelt in her efforts. Largely professional women interested in reform, they especially hoped to improve women's condition in the family and in the labor force. Whether purposefully or not, they laid the foundation for the eventual resurgence of women's rights and feminism.

One New Deal woman was Frances Perkins, a social reformer and the first female cabinet member in the nation's history. As secretary of labor, Perkins helped draft such New Deal legislation as the Federal Emergency Relief Act, the Social Security Act, and the National Labor Relations Act. Perkins also helped President Roosevelt make appointments, maintain harmonious relations with union leaders, and bring the United States into the International Labor Organization in 1934. As a woman, Perkins's leadership of the Labor Department through the nation's most severe economic crisis helped establish an image of women as competent, trustworthy individuals. Perkins herself once said that "doing" means "digging your nails in and working like a truck horse," which she herself regularly did.

Another important New Deal woman was social-worker Molly Dewson, who had long campaigned for minimum wages for women. When in 1933 Dewson became a top echelon New Deal politician—director of the women's division of the Democratic party—she urged the equal representation of women in party membership and leadership positions. Partially as a result of Dewson's efforts, women campaign workers numbered 73,000 in 1936 and 109,000 in 1940. Dewson also helped secure an unemployment insurance act in the State of New York in 1935 and minimum-wage laws in Illinois and Ohio. She served on the President's Commission on Economic Security and had a hand in shaping the Social Security Act of 1935. As a member of the Social Security Board in 1937 and 1938, Dewson helped improve federal-state relations in the administration of the Social Security Act.

A lesser-known female figure of the New Deal was Ellen S. Woodward, the director of women's work under the Federal Emergency Relief Administration. Woodward also contributed programs to the Civil Works Administration and, in 1935, became the director of Women's and Professional Projects of the WPA. At the time, many political commentators viewed Woodward as President Roosevelt's most important noncabinet female appointment. She worked diligently to reeducate the American public to view women as heads of families, and to create programs that would train women as mattress makers, bookbinders, seamstresses, and household workers. Unlike most New Deal officials, Woodward emphasized the importance of reaching both white and black women with federal programs.

Black women leaders also gained prominence during the New Deal. Mary McLeod Bethune played a critical role between 1935 and 1943 as director of the Division of Negro Affairs of the National Youth Administration (NYA). As a member of President Roosevelt's so-called black cabi-

net—those advisers who assisted in the implementation of black programs in New Deal projects—Bethune exercised great influence. Yet she
seldom forcefully challenged segregation, apparently hoping to offend no
one while extending her vision of racial equality to all. When necessary,
however, Bethune proved a strong advocate for the rights of blacks. In
1937, she told the director of the National Youth Administration (NYA)
in no uncertain terms that "it is about time that white folks recognize
that Negroes are human too, and will not much longer stand to be the
dregs of the work force."

A more outspoken black woman was Juanita J. Sadler, also an admin-
istrator in the Division of Negro Affairs during the organization's forma-
tive period. Unlike Bethune, Sadler openly questioned the NYA's and
President Roosevelt's stands on desegregation. She argued for the total
integration of blacks into New Deal programs in particular and American
society in general.

Other New Deal black women strove to improve the condition of their
communities, their race, and themselves. In 1935, many of these black
women activists formed the National Council of Negro Women and
elected Bethune its first president. The council coordinated the efforts of
over twenty national and ninety-five local groups representing almost
850,000 black women. Black women activists also continued to pressure
the YWCA to open its doors and its programs to black women, and the
activists maintained during the 1930s their crusade to abolish lynching in
the South.

Unionization

The New Deal disappointed many women, especially those who
worked for wages or who fell outside the purview of the New Deal because they were not yet citizens. Consequently, women continued to view
unionization as the solution to at least some of their problems. After the
passage of the National Industrial Recovery Act in 1933, the International Ladies' Garment Workers' Union (ILGWU) mounted a membership
drive headed by such organizers as Pauline Newman and Rose Pesotta. In
the Southwest, leaders organized Chicana garment workers, who accounted for approximately one-third of the labor force in the nation's garment industry. By late 1934, membership of the ILGWU reached 200,000.

Among Chicano wage-workers, women actively participated in labor
protests and unions at a far greater rate than did men, even though they
faced firings and possible deportation. During the 1930s, for example,
Manuela Solis Sager organized garment and agricultural workers in
Laredo, Texas. Sager helped establish a statewide Mexican labor movement, and in 1935 assisted the formation of the South Texas Agricultural
Workers' Union (STAWU). She then joined ranks with San Antonio organizers, notably Emma Tenayuca.

Tenayuca's grandfather was a Socialist, her husband a Communist, and she herself an effective speaker who blended ideologies. When Tenayuca tried but failed to organize workers of Spanish heritage into a single union, she instead established the Workers' Alliance to distribute civil rights literature, stage demonstrations, and protest the deportation of Chicanos under Operation Wetback. During a 1937 sit-in at San Antonio city hall, Tenayuca was arrested. The following year, during the Pecan-shellers' Strike, Tenayuca again played a central role and was nicknamed "La Paionariea" after Dolores Ibarrui of the Spanish Civil War. When a rally ended with a violent attack from Anglo opponents, it spurred Tenayuca's resignation and retirement.

Other women also continued their efforts to unite women workers. The Women's Trade Union League and such female members of the Communist party as Ella Reeves "Mother" Bloor energetically urged female workers to join unions. These workers labored in such heavily female-employed industries as canneries, clothing, paper products, cigar and candy making, restaurants, and laundries.

During the 1930s, despite resulting internal dissension, the AFL also concentrated on organizing skilled workers and craftspeople. One especially effective AFL organizer was Luisa Moreno, a Guatemalan who emigrated to the United States in 1928 with her Mexican husband. Moreno had begun her career in the fertile ground of Puerto Rican *colonias* in New York's Spanish Harlem. Here, Moreno built on the many existing associations and reform movements to begin unifying Puerto Rican women garment workers. In 1936, the AFL hired Moreno to work a wider field. She also established the first Congress of Spanish Speaking People, dedicated to bringing together Mexican, Chicano, and other Spanish-speaking laborers throughout the United States.

During the 1930s, a new labor union entered the scene. Led by John L. Lewis, in November of 1935 a splinter group of the AFL, which called itself the Committee for Industrial Organization, formed to organize workers without regard to gender, race, or skills. In 1938, this group took the name Congress of Industrial Organizations (CIO). The CIO focused on all workers in a particular industry, such as automobiles, steel, and textiles, in which 40 percent of the workers were women.

Increasingly, union women, as well as wives and daughters of male workers, participated in strikes as marchers, picketers, and providers of support services. Women also spontaneously formed themselves into groups known as the Women's Emergency Brigade and into women's auxiliaries. During strikes, these women's groups created diversions to aid pickets, broke windows to prevent strikers from being gassed inside plants, cared for injured picketers, provided food, distributed literature, and swelled the numbers of marchers. That women proved their worth is unarguable; when Minnesota writer Miradel La Sueur participated in her first strike during the mid-1930s she heard union men guarding the doors declare, "Let the women in—we need women."

Women's efforts proved especially important in the Flint (Michigan) Auto Workers' Strike between December 1936 and February 1937. This strike, the most famous of "sit-down" actions, erupted over such issues as employers' refusal to negotiate with union representatives and speed-ups on the assembly line. Male workers sat down at their machines and refused to leave the factories, while women, who protested their exclusion from the occupation of factories, established aid organizations that provided food, clothing, and medical supplies.

When police threatened the men with violent action, women formed a Women's Emergency Brigade. Soon, 350 women established a picket line between the police and the strikers. Then, one January day, police shot into the milling crowd and hit fourteen people. As the crowd surged forward and threw stones, coal, milk bottles, and whatever else they could lay their hands on, the police broke and ran. Later, the event took the name of the Battle of Bulls' (police) Run. In February, the final crisis occurred when women's brigades came from all over the area on a single day designated as Women's Day. As they congregated, a woman's voice boomed over the loudspeaker: "We don't want any violence; we don't want any trouble. . . . But we are going to protect our husbands."

The Flint Auto Workers' Strike succeeded in getting General Motors to recognize unions and agree to negotiate with their representatives. For the United Auto Workers this meant a huge increase in membership, but for women it indicated an important coming of age as labor activists. As one female participant said, "women who only yesterday . . . felt inferior to the task of organizing, speaking, leading, have, as if overnight, become the spearhead in the battle of unionism."

The Pecan-shellers' Strike of 1938 in San Antonio marked another turning point for women. In this Chicana-heavy industry, women earned an average of $2.73 a week by sitting and shelling pecans, "crowded elbow to elbow on long wooden benches without backs." The United Cannery, Agricultural, Packing, and Allied Workers of America, a CIO-chartered union, had begun organizing these women. Then, in 1938, workers in 130 plants struck. Employers and police used tear gas and beatings to halt the strike, and arrested hundred of picketers. As many as thirty-three women filled cells meant for six, and often shared quarters with venereal-disease infested prostitutes. Although some of the plants hired other workers or closed entirely, women now recognized the potential power of unity.

By 1938, an estimated 800,000 women, an increase of 300 percent from 1928, had joined unions. Yet, women remained underrepresented, for the idea that women belonged in the home continued to carry weight among most male union leaders. Consequently, women workers were usually expected to join gender-segregated locals. In addition, only a few women served as union organizers and leaders, union-approved contracts often allowed unequal pay scales, and fourteen of every fifteen female laborers remained outside the union structure. In other words, union leadership overlooked some five million women workers.

Yet other working women could not have joined unions even if they had chosen to do so. Few unions existed for white rural women laborers in the South and West, or for American Indian women workers. In both regions, women continued to serve as unpaid domestic artisans and field workers on family farms. In the South, they participated in sharecropping and other tenant farming operations, while in the West they worked as day- and migrant-laborers. Poverty, farm mortgages, and hard work characterized these women's lives.

Black women composed another group which unions largely overlooked. In 1930, 90 percent of black women workers performed domestic or farm labor, areas of employment seldom covered by labor organizations. Throughout the decade, only 10 percent of black women worked in industry. In addition, because they worked separately from white co-workers they had little opportunity to develop unity. In the cotton mills of Durham, North Carolina, black women labored in separate areas, earned lower wages, and were considered inferior to white women performing similar tasks.

Black women developed cohesion among themselves, however, and attempted to form their own unions. In 1934, Dora Jones helped organize household workers in New York into their own Domestic Workers' Union. Three years later, the National Negro Congress recognized the plight of household workers by sponsoring a Domestic Workers' Association in New York.

LIFE DURING THE 1930s

The Feminine Ideal

In 1930, journalist Paul W. White remarked that American women spent two billion dollars a year on cosmetics. In their pursuit to appear "feminine," White said, women consumed 52,500 tons of cleansing cream, 6,562 tons of bath powder, and 2,375 tons of rouge each year. The 1930 Sears Roebuck catalogue encouraged and confirmed women's interest in looking feminine. Fashion advertisements emphasized long, flowing skirts, defined bustlines, tiny waistlines, and a modernized version of the corset. The catalogue explained that "the new mode calls for a definitely higher indented waistline, long tapering hips and the molded bust. To wear the new frocks, you must wear the smart, new corsetry."

Moreover, movie stars and the characters they created both set and reinforced these trends. Jeanne Harlow bleached her hair, thus metamorphosing into the screen's original blond temptress. Such others as

Marlene Dietrich, Bette Davis, and Greta Garbo became models of steamy sensuality, with "bedroom eyes," painted lips, and camellia-like complexions. But Mae West carried the style to a new high; she not only exuded sexuality but also loved in a supposedly "masculine" style, committing herself neither to one man nor to the idea of marriage.

Dating During the 1930s

Given such role models, it is unsurprising that relationships between women and men continued to alter. During the 1930s, the traditional custom of a man "calling" upon a woman in her family's home for the purpose of courting virtually disappeared. Instead, continuing a pattern that had emerged during the 1920s, men now invited women to accompany them to such public places as amusement parks and bowling alleys with the understanding that the men would pay the cost of such entertainment. The proliferation of the automobile further accelerated the development of dating, for it provided mobility and privacy to courting couples.

Hundreds of articles and books appeared spelling out the new etiquette of dating. The prevailing ideal of the time prescribed that an individual "date" as many people as possible, both to demonstrate his or her popularity and to search out the perfect mate. No one, however, discussed the issue of changing power relationships between women and men. In the day of the formal "call," women had controlled courting by inviting men to their homes and exposing them to their families' assessment. Now, men invited women to share their company away from family homes, out of sight of family members, and in situations funded by men.

Women, who now felt free to do as they pleased and also indebted to their suitors, increasingly participated in premarital sexual activity. Although most women expected to marry the man with whom they were involved, many ended up pregnant and unwed instead. During the 1930s, the Florence Crittenton Home for Unwed Mothers established additional branches all over the United States. Now staffed by professional social workers rather than benevolent middle- and upper-class ladies, the Crittenton homes offered pregnant women vocational training so they could find employment as domestics and in other jobs. Perhaps domestic service was not the ideal position for a young and already "fallen" woman, but it allowed mother and child to remain together, a Crittenton policy.

Marriage and Family

Given such changes, educators and social scientists came to believe that Americans required practical training in courtship, marriage, and family life. Because educators and counselors had concluded that parents could no longer cope with such matters as dating and premarital sex, they decided to bring young women and men under the guidance of experts. In turn, it was hoped that such training would bring about more functional behavior and lasting marriages. Accordingly, during the 1930s colleges and universities, as well as some high schools, introduced "marriage and family" courses. Enrollments climbed and research proliferated, but unfortunately teachers tailored their ideas to the needs of Anglo middle- and upper-class students, while researchers interviewed Anglo, middle-class subjects. Thus, the information dispensed and the societal norms established reinforced gender differences traditional to the dominant Anglo middle class and offered little of use to the majority of Americans.

For the bulk of the American population, harsh economic times dictated family lifestyles and decisions to a far greater extent than did so-called expert advice. For women, sustaining family life during the depression years often meant learning how to "make do." The slogan "Use it up, wear it out, make it do or go without" became words to live by. Consequently, women put their pride aside, sought welfare for their families, and took whatever jobs they could find to help keep themselves and their families afloat.

During the 1930s, over half of American families lived on incomes of between $500 and $1,500 per year. Under such conditions, conspicuous consumption declined, but consumerism itself remained strong. The goods and products that women had once produced in their homes now came from factories, shops, and department stores. Because women controlled approximately 80 percent of families' spending, they served as the primary consumers for their families.

It also fell to women to stretch the twenty to twenty-five dollars allotted each week for food, clothing, and shelter. In northern cities, milk sold for ten cents a quart, butter for twenty-three cents per pound, bread for seven cents a loaf, and hamburger for twelve cents a pound. With careful shopping and such deflated prices, a woman could feed a family of six for five dollars a week. Even formerly wealthy women soon grasped the nuances of economizing; they bought day-old bread, relined coats with old blankets, bought meats of a cheaper cut, and moved to smaller living quarters.

On such limited budgets, divorce soon became an expensive luxury for most dissatisfied couples. In "Middletown" (Muncie, Indiana), the divorce rate fell 43 percent between 1929 and 1933, and a similar drop occurred on the national level. In some areas of the country, however, the divorce rate remained level or rose. In Cedar Rapids, Iowa, an industrial city in the center of an agricultural area, the divorce rate climbed during the 1930s. Moreover, anecdotal evidence suggests that even though overall divorce rates declined, desertion rates increased. Many of these people planned to obtain a formal divorce when the economy improved and they could afford the cost.

At the same time, the marriage and birth rates fell because many people who felt they could not afford to get married or have another child simply postponed these events. By the mid-1930s, the birth rate dropped below replacement level for the first time in the nation's history.

Women and Reform

The climate of the depression era promoted economic and political reforms, rather than social causes. For instance, the 1930s ended a century of concern over women's prisons. Partly because women had gone to jail in large numbers as bootleggers and prostitutes during the prohibition years, sentiment on behalf of female offenders decreased. In addition, most women reformers now turned their attention from social evils to the more immediate concerns of food, shelter, and employment. Also, prison philosophy was moving away from a belief in the possible reform of offenders and toward custodianship, thinking which did little to stimulate innovative prison strategies.

As early as November of 1930, the Young Women's Christian Association reordered its usual priorities and began to offer food, shelter, clothing, medical care, job skills classes, and an employment service. The YWCA also assisted single women, who were routinely denied relief, and tried to alleviate the suffering of thousands of homeless women, who lived in city streets and on the open road as hoboes, or "sisters of the road," as they were called.

Journalist and activist Dorothy Day pursued a slightly different angle of reform. After her conversion to Roman Catholicism in 1927, Day helped organize the Catholic Worker Party and edit its journal, the *Catholic Worker*. Day described herself as a "Christian anarchist," which meant she often opposed church policy, yet she strove to carry the spirit of love and assistance to those in need.

Despite the clear trend toward economic rather than social reform, black women refused to abandon their antilynching campaign. Although especially hard-hit by the depression, they continued to dedicate whatever resources they could toward eradicating this racially motivated crime. White southern women also exerted great efforts to stop the lynching. In 1930, Texas reformer Jessie Daniel Ames founded the Association of Southern Women for the Prevention of Lynching (ASWPL). Ames, widowed in 1902 when she was thirty-one years old and with three small children to support, had learned the hard way about the importance of self-confidence, economic independence, and civil rights. As an ardent suffragist, Ames had objected to the movement's general exclusion of black women, calling instead for an end to the racist stereotypes that separated black and white women in their reform efforts.

With the formation of the ASWPL, Ames hoped to devise some means to prevent lynching in the South and to mobilize southern white women on behalf of the antilynching cause. Appalled that American society rationalized lynching as a necessary step to protect white womanhood, Ames's group issued a public statement disclaiming any connection with lynchings: "Women dare no longer allow themselves to be the cloak behind which those bent upon personal revenge and savagery commit acts of violence and lawlessness." By attacking the dual concepts of paternalism and chivalry, Ames's followers asserted themselves as antilynching advocates and "new women."

Achievement-minded Women

This bleak picture is not meant to suggest that women sacrificed every shred of opportunity during the depression era, for they did not. Ruth Fulton Benedict, for example, achieved distinction as the country's first female professional anthropologist. In 1930, Benedict went to Columbia University as an assistant professor. Four years later, she published her renowned *Patterns of Culture* (1934), an analysis of Zuni, Dobu, and Kwakiutl cultures. During subsequent years, Benedict worked in the southwestern United States, studying Serrano, Zuni, Pima, Apache, and Blackfoot Indians. At the end of the decade, another of Benedict's best-known works, *Race, Science, and Politics* (1940), attempted to refute Nazism and other racist philosophies by demonstrating that differences between groups of people originated with their cultures rather than from biological characteristics.

Another anthropologist, Margaret Mead, became world-famous. Mead, the first American woman to earn a Ph.D. in anthropology, published her acclaimed *Coming of Age in Samoa* in 1928 and her equally celebrated *Sex and Temperament* in 1935. In combination with Benedict's pioneering work, Mead's studies encouraged further culture and personality studies in the United States. Like Benedict, Mead hoped to demonstrate that culture shaped personality, and that characteristics resulted more from cultural patterning than genetic determinants. As Curator of Ethnology at the American Museum of Natural History when not in Samoa and New Guinea on field trips, Mead also popularized and legitimized the study of anthropology and the concept of culture.

Outside academia, women achieved success as well, at least partly as a result of support from federal programs. The Resettlement Administration and the Farm Security Administration employed photographer Dorothea Lange to document the harsh conditions that rural Americans endured. By lighting, angle of shot, and pose, Lange could reveal the tragedy of the depression in a southern woman's face. Lange also captured with her camera bread lines, the unemployed, and especially migrant workers in the West. Lange's best-known work, *The Migrant Mother* (1936), laid bare the emotion of a young woman in despair.

Also in photography, Margaret Bourke-White became a daring and innovative photojournalist. She joined the original staff of *Life* magazine in 1936, where she helped develop the photographic essay as a separate and significant genre. Bourke-White's photographs not only captured an event, but commented on it. She especially chose to explore with her photographic techniques the topics of war and industry, and traveled to places were few men dared go. She also journeyed across the United States photographing such scenes as the Fort Peck Dam in Montana for *Life, Fortune,* and other major magazines, as well as collaborating with novelist Erskine Caldwell on *You Have Seen Their Faces,* a 1937 study of southern sharecroppers.

Another photographer, Louise A. Boyd, led scientific expeditions to Greenland. In 1935, the American Geographical Society published Boyd's *The Fiord Region of East Greenland.* Public response proved enthusiastic, and the Swedish government even presented the Order of Saint Olaf to Boyd in recognition of her courageous Arctic journeys. When asked how she preserved her femininity under such trying conditions, Boyd responded that it was not a pressing concern. She added that her primary worry was averting frostbite rather than preserving smooth hands.

In politics, Reva Beck Bosone, a Mormon, lawyer, and Democrat, also helped open new frontiers for women. In a coal-mining town in central Utah named Helper, Bosone assisted Italian and Greek miners, and on occasion gave legal advice to prostitutes. In 1932, the socially sensitive Bosone won election to the Utah state legislature. During two terms, Bosone sponsored minimum-wage and maximum-hour laws for women and children. She later moved to the judicial bench as Utah's first woman judge.

Yet another achievement-minded woman of the era was Bonnie Parker, although she had a very different kind of achievement in mind. Parker grabbed headlines for her violent crime binges with her partner, Clyde Barrow. In 1932, Parker spent three months in jail, then rejoined Barrow and began a crime spree in which the couple took a New Mexico sheriff hostage and left him in Texas; raided a National Guard Armory in Fort Worth, Texas, taking machine guns, automatic rifles, and shotguns; then moved across the South and Midwest using their new weaponry. Because Parker and Barrow primarily robbed grocery stores and small businesses, their biggest take was only fifteen hundred dollars. In the process, however, Bonnie and Clyde brutally shot and killed fifteen people, including several police officers. Their rampage, and their press coverage, came to an abrupt end in May of 1934 when a posse killed them in a roadside ambush near Gibland, Texas.

Women and Literature

Although the depression had nearly silenced the Harlem Renaissance and New Deal programs did little to stimulate black writers and artists, women distinguished themselves in literature. African American author Zora Neale Hurston continued to write. During the 1930s, Hurston turned from the short story to the novel, publishing her first novel, *Jonah's Gourd Vine*, in 1934. In 1937, Hurston's masterpiece, *Their Eyes Were Watching God*, stunned its readers with a skillfully constructed story in which race and gender exerted critical influence yet were not overtly discussed. Hurston exhibited her genius in exploring African American culture and authenticating it.

During the 1930s, a number of other women writers also made an impact on the public. Federal employment projects frequently encouraged and funded their work. A number of Latinas, especially in New Mexico, wrote books dealing with their history, folklore, and customs for the Federal Writers Project. For example, Nina Otero Warren's *Old Spain in Our Southwest* (1936) tied Mexican culture to its Spanish roots.

In addition, in 1932 Pearl Buck's *The Good Earth*, the poignant story of a Chinese family, became the most widely read novel of the year. In that same year, Gertrude Stein published her bestseller, *The Autobiography of Alice B. Toklas*. Although Stein usually attracted a limited audience due to her unconventional style, length of her works, and repetition for effect as in her famous sentence "A rose is a rose is a rose," the *Autobiography* of Toklas, Stein's companion and lover, enjoyed huge sales. And, of course, Margaret Mitchell's Civil War tale of suffering and love, *Gone with the Wind*, became a bestseller in 1936 and a hit movie in 1939.

Most of these writers restricted their feminism to their personal lives and interviews. Often personally supporting women's rights, female authors found themselves bound by cultural expectations of "women's fiction" if they wanted their works to sell. But women journalists tended to be more outspoken. Freda Kirchwey, Anne O'Hare McCormick, and Dorothy Thompson used their wide-ranging influence to support a number of causes, including women's issues.

Of these, Thompson was the most prominent. Through her lectures, radio broadcasts, columns, and books, the sharp-tongued and witty Thompson commented on the American scene, supported women's issues, and opposed Nazism. After interviewing Hitler in 1931, Thompson especially focused on the plight of European Jews. Five years later, Thompson began her "On the Record" column for the *New York Herald Tribune*, and in 1936, began to write for the *Ladies' Home Journal*. Although briefly married to writer Sinclair Lewis and the mother of one son, Thompson later garnered attention as a candid lesbian.

A number of women poets also examined the world during the 1930s from various perspectives. Edna St. Vincent Millay gained renown for her poem, "Say That We Saw Spain Die," while Genevieve Taggard achieved notice with her collection of poems, *Calling Western Union* (1936).

Women and Art

New Deal programs also encouraged women artists. The Federal Art Project helped to support the work of sculptor Louise Nevelson, while WPA murals projects both revised images of women and displayed women's artistic talents in post offices and other public buildings. These murals typically represented strong, courageous women surviving economic reversals, drought, and other hardships. Painter Agnes Tait was part of a collaborative team that in 1937 created a decorative mural in Bellevue Hospital in New York, but her best-known mural was *Fruits of the Land*, a frieze she painted in 1941 in a North Carolina post office.

Folk art also attracted a growing number of devotees during the 1930s. As the home once again became the focal point for American families, quilting reappeared. Quilts, which reflected new technology in their fabrics, printed patterns, and dyed colors, contributed social documentation through their scenes. Chicana and Indian artists also attracted attention, especially *Santeros* (saint-makers), tin-workers, potters, and weavers.

Meanwhile, folk painters experienced a revival. A renewed interest in the life of common folk led to an appreciation of the simple and primitive approach of the folk artist. The most famous of these was Anna Mary Robertson Moses, better known as "Grandma Moses," who began her career as a painter in 1933 at the age of seventy-seven, and whose works did much to popularize the genre of folk art.

In the fine arts, Romaine Brooks first achieved notice for her paintings of lesbians during the 1920s. During the 1930s, Brooks experimented with drawings composed from a single, unbroken line. Undoubtedly, however, the most important artist of the period was Georgia O'Keefe. Although art critics often dismissed O'Keefe's lucid, colorful works as "feminine" because of their use of color, flowing forms, and parts of the female body, others described O'Keefe's watercolors and other works as epic, vast, clean-cut, and pristine. O'Keefe gradually became a major figure in American art during the twentieth century, and, because of her unorthodox style, served as a role model for other innovative women artists.

Black women artists also gained notice during the 1930s. They produced a good deal of folk art, including quilts, textiles, and handcrafts in the black folk tradition. But black women artists produced more formal works as well. An outstanding case was Minnie Evans, a domestic worker, who in 1935 began to create pen, ink, and crayon drawings. Turning later to oils, Evans gained a reputation as a visionary artist through her powerful imagery and the provocative depiction of her figures' eyes.

Women and Music

During the 1930s, the musical work of women also proved prolific and diverse. A widespread interest in ethnomusicology emerged; that is, the collection, writing down, and arrangement of folk music. Women musicians and composers actively participated in this movement, traveling through the Appalachian Mountains, the South, and the Southwest searching out the music of the "hillbilly," the cowboy, African American, Creole, Chicano, American Indian, and others. Ruth Crawford Seeger collaborated with her husband Charles in transcribing and arranging more than a thousand folk songs, while such groups as *"El Despertador y Los Chicos"* performed on KFOX radio in Los Angeles during the early 1930s and Adelina García recorded with Columbia Records in Los Angeles during the late 1930s.

Other women incorporated folk music into their work. In 1936, composer and pianist Julia Frances Smith presented her first important composition, *American Dance Suite*, based on four folk songs. Smith later wrote several operas based on folk music as well as the *Folkways Symphony*, derived from folk and cowboy tunes.

In the area of classical music, Marion Bauer composed symphonies, chamber pieces, and works for piano and voice, while Ruth Seeger became an early leader of avant-garde twentieth-century music. Moreover, Florence Price was the first black woman to have her work performed by a major American orchestra.

Other women formed their own orchestras. Rejected time and time again by major, male-dominated orchestras, composer Mary Howe helped to organize the National Symphony orchestra, while conductor Antonia Brico formed a women's orchestra in New York. Brico explained that an orchestra comprised her instrument. If orchestra companies denied her work, they denied her the opportunity to practice and perform. Brico effectively fought back by assembling her own female musicians, which attracted a significant proportion of symphony-goers to their excellent performances.

Marian Anderson, one of the finest operatic singers in the world, faced a different type of barrier: racism. During the 1930s, Anderson sang in Europe to escape racist policies and segregated audiences, but in 1935 she returned to the United States. Anderson toured with a white pianist, an unthinkable act at the time, and in 1939 became the first black performer to appear at the Metropolitan Opera. When later that year the Daughters of the American Revolution barred Anderson from singing in Washington, D.C.'s Constitution Hall, Eleanor Roosevelt resigned from the DAR and helped Anderson stage an outdoor concert in front of the Lincoln Memorial. Although Anderson initially hesitated to appear, she later admitted: "I had become, whether I liked it or not, a symbol, representing my people. I had to appear." In a groundswell of appreciation and respect, seventy-five thousand people attended the concert.

Women and Theater

Women proved every bit as prolific and energetic in theater during the 1930s. The Harlem Experimental Theatre Company and the American Negro Theatre employed and encouraged black writers and actors in a wide variety of productions. In 1932, the first opera by black writers, *Tom-Toms: An Epic of Music and the Negro*, utilized a cast of five hundred people to trace black history from Africa to America.

Meanwhile, Martha Graham, a dancer and choreographer, developed a new dance technique. She explained that her style of dancing was "an affirmation of life through movement." Graham also founded her own dance company, creating over 150 dances and 25 plays for its members. One of her dance masterpieces was *Primitive Mysteries* (1931). Graham also inspired other dancers, as well as composers, choreographers, poets, and sculptors.

Also during the 1930s, playwright and director Hallie Mae Ferguson Flanagan administered the Federal Theater Project, while playwright Lillian Hellman dealt with a very controversial subject in her 1934 Broadway hit, *The Children's Hour*, a chilling story about two teachers accused of lesbianism. In this, her first play, Hellman produced an incredibly successful, sensitive probing of the issue. Hellman, a political activist and antifascist during the 1930s, also wrote for films, but Hollywood eventually blacklisted her for her political activities. Although many thought of Hellman as America's greatest female playwright, others were clearly unprepared for her searching honesty.

Women and Sports

Women distinguished themselves in the sports world as well. Alice Marble and Helen Wills set records in tennis, while Eleanor Holm and Helen Madison established new swimming distances. In women's bowling, Floretta McCutcheon predominated. But the most famous woman athlete of the period was Mildred "Babe" Didrikson Zaharias. In the 1932 Los Angeles Olympics, Zaharias not only won gold medals in the javelin throw and hurdles but captured the silver medal in the high-jump competition. Zaharias also excelled in women's basketball and softball, thus revealing women's athletic potential and providing a model for other talented female athletes.

For average women the most popular sports of the era were basketball, swimming, bowling, tennis, golf, and ice-skating. Women's softball and basketball teams, often sponsored by industrial organizations and businesses, flourished. While women's choice of sports was not particularly innovative, their sports clothing was. Lighter tennis dresses, tennis shorts, and satin shorts for basketball players exposed both women's athletic skills and their bodies.

Popular Culture

Clearly, despite the depression, American women continued to seize and magnify their opportunities. Popular culture frequently reflected, and reinforced, the changes taking places in women's lives. For instance, moving picture films often featured successful businesswomen, reporters, attorneys, detectives, and even spies. Sounding a new note, these films presented characters of wit, intelligence, and sophistication. Dressed in mannish suits with padded shoulders, these women were strong-minded, aggressive, and forceful leaders who ran empires and amassed fortunes.

In virtually every case, however, these successful women learned that marriage and family were all that really mattered. In film after film, such stars as Joan Bennett, Rosalind Russell, Ginger Rogers, Claudette Colbert, Joan Crawford, and Katharine Hepburn gave up thriving careers for the men of their dreams. Such films usually stopped short of revealing how these superwomen reconciled their achievements with the demands of traditional marriage and family. Only one of the few female feature-film directors of the era, Dorothy Arzner, did explore during the 1930s such paradoxes of women's lives. In *Merrily We Go to Hell* (1932), *Christopher Strong* (1933), *Craig's Wife* (1936), and *Dance, Girl, Dance* (1940), Arzner not only achieved a reputation as a major director but established her feminist work as legitimate culture criticism.

At the same time, in such popular press magazines as the *Saturday Evening Post*, women also appeared as contradictory creatures. The idealized Anglo woman, for example, often exhibited feminist overtones. Clever, achieving, and assertive, she frequently had to cope with gender prejudice and male chauvinism. But here, too, the modern image of woman was offset by other representations of the vain and silly woman and the married woman who happily sacrificed her career in favor of her husband's vocation.

The newly popular comic strips also featured conflicting views of women. In 1930, Chic Young's Blondie began to manipulate the inept Dagwood, and, in 1940, female cartoonist Dale Messick (who was actually a woman, Dalia Messick) created "girl reporter" Brenda Starr. The new radio soap operas, including "Our Gal Sunday," "Backstage Wife," and "Romance of Helen Trent," similarly vacillated between women who could make their own way in the world and those who found their fulfillment solely through men.

Even the modest gains made in views of white women did not usually extend to women of color. Asian women, for example, found themselves limited to stereotyped film roles during the 1930s. Anna May Wong, who entered films against the wishes of her traditional parents, discovered that Hollywood reserved major Asian roles in Class A films for Anglo actresses. Directors repeatedly cast Wong to play Asian female villains in such films as *Limehouse Blues* (1934). In fact, *Time* magazine once called Wong the "foremost Oriental villainess. The film *Daughter of Shanghai* (1937) was among the very few Wong made that took a sympathetic approach to Asian women.

Moreover, directors and producers continued to cast black women as artless and affectionate mother-figures. Louise Beavers projected the lovable, wholesome "Aunt Jemima" image in a number of films, including *Imitation of Life* (1934), and later went on to become Beulah the maid on television. Hattie McDaniel won an Academy Award for her version of the simple-minded and loyal, yet tough, black servant in *Gone with the Wind* (1939). Metro Goldwyn Mayer signed such talented and beautiful black women as Nina Mae McKinney but never gave them leading roles.

More visible among black performers was Ethel Waters, a 1920s blues singer who during the 1930s rolled blues over into jazz. As the first important jazz singer, Waters experimented with numerous new forms, including adding "scat" to such hits as "Dinah," "Heat Wave," and her trademark "His Eye Is on the Sparrow." Waters also appeared on Broadway and in 1939 in *Mamba's Daughter* achieved the distinction of being the first black woman to appear on Broadway in a dramatic role.

Billie Holiday also became a celebrity, gaining the title "greatest jazz singer of the era." Although Holiday suffered physical abuse as a child and was arrested for prostitution as a teenager, her talent and determination triumphed. As the first singer to use a microphone to carry vocal subtleties, Holiday recorded such hits as "Me, Myself and I" and "Sailboat in the Moonlight" during the 1930s. Beginning in 1934, jazz saxophonist and great improvisationist Lester Young encouraged Holiday to improvise. Holiday also appeared with Teddy Wilson and his women's jazz orchestra; with Count Basie's all-black band where she had to tint her skin to appear darker; and with Artie Shaw's all-white band where she had to lodge and eat separately from Anglo band members.

Dinah Washington, who became known as "Queen of the Blues," idolized Holiday and modeled herself after the jazz great. In 1940, Washington joined the first all-women gospel group, the Sallie Martin Colored Ladies Quartet. Three years later, she began playing in Chicago nightclubs where she met her first husband and agent John Young. She recorded for Mercury Records, soon becoming famous for such hits as "What a Difference a Day Makes" and "Baby, Get Lost."

Losses and Gains

Overall, between 1929 and 1941 American women lost ground in some areas and gained it in others. On the one hand, the harsh economics of the depression underwrote a reemphasis on women's domestic roles as wives and mothers and an erosion of many earlier gains in job and professional areas. On the other, the New Deal furnished beneficial legislation and brought women into prominence in government positions. New Deal programs and the public's desire to escape the stress of difficult times through such entertainment avenues as films, music, and comic strips also created a receptive atmosphere for women in literature, the arts, and popular culture. Consequently, even though feminism may not have been highly visible during the 1930s, it was present and in a healthier state than usually thought.

WORLD WAR II, 1941–1945

Pearl Harbor

On 7 December 1941, the Japanese bombing of the U.S. fleet in Pearl Harbor catapulted the United States into World War II. The war introduced much-appreciated prosperity into the United States during the 1940s, but it brought overwhelming problems as well. One of the first was mobilization of manpower for the front and womanpower for home production. Under the leadership of President Roosevelt, now in his third consecutive term, the government turned its attention to these tasks.

The course of American history had made it obvious that Americans regarded women as a flexible labor supply to be pulled out of the home when needed and pushed back when not. But in 1941 an enigmatic situation existed; women had been lectured for better than a decade on their responsibilities as wives and mothers, and had been advised to avoid paid employment unless it was an absolute necessity. Now the government had to recast the image of women as potential workers.

Thus, the War Manpower Commission (WMC) and the Office of War Information (OWI) faced a huge challenge in mobilizing women workers. Created in April of 1942 to plan placement, training, program review, labor utilization, and selective services, the WMC launched three public-message campaigns to attract women into the workforce. Especially in areas of the country experiencing labor shortages, the WMC used propaganda films, posters, billboards, and radio personalities.

Rosie the Riveter

Initially, the War Advertising Council, an agency of the WMC, and the OWI emphasized the good wages women could earn. Next came the character of "Rosie the Riveter." Much like the famous "Uncle Sam Wants You" poster, Rosie the Riveter posters soon plastered walls and sides of buildings everywhere. Rosie also appeared in newspapers, magazines, and advertisements. Dressed in overalls, her hair covered by a bandanna,

Rosie called out to housewives across the land to join the army of the employed.

Rosie quickly fired the public's imagination. Movies appeared with such titles as *Swing Shift Maisie*. Magazines ran articles proclaiming, "I Take Part in the War Effort," while advertisements declared, "There's a new woman today doing a man's job so that he may fight and finish this war sooner." Songs called "Rosie the Riveter" and "We're the Janes Who Make the Planes" became instant hits.

Because the OWI believed that effective propaganda included "highly emotional, patriotic appeals," the campaign also developed a "feminine" dimension. Advertisements compared acetylene torches to vacuum cleaners, arguing that women could handle any kind of machinery. The agency encouraged the design of special fashions to guarantee "vain" women the ability to look glamorous while working. It distributed war recruitment literature and posters that stressed a woman's patriotic duty to her country: "The More Women at Work—The Sooner We'll Win," but it also played on a woman's sense of loss and her duty to her man: "Longing Won't Bring Him Back Sooner—Get A War job!"

The wartime propaganda directed at women had two major effects; it created an image of women as dynamic citizens, and it helped to persuade millions of them to go to work. Lured by high wages and the nation's new image of women, American women poured into the labor force. Between 1940 and 1945, female workers increased by slightly more than 50 percent. In 1940, 11,970,000 women worked outside of their homes; in 1945, 18,610,000 did so. In other words, the proportion of women working for wages, three-fourths of whom were married, rose from 17.6 to 37 percent in this period.

Women with small children also took wartime jobs. To assist them, in 1942 the Lanham Act established Child Care Centers in forty-one states. The government intended these centers only as an emergency wartime measure rather than a sign of women's acceptance into the labor force or a permanent perquisite for women. After the war, the centers were closed or converted to other uses.

During the war, women replaced male workers in ordnance plants, shipyards, aircraft factories, and steel mills. But they also seized newly opened opportunities as musicians, scientists, doctors, attorneys, university professors, governmental officials, athletes, and teachers. The federal government itself hired a huge number of women. In 1939, less than 200,000 women worked in civil service jobs; in 1940 they totaled more than one million—an increase of 540 percent.

For their labor, women received high wartime wages, regulated hours, decent working conditions, and such support services as canteens and the day care provided through the Lanham Act. Moreover, the Women's Bureau, the War Production Board, and the War Manpower Commission all endorsed the principle of equal pay. In 1942, the one agency that had the power to enforce equal pay—the National War Labor Board—ordered equal wages for women who performed "work of the same quality and quantity" as male laborers. Although women continued to suffer inequitable pay because of lack of enforcement, the NWL had established the ideal of equal pay.

In addition, wartime gains for women included the end of age requirements for teachers and bans against hiring married women teachers. Also, approximately half of black domestic servants found jobs with higher pay and more status, while other women of color and disabled women also obtained employment in factories.

Unions also began to open memberships to women workers. Although many male workers still resisted working with women, some union leaders began to accept the idea of women wageworkers. From its inception in 1935, the CIO had admitted all workers and the AFL had long included the ILGWU as an affiliate, but now the AFL began to open membership in craft-oriented affiliates to women as well. By the end of the war, between 3 and 3.5 million women (including women of color) belonged to unions, an increase of over 12 percent since 1940. Yet the struggle for access to unions was not over for women; they still faced prejudice of male members, restricted membership, and exclusion from positions of leadership.

Black Women

For black women, the war brought a welcome respite. As jobs long closed to them suddenly opened, black women inched up the economic ladder. Approximately 600,000 entered the labor force between 1941 and 1945, while many of those already employed bettered their positions. Aided by the Fair Employment Practices Commission (created in 1941), the National Council of Negro Women, and the NAACP, the number of black factory operatives more than doubled, increasing between 1940 and 1944 from 6.8 to 18.0 percent. Black clerical, sales, and professional workers also increased substantially by 1945, while the percentage of black women in domestic service fell from 59.9 to 44.6.

These developments encouraged black women to migrate from the rural South to the urban North and West in search of employment. Here they discovered that although they might find jobs, they had to live in crowded black neighborhoods served by little or no public transportation or available childcare. They also earned lower wages than white women and remained segregated in heavy, dirty, and hazardous tasks with lower pay. In Detroit and St. Louis defense factories, black women worked in segregated plants and workshops. In the federal civil service, they not only labored in separate offices but were denied opportunities for advancement.

Black women increasingly looked to labor unions to protect them. In 1941, black union organizer Sabina Martinez encouraged black women workers to have confidence in "the principles of organized labor" and to join the union appropriate to their field of employment. Martinez organized for the Amalgamated Clothing Workers of America, while other black union women worked to organize the southern tobacco industry, domestic laborers, and black factory operatives.

Women in Uniform

Another large group of women chose to combine employment and patriotic support of the war effort by joining the armed services. Women continued to serve as nurses; Helen Pon Onyett, for example, endangered her owned life caring for injured soldiers on landing ships. After Pearl Harbor, women also participated in non-nurse corps for the first time. The U.S. Army organized the Women's Army Auxiliary Corps (WAAC) in May 1942, but granted women only partial military status and no benefits.

The mobilization crisis reached such a high point that government and military officials soon found themselves calling upon black women as well, even though many officials continued to believe black women would be best employed in cooking, cleaning, and other maintenance work. These black women staged sit-down strikes and filed complaints asking for more than menial duties, but they performed well and had high morale despite the restrictions upon them.

In response to the pressure of the black press, civil rights groups, and black women's organizations, the war department finally agreed that black women should account for 10 percent of total WAAC female officer candidates, approximately the same proportion as in the general U.S. population. A 1942 press release reported that "forty negro women, successful in a nationwide competition for enrollment in the Officer Candidate School of the Women's Army Auxiliary Corps, are scheduled to report today." These women, virtually all college graduates, were among 440 women who comprised the first class of WAAC officer candidates.

Sexism, predictions of failure, stories of sexual liaisons with military men, and rumors of lesbianism plagued both white and black WAAC units, yet these women proved themselves effective and efficient military personnel who handled a wide variety of duties. Soon, Army commanders asked for more WAACs, primarily to fill such traditionally female jobs as typing and filing. In July 1943, the WAAC became the Women's Army Corps (WAC), which offered women recruits the additional enticements of the same rank, titles, and pay as male reservists.

The WAC built an even finer reputation than the WAAC. According to a WAC publication these women were proud to "do every job—little or big—with a thrilling competence that awakens respect in the eyes of even the ablest G.I. Wherever they serve, Wacs are doing a gallant, soldier's job." The WAC also distinguished itself by commissioning the first African American woman officer, Charity Early Adams, who led thirty-nine black women, the first all-black female unit to serve overseas. At the same time, however, the WAC required black officers to live separately and lead only segregated WAC companies.

Despite its prejudicial attitudes, the WAC offered women better salaries and more chance for advancement than did their peacetime employment. By mid-1942, largely due to the lobbying efforts of Dr. Margaret Chung, the first Chinese American woman physician, the Navy created the Women Accepted for Volunteers Emergency Service (WAVES). Established in July 1942, the WAVES immediately offered pay and benefits comparable to male reservists. None of these women served overseas but instead performed clerical and administrative jobs in the United States. One-third of the women trained pilots, packed parachutes, and operated weather stations. The WAVES excluded black women until 1944, when President Roosevelt ordered their admission, but it was then so late in the war that less than one hundred black WAVES actually served.

The Marines were the last military branch to establish a woman's corps. Known simply as women marines, these women took pride in performing state-side duties so that men could fight at the front. Women marines provided one-third to one-half of post troops, mechanics, and aviation personnel. At Cherry Point, North Carolina, the flight instructors were all female, while women marines also packed parachutes and largely ran the control tower.

During World War II, a total of 350,000 women served in the U.S. armed forces. For the first time, women engaged in every military activity except combat. Furthermore, they achieved regular status in women's military units, which in turn opened new employment options for women. Women's military record, combined with the authoritative and tailored uniforms they wore, created a new public image of women.

The women's armed forces also achieved a measure of racial integration. During the war, black women created many of their own opportunities and raised awareness of the restrictions on them by filing complaints with the Fair Employment Practices Committee or enlisting the aid of civil rights groups. Early in 1945, the efforts of black activists and civil rights proponents led to the end of segregated assignments. In addition, Asian American women distinguished themselves in the service. Among them, pilot Maggie Gee served with the Women's Airforce Service Pilots Program, transporting military aircraft in the United States.

Wartime Entrepreneurs and Consultants

Women served their nation in other ways as well. Olive Ann Beech turned her small commercial airline company into a major defense contractor. During the war, Beech supplied 90 percent of the planes used to train American bombardiers and navigators.

Tillie Lewis helped refine the canned-food industry, so necessary to supply food to the front. Lewis also brought the Italian tomato industry to California and developed the first artificially sweetened canned fruit. By the end of the war, Lewis had become the first woman director of the multibillion dollar Ogden Corporation.

Lillian Evelyn Gilbreth contributed scientific management techniques to wartime industry. The holder of a Ph.D. in industrial psychology from Brown University, Gilbreth married and eventually bore twelve children. When widowed, Gilbreth not only raised her family on her own but developed efficiency techniques for the home. These were later applied to industry and eventually used in World War II plants.

Women at Home

Clearly, women played active and public roles in World War II, yet nearly two-thirds of the adult female population did not hold employment outside their homes or serve in the military. Instead, they worked on behalf of the war through their own communities. For example, women in Chinese communities formed chapters of the New Life Movement to organize women for war relief efforts. These and millions of other women gave their time and energy to the Red Cross and the Office of Civil Defense. They provided entertainment for military men and women at USO canteens. And they sold war bonds, raised victory gardens, canned their own foods, collected tin cans and newspapers for recycling, and stretched their families' food and gasoline rationing stamps as far as they would go.

Moreover, war brides provided a generally unrecognized support system for the armed forces. Between 1940 and 1943, one million more marriages occurred than prewar rates would have predicted. Some 8 percent, or four to five million women married servicemen. As war brides, the women traveled all over the country to live on or near bases, where they joined the Red Cross, volunteered as motor pool drivers, worked in hospitals and United Service Organizations (USOs), and supplied myriad other services. In 1944, one journalist described war brides as "wandering members of a huge unorganized club" but neglected to comment on their invaluable contributions to the war effort.

The Debate Regarding the Nature of Women

The varied efforts of American women during the war years raised basic questions regarding their supposedly "inherent" nature. Were women really "natural" mothers who were at their happiest and most fulfilled when surrounded by children? Certainly, childbearing statistics disputed this long-held belief, for the average number of children dropped to two to three children per woman.

Furthermore, many women now held a more limited, sanitized view of pregnancy and childbirth. Women often shopped for the latest in birth-control technology and advisors. In 1942, the American Birth Control League transformed itself into the Planned Parenthood Federation of America. Officers, who now preferred the term "planned parenthood" over "birth control" because they thought it had more public appeal, no longer targeted working-class women but hoped to serve all classes. In addition, expectant women less frequently called upon immigrant mid-wives, except in ethnic communities and rural areas. In most states, regu-lations surrounding birth tightened, further excluding midwives, but women themselves increasingly preferred "physician-managed" child-birth in their homes or in hospitals.

During the war years, psychologist Helene Deutsch attempted to re-vise the traditional Freudian image of women to match such contempo-rary realities as a decreasing birthrate and increasing hospital deliveries. As a disciple of Freud, Deutsch recognized Freud's hypothesis that women became hysterical because of sexual repression and accompany-ing hypermoralism. In her classic two-volume *Psychology of Women* (1944), however, Deutsch anticipated feminist psychoanalysis by some thirty years; she argued that women's dependency grew out of their learned dependence on their mothers as small children. Women thus had re-pressed rage, Deutsch explained, which put them in danger of developing neuroses. Deutsch stopped short of her promise, however, because she continued to describe women as basically passive and even masochistic. Thus, although Deutsch contributed to the ferment of thought regarding women and their innate natures, she also reinforced some traditional ideas.

By the time that the war came to a welcome end in 1945, American women had indeed experienced many modifications in their images, roles, and lifestyles. The war years had dramatically broken women's usual life cycle of childhood, schooling, employment, marriage, mother-hood, and widowhood. Instead, it offered them paid employment, mili-tary service, travel, and patriotic service. That the war proved a critical life stage for many women was revealed in an army nurse's assessment of herself: "More mature, more realistic, more open-minded."

Demobilization

In 1945, the Women's Bureau reported that a significant number of women workers hoped to keep their jobs after the war's conclusion. Probably motivated more by high pay than feminist goals, fully 80 percent of working women wanted to continue working. Of these, 57 percent were single, 34 percent married, and 15 percent widowed or divorced. In that same year, however, a study of women workers in Michigan defense plants revealed that a significant number had no desire for fundamental alterations in their lives. Rather than interpreting the war as an opportunity for emancipation, they, like men, saw it as a temporary emergency and intended to return to their domestic duties.

U.S. government agencies, which favored the latter group of women, now reversed Rosie's image; postwar propaganda showed Rosie abandoning her welding torch as she retreated to the suburbs. The media cooperated in this effort, encouraging women to marry and to bear children, to create the warm home life that the national emergency had interrupted, and to act sweet, supportive, and motherly to their returning veterans.

Accordingly, layoffs of women workers came quickly and day-care centers closed abruptly. In early 1946, a *New York Times* reporter commented that "the courtship of women workers has ended." Employers initially fired women of color, then Anglo women. After losing their wartime jobs, women often sought others—in department stores, offices, or service industries. Women of color took clerical, retail, and other similar positions rather than return to domestic or agricultural labor. One million other women withdrew from the labor pool, but half of these listed themselves as unemployed—that is, wanting to work and actively seeking employment.

SURVIVAL OF REGIONALISM DURING THE DEPRESSION AND WORLD WAR II

The South, 1930–1945

In the South during the depression and war years, some aspects of women's lives altered while others remained much the same, especially among working-class women. During the depression, the government identified the South as "the nation's economic problem Number 1." Farm tenancy, sharecropping, eroding land, illiteracy, and the highest birthrate in the country plagued the region. When sociologist Margaret Jarman Hagood studied black and white farm-tenant women in North Carolina, Georgia, and Alabama during the late 1930s and published her results in *Mothers of the South* (1939), she repeatedly remarked on women's powerlessness, poverty, and the debilitating demands of raising too many children.

Of course, poor southern women took paid employment outside their homes when available, especially during the war years. But white and black southern women continued to work at different tasks for unequal pay. In North Carolina's tobacco industry, for example, black women earned the lowest wages of all workers. In addition, employers hired them only for certain types of jobs. Much like the days of slavery, supervisors created an auction setting, lining the women up against walls and choosing the sturdy-looking ones. One woman remembered that she had "to hold up one leg at a time and then bend each backwards and forwards."

Once hired, women toiled in incredible discomfort. White and black women worked separately, with the black women performing dirtier, heavier jobs. Each group tried to organize its own local unions, establishing racial and gender unity among themselves rather than among women workers as a whole. Also much like slave times, black women viewed their homes as the only place they commanded respect and wielded influence. Raising children and participating in church activities gave them an additional sense of dignity and strength.

The West, 1930–1945

In the West, because of the many different cultures represented, the situation was even more complicated during the depression and war years. American Indian women, largely sequestered now on western reservations, received attention from New Deal reformers. The Indian Reorganization Act of 1934, designed primarily by John Collier, Commissioner of Indian Affairs between 1933 and 1945, encouraged a revitalization of Indian culture. Under Collier's administration, the Bureau of Indian Affairs (BIA) offered improved education and medical services, religious freedom, and the potential for an American Indian artistic and cultural revival. The Indian New Deal was widely disputed, woefully underfunded, and poorly enforced, yet it broke sharply with the customary belief that Indians should be pseudo-whites.

The Indian New Deal also included a number of programs and activities designed to aid American Indian women. Native women could apply for relief and social service jobs; they worked as supervisors and laborers in CCC Indian Work Camps, as file clerks for the WPA, and as clerks and seamstresses for the Civil Works Administration. They were also eligible for extension services that provided training in cooking, sewing, canning, handcrafts, and childcare.

Moreover, the Indian New Deal included a conscious attempt to encourage native women's renewed participation in Indian affairs. John Collier was especially pleased that, of the 135 native constitutions drawn up under the Reorganization Act, not one denied women the right to vote or to hold office. In 1936, one Assiniboine woman and one Gros Ventres woman were elected to the Fort Belknap tribal council. Other women, customarily limited to the domestic realm, now moved into leadership positions among the Colorado River tribes, the Oneida and the

Blackfeet. Collier proudly noted that Indian women "are increasingly interested in tribal affairs, and are being given every opportunity to vote and hold office" under the act.

During World War II, Collier broke further with tradition in designing educational programs for young native women. In 1942, he explained that "in the earlier days, white teachers refused to recognize Plains Indians customs which assigned work with the farms, gardens or small livestock to the women. . . . we are recognizing that in many Indian homes there will be no garden, no chickens, and no goats if the woman doesn't provide them—we are training girls to do these things well." The BIA also offered courses in secretarial work and nursing so that native women could support themselves off reservations. Then, in 1944, Collier urged women delegates to participate in the first National Congress of American Indians.

Native women also worked on their own behalves. A Dakota Sioux, Ella Deloria, assisted anthropologist Ruth Benedict in studying and recording Sioux culture. Deloria performed a great deal of field work, especially interviewing elders on her home reservation, the Yankton Indian Reservation in South Dakota. In 1932, Deloria published in *Dakota Texts* the myths and tales she had collected, and, in 1944, her *Speaking of Indians* offered a popular description of Dakota culture and life. Perhaps Deloria's greatest achievement was to show for the first time Dakota culture through women's perspectives.

In Southeast Alaska, another energetic woman, a Tlingit Indian named Elizabeth Peratrovich, served as president of the Alaska Native Sisterhood during the war years. Peratrovich frequently inveighed against the discriminatory treatment of native peoples in movie theaters, restaurants, and other Juneau businesses. As Peratrovich spoke, lobbied, and petitioned, she attacked the prevalence of "un-American" prejudice at home, even as Tlingit men fought at the front. She was largely responsible for Alaska's Anti-Discrimination Bill of 1945, and also traveled at her own expense to locate markets for Indian- and Eskimo-produced items.

Chicanos, however, received less attention from the government and reformers during these years. During the depression, President Roosevelt's short-lived Good Neighbor Policy of 1933–1934 en- couraged friendly relations in the western hemisphere and inspired an interest in Spanish-style art, architecture, and culture. The CCC and WPA also hired Chicanos and other Latinos, but usually segregated them in menial jobs. Consequently, Chicanas faced myriad difficulties. In 1930, 15 percent were wageworkers who typically earned inadequate pay as field workers, domestics, and unskilled service and factory workers. In 1931, a sociologist who studied Chicanas noted that women workers often turned over their wages to husbands, for the "supremacy of the male is seldom disputed." More recent evidence refutes this observation, indicating instead that Chicanas were far from passive.

During World War II, even though 375,000 to 500,000 Latinos served in the U.S. armed forces, prejudice against them continued, but Asians and Asian Americans fared even worse. During the depression, racism barred Japanese American women in California from office and sales jobs. Restricted primarily to domestic service, women nevertheless used their minimal wages as a lever to achieve small gains in American society as well as in the traditional Japanese family structure.

During World War II, however, groundswells of fear against Japan, America's primary opponent in the war, led to policies depriving 120,000 Japanese Americans of their civil rights, investments, and possessions. Although thousands of Japanese American men and women served with the U.S. armed forces, their families spent the war years in western detention camps. Here, people lived in noisy barracks with small spartan rooms furnished with wooden tables and steel army cots. Under the duress of communal bathrooms and mess halls, family unity disintegrated.

In some ways, Japanese American women took advantage of the situation. They strengthened their roles as conservator of families and of Japanese culture. Also, because women held camp jobs, such Japanese customs as arranged marriages disappeared. Still, the detention experience hurt women tremendously. As one explained, "it is the effect on the spirit." Another, who was sixteen years old at the time, admitted, "I relive and re-experience the terror, the frustration, and total helplessness of those times."

Often mistaken for Japanese, other people of Asian heritage also suffered discrimination during the war years. Only the Chinese commanded any respect. Because China joined the United States as an ally in World War II, people of Chinese heritage were now acceptable. Thus, such women as Gertrude Wong and Margaret Chow worked in Detroit, Michigan, and other defense plants. In 1942, the California League of Women Voters initiated an educational campaign to revise immigration laws.

Between 1930 and 1945, the flapper of the 1920s gave way to the strong woman of the depression and New Deal years. She in turn prepared the way for Rosie the Riveter, a heroine not so easy to discredit as she was to create. In 1945, women began to stand on the edge of the nest ready to fly, bolstered by an emerging consciousness of themselves as women and as people of ability and strength.

But what they saw before them was disheartening. Changes implemented during times of national crisis appeared easily reversible. Americans who nostalgically longed for an old-fashioned America, which they imagined as simple and family oriented, urged a return to prewar ideals.

Thus, once again, two steps forward would be accompanied by one step backward in the agonizingly slow dance known as "progress."

Suggestions for Further Reading

Ammer, Christine. *Unsung: A History of Women in American Music.* Westport, CT: Greenwood Press, 1980.

Anderson, Karen Tucker. *Wartime Women: Sex Roles, Family Relations, and the Status of Women during World War II.* Westport, CT: Greenwood Press, 1981.

———. "Last Hired, First Fired: Black Women during World War II," *Journal of American History* 69 (June 1982): 82–97.

Babbitt, Kathleen R. "The Productive Farm Woman and the Extension Home Economist in New York State, 1920–1940," *Agricultural History* 67 (Spring 1993): 83–101.

Bailey, Beth L. "Scientific Truth . . . and Love: The Marriage Education Movement in the United States," *Journal of Social History* 20 (Summer 1987): 711–32.

Bailey, Beth L., and David Farber. *The First Strange Place: The Alchemy of Race and Sex in World War II Hawaii.* New York: Free Press, 1992.

Banner, Lois W. *Women in Modern America: A Brief History.* New York: Harcourt Brace Jovanovich, Publishers, 1984.

Baxandall, Rosalyn, Linda Gordon, and Susan Reverby, eds. *America's Working Women.* New York: Random House, 1976.

Beasley, Maurine. "Eleanor Roosevelt's Vision of Journalism: A Communication Medium for Women," *Presidential Studies Quarterly* 16 (Winter 1986): 66–75.

———. *Eleanor Roosevelt and the Media: A Public Quest for Self-Fulfillment.* Urbana: University of Illinois Press, 1987.

Berger, Jason. *A New Deal for the World: Eleanor Roosevelt and American Foreign Policy, 1920–1962.* New York: Columbia University Press, 1982.

Bergman, Andrew. *We're in the Money: Depression America and Its Films.* Chicago: Ivan R. Dee, Inc., 1993.

Berkin, Carol Ruth, and Mary Beth Norton, eds. *Women of America: A History.* Boston: Houghton Mifflin Company, 1979. Part IV.

Bernstein, Alison. "A Mixed Record: The Political Enfranchisement of American Indian Women during the Indian New Deal," *Journal of the West* 23 (July 1984): 13–20.

Blackwelder, Julia Kirk. "Women in the Work Force: Atlanta, New Orleans, and San Antonio, 1930 to 1940," *Journal of Urban History* 4 (May 1978): 331–53.

———. *Women of the Depression: Caste and Culture in San Antonio, 1929–1939.* College Station: Texas A & M Press, 1984.

Bogle, Donald. *Brown Sugar: Eighty Years of America's Black Superstars.* New York: Harmond, 1980.

Boris, Eileen. "Regulating Industrial Homework: The Triumph of "Sacred Motherhood,'" *Journal of American History* 71 (March 1985): 745–63.

Calderón, Roberto R., and Emilio Zamora. "Manuela Solis Sager and Emma Tenayuca: A Tribute," 30–41, in *Chicana Voices: Intersections of Class, Race, and Gender,* edited by Teresa Córdova et al. Albuquerque: University of New Mexico Press, 1990.

Campbell, D'Ann. "Was the West Different? Values and Attitudes of Young Women in 1943," *Pacific Historical Review* 47 (August 1978): 453–63.

———. *Women at War with America: Private Lives in a Patriotic Era.* Cambridge, MA: Harvard University Press, 1984.

———. "Servicewomen of World War II," *Armed Forces and Society* 16 (Winter 1990): 251–70.

———. "Women in Combat: The World War II Experience in the United States, Great Britain, Germany, and the Soviet Union," *Journal of Military History* 57 (April 1993): 301–23.

Chacón, Ramón D. "The 1933 San Joaquín Valley Cotton Strikes: Strike-breaking Activities in California Agriculture," 33–70, in *Work, Family, Sex Roles, Language*, edited by Mario Barrera, Alberto Camarillo, and Francisco Hernández. Berkeley: Tonatiuh-Quinto Sol Press, 1980.

Chan, Sucheng, Douglas Henry Daniels, Mario T. García, and Terry P. Wilson, eds. *Peoples of Color in the American West*. Lexington, MA: D.C. Heath & Co., 1994.

Chaudhuri, Nupur. "'We All Seem Like Brothers and Sisters': The African-American Community in Manhattan, Kansas, 1865–1940," *Kansas History* 14 (Winter 1992–92): 270–88.

Christian, Barbara. *Black Women Novelists: The Development of a Tradition, 1892–1976*. Westport, CT: Greenwood Press, 1980.

Clive, Alan. "Women Workers in World War II: Michigan as a Test Case," *Labor History* 20 (Winter 1979): 44–72.

Cobble, Dorothy Sue. *Dishing It Out: Waitresses and Their Unions in the Twentieth Century*. Urbana: University of Illinois Press, 1991.

Coburn, Carol K. *Life at Four Corners: Religion, Gender, and Education in a German-Lutheran Community, 1868–1945*. Lawrence: University Press of Kansas, 1992.

Cook, Blanche Wiesen. *Eleanor Roosevelt, 1884–1933*. New York: Viking Press, 1992.

Daniel, Cletus E. *Bitter Harvest: A History of California Farmworkers, 1870–1914*. Ithaca, NY: Cornell University Press, 1981.

Durón, Clementina. "Mexican Women and Labor Conflict in Los Angeles: The ILGWU Dressmakers' Strike of 1933," *Aztlan* 15 (Spring 1984): 365–75.

Evans, Sara M. *Born for Liberty: A History of Women in America*. New York: Free Press, 1989. Chapters 9–10.

Faulkner, Mara. *Protest and Possibility in the Writing of Tillie Olsen*. Charlottesville: University Press of Virginia, 1993.

Fink, Deborah. *Agrarian Women: Wives and Mothers in Rural Nebraska, 1880–1940*. Chapel Hill: University of North Carolina Press, 1992.

García, Richard A. *The Rise of the Mexican American Middle Class: San Antonio, 1923–1941*. College Station: Texas A & M University Press, 1991.

Glenn, Evelyn Nakano. "The Dialectics of Wage Work: Japanese-American Women and Domestic Service, 1905–1940," *Feminist Studies* 6 (Fall 1980): 432–71.

Gluck, Sherna Berger. *Rosie the Riveter Revisited: Women, the War, and Social Change*. Boston: Twayne, 1987.

Gonzalez, Rosalinda M. "Chicanas and Mexican Immigrant Families 1920–1940: Women's Subordination and Family Exploitation," 59–84, in *Decades of Discontent: The Women's Movement, 1920–1940*, edited by Joan M. Jensen and Lois Scharf. Westport, CT: Greenwood Press, 1983.

Green, George N. "ILGWU in Texas, 1930–1970," *Journal of Mexican-American History* I (Spring 1971): 144–69.

Harris, Ann Sutherland, and Linda Nochlin. *Women Artists, 1550–1950*. New York: Alfred A. Knopf, 1979.

Hartmann, Susan M. *The Home Front and Beyond: American Women in the 1940s*. Boston: Twayne Publishers, 1982.

Harvey, Lola. *Derevinia's Daughters: Saga of an Alaskan Village*. Manhattan, KS: Sunflower University Press, 1991.

Heacock, Nan. *Battle Stations! The Homefront in World War II*. Ames: Iowa State University Press, 1992.

Hewitt, Nancy A., ed. *Women, Families, Communities: Readings in American History*. Glenview, IL: Scott, Foresman, 1991. Part 5.

Hirshfield, Deborah Scott. "Women Shipyard Workers in the Second World War: A Note," *International History Review* 11 (May 1989): 278–85.

Honey, Maureen. "Images of Women in *The Saturday Evening Post*, 1931–1936," *Journal of Popular Culture* 10 (Fall 1976): 352–58.

———. *Creating Rosie the Riveter: Class, Gender, and Propaganda during World War II*. Amherst: University of Massachusetts Press, 1984.

Janiewski, Dolores. "Flawed Victories: The Experiences of Black and White Women Workers in Durham during the 1930s," 85–109, in *Decades of Discontent: The Women's Movement, 1920–1940*, edited by Joan M. Jensen and Lois Scharf. Westport, CT: Greenwood Press, 1983.

———. *Sisterhood Denied: Race, Gender, and Class in a New South Community*. Philadelphia: Temple University Press, 1985.

Jellison, Katherine. "Women and Technology on the Great Plains, 1910–40," *Great Plains Quarterly* 8 (Summer 1988): 145–57.

———. *Entitled to Power: Farm Women and Technology, 1913–1963*. Chapel Hill: University of North Carolina Press, 1993.

Jones, Beverly W. "Race, Sex, and Class: Black Female Tobacco Workers in Durham, North Carolina, 1920–1940, and the Development of Female Consciousness," *Feminist Studies* 10 (Fall 1984): 441–52.

Jones, Jacqueline. *Labor of Love, Labor of Sorrow: Black Women, Work, and the Family from Slavery to the Present*. New York: Basic Books, 1985.

Kennedy, Susan Estabrook. *If All We Did Was to Weep at Home: A History of White Working Class Women*. Bloomington: Indiana University Press, 1979.

Kerber, Linda K., and Jane DeHart Mathews, eds. *Women's America: Refocusing the Past*. New York: Oxford University Press, 1982. Part III.

Kessler-Harris, Alice. *Out to Work: A History of Wage-Earning Women in the United States*. New York: Oxford University Press, 1982.

Korrol, Virginia E. Sánchez. *From Colonia to Community: The History of Puerto Ricans in New York City, 1917–1948*. Westport, CT: Greenwood Press, 1983.

Kunzel, Regina G. "The Professionalization of Benevolence: Evangelicals and Social Workers in the Florence Crittenton Homes, 1915 to 1945," *Journal of Social History* 22 (Fall 1988): 21–43.

———. *Fallen Women, Problem Girls: Unmarried Mothers and the Professionalization of Social Work, 1890–1945*. New Haven, CT: Yale University Press, 1993.

Lash, Joseph P. *Eleanor: The Years Alone*. New York: W. W. Norton & Company, Inc., 1972.

Laslett, John H. M. "Gender, Class, or Ethno-Cultural Struggle? The Problematic Relationship Between Rose Pesotta and the Los Angeles ILGWU," *California History* 72 (Spring 1993): 20–39.

Lewandowski, Michael J. "Democracy in the Workplace: Working Women in Midwestern Unions, 1943–1945," *Prologue* 25 (Summer 1993): 157–69.

Linden-Ward, Blanche, and Carol Hurd Green. *Changing the Future: American Women in the 1960s*. New York: Twayne Publishers, 1992.

Litoff, Judy Barrett, and David C. Smith. *Since You Went Away: World War II Letters from American Women on the Home Front*. New York: Oxford University Press, 1991.

Madsen, Carol Cornwall. "'Sisters at the Bar': Utah Women in Law," *Utah Historical Quarterly* 61 (Summer 1993): 208–32.

Matsumoto, Valerie. "Japanese American Women During World War II," *Frontiers* 8 (1984): 6–14.

———. "Desperately Seeking 'Deirdre': Gender Roles, Multicultural Relations, and Nisei Women Writers of the 1930s," *Frontiers* 12 (1991): 19–32.

Melosh, Barbara. *Engendering Culture: Manhood and Womanhood in New Deal Public Art and Theater*. Summit, PA: Smithsonian Institution Press, 1991.

Meyer, Leisa D. "Creating G.I. Jane: The Regulation of Sexuality and Sexual Behavior in the Women's Army Corps during World War II," *Feminist Studies* 18 (Fall 1992): 581–601.

Milkman, Ruth. *Gender at Work: The Dynamics of Job Segregation by Sex during World War II.* Urbana: University of Illinois Press, 1987.

Morton, Marian J. "Seduced and Abandoned in an American City: Cleveland and Its Fallen Women, 1869–1936," *Journal of Urban History* 11 (August 1985): 443–69.

Nelson-Cisneros, Victor B. "UCAPAWA and Chicanos in California: The Farmworker Period, 1937–40," *Aztlan* 7 (Fall 1976): 453–77.

———. "UCAPAWA Organizing Activities in Texas, 1935–50," *Aztlan* 9 (Spring/Summer/Fall 1978): 71–84.

Newman, Debra L. "The Propaganda and the Truth: Black Women and World War II," *Minerva: Quarterly Report on Women and the Military* 4 (Winter 1986): 72–92.

Ogden, Annegret S. *The Great American Housewife: From Helpmate to Wage Earner, 1776–1986.* Westport, CT: Greenwood Press, 1986.

Orleck, Annelise. "'We Are That Mythical Thing Called the Public': Militant Housewives during the Great Depression," *Feminist Studies* 19 (Spring 1993): 147–72.

Patterson, James I. "Mary Dewson and the American Minimum Wage Movement," *Labor History* 5 (Spring 1964): 134–52.

Patterson, Victoria D. "Indian Life in the City: A Glimpse of the Urban Experience of Pomo Women in the 1930s," *California History* 71 (Fall 1992): 402–31.

Peterson, Susan C., and Amy K. Rieger. "'They Needed Nurses at Home': The Cadet Nurse Corps in South Dakota and North Dakota," *South Dakota History* 23 (Summer 1993): 122–32.

Reverby, Susan M. *Ordered to Care: The Dilemma of American Nursing, 1850–1945.* Cambridge: Cambridge University Press, 1987.

Rosenfeld, Rachel Ann. *Farm Women: Work, Farm, and Family in the United States.* Chapel Hill: University of North Carolina Press, 1985.

Ross, B. Joyce. "Mary McLeod Bethune and the National Youth Administration: A Case Study of Power Relationships in the Black Cabinet of Franklin D. Roosevelt," *Journal of Negro History* 60 (January 1975): 1–28.

Rupp, Leila J. *Mobilizing Women for War: German and American Propaganda, 1939–1945.* Princeton: Princeton University Press, 1978.

Scadron, Arlene, ed. *On Their Own: Widows and Widowhood in the American Southwest, 1848–1939.* Urbana: University of Illinois Press, 1988.

Schackel, Sandra. *Social Housekeepers: Women Shaping Public Policy in New Mexico, 1920–1940.* Albuquerque: University of New Mexico Press, 1992.

Scharf, Lois. *To Work and to Wed: Female Employment, Feminism, and the Great Depression.* Westport, CT: Greenwood Press, 1980.

———. *Eleanor Roosevelt: The First Lady of American Liberalism.* Boston: G. K. Hall, 1987.

Schwieder, Dorothy, and Deborah Fink. "Plains Women: Rural Life in the 1930s," *Great Plains Quarterly* 8 (Spring 1988): 79–88.

Sklar, Kathryn Kish, and Thomas Dublin, eds. *Women and Power in American History: A Reader.* Vol. II. Englewood Cliffs, NJ: Prentice-Hall, 1991. Parts 14–15.

Shukert, Elfrieda B., and Barbara S. Scibetta. *War Brides of World War Two.* New York: Penguin, 1989.

Sochen, June. "Mildred Pierce and Women in Film," *American Quarterly* 30 (Spring 1978): 3–20.

———. *Mae West: She who Laughs, Lasts.* Wheeling, IL: Harlan Davidson, Inc., 1992.

Spickard, Paul R. "Work and Hope: African American Women in Southern California during World War II," *Journal of the West* 33 (July 1993): 70–79.

Swain, Martha H. "'The Forgotten Woman': Ellen S. Woodward and Women's Relief in the New Deal," *Prologue* 15 (Winter 1983): 200–13.

Taylor, Sandra C. "Leaving the Concentration Camps: Japanese Americans and Resettlement in the Intermountain West," *Pacific Historical Review* 60 (May 1991): 169–94.

Todd, Ellen Wiley. *The 'New Woman' Revised: Painting and Gender Politics on Fourteenth Street*. Berkeley: University of California Press, 1993.

Tsuchida, Nobuya, ed. *Asian and Pacific American Experiences: Women's Perspectives*. Asian/American Learning Resource Center, University of Minnesota, 1982.

Wagner, Lilya. *Women War Correspondents of World War II*. Westport, CT: Greenwood Press, 1989.

Wandersee, Winifred D. *Women's Work and Family Values, 1920–1940*. Cambridge: Harvard University Press, 1981.

Ware, Susan. *Beyond Suffrage: Women and the New Deal*. Cambridge: Harvard University Press, 1981.

———. *Holding Their Own: American Women in the 1930s*. Boston: Twayne Publishers, 1982.

———. *Partner and I: Molly Dewson, Feminism, and New Deal Politics*. New Haven, CT: Yale University Press, 1987.

Westin, Jeanne. *Making Do: How Women Survived the Depression*. Chicago: Follett Publishing Company, 1976.

Whaley, Charlotte. *Nina Otero-Warren of Santa Fe*. Albuquerque: University of New Mexico Press, 1994.

Woloch, Nancy. *Women and the American Experience*. New York: Alfred A. Knopf, 1984. Chapters 17–18.

Wortman, Roy. "Gender Issues in the National Farmers Union in the 1930s," *Midwest Review* 15 (1993): 71–83.

Youngs, J. William T. *Eleanor Roosevelt: A Personal and Public Life*. Boston: Little, Brown and Co., 1985.

IMAGES
AND
REALITIES

Right:
A young Latina,
c. 1890.

Below: Tejanas and
Anglos (French)
among this class, El
Carmen, Texas,
ca. 1896.

Left: Inside a frame homestead, Montana, ca. 1900.

Below: Homestead, Montana, ca. 1890s.

Right: Breaking down cotton stalks, Uniontown, Alabama, 1905.

Below: A courting couple near Sioux City, Iowa, ca. 1900.

*Gathering cotton near
Dallas, Texas, 1907.*

*Opposite top: Spring
plowing, Mandan,
North Dakota,
1906.*

*Middle: Sawmill crew
near Pekin, North
Dakota, ca. 1897.*

*Bottom: Martha
Stoecker in front of
her homesteading
shack, ca. 1904.*

Top: Polly Bemis of Warrens, Idaho.

Bottom: California Maidu woman with traditional seed beater for gathering food, early twentieth-century photo.

Opposite top: Trimming currency, Bureau of Engraving and Printing, Washington, D.C., 1907.

Opposite bottom: A physical education class in the Armory, University of North Dakota, Grand Forks, 1904.

Right: Bertie Lord with coyote she shot, after 1900.

Below: A teacher with her Flathead Indian pupils in Montana, 1910.

Right: African American pioneer in Minnesota, c. 1905.

Below: Zambrano family and others at baby's funeral in early 1900s, Texas.

Left: Doctors Tai Heong Kong (Li) and Kai Fai Li.

Below: Washing clothes in a stream near Ft. Pierre, 1911.

Opposite top: Working for national woman suffrage.

Opposite bottom: Woman suffrage comes early to Oregon—Abigail Scott Duniway at the polls.

Left: Latina in New Mexico, c. 1915.

Below: Black family among thousands to migrate from the South to northern cities during the early twentieth century.

Opposite top: Working in the dry goods store, Lakota, North Dakota.

Opposite bottom: Confirmation Class of 1905 at Temple B'nai Israel, Galveston, Texas.

Top: Washing clothes with the
aid of a mechanical wringer,
Hinsdale, Illinois, 1919.

Bottom: Nancy Hendrickson,
planting corn, Morton
County, North Dakota,
ca. 1918.

*Top: Red Cross post card,
First World War.*

*Bottom: Kansas showgirls
receive a Gideon Bible, 1927.*

Top: Creating beauty in the
barrio, Rio Grande Valley.

Bottom: Creole women in
Plaquemines Parish,
Louisiana, 1939.

Opposite top: Migrant family
on the road, 1939. Dorothea
Lange.

Opposite bottom: Cigar
factory strike, August 1933.

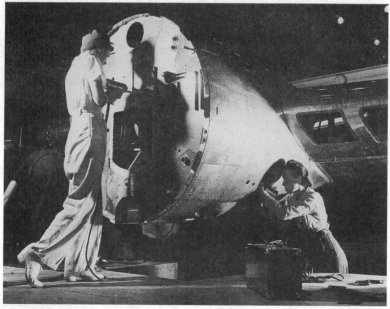

*Top: Women's Air Force
service pilots at Scott Field,
Illinois, 1943.*

*Bottom: Riveters in the Long
Beach plant of Douglas
Aircraft Co., 1942.*

*Right: On the way to one of
seven internment camps for
Japanese Americans, 1942.*

*Bottom: Welding pipe outlets
for a ship in Baltimore.*

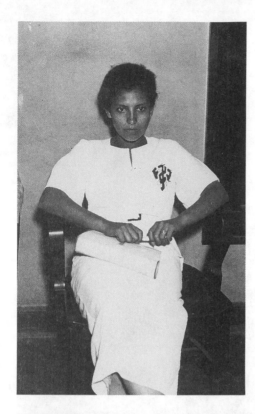

Left: Emma Tenayuca, union organizer, at age 19.

Below: Eleanor Roosevelt greeting Mary McLeod Bethune at a women's dormitory for black war workers, May 1943.

Opposite top: Woman of courage at 15, Elizabeth Echford, during the Little Rock school crisis, 1957.

Opposite bottom: Dolores Huerta signaling to strikebreakers in fields near Delano, September 24, 1965.

Left: Maggie Kuhn at Gray Panther convention, 1977.

Bottom left: Barbara Jordan, as Democratic National Convention keynote speaker, 1977.

Bottom right: Joyce Miller, Vice President and Director of Social Services of ACTWU, and first woman on executive council of AFL-CIO.

Opposite top: National Women's Conference, Houston, 1977.

Opposite bottom: Betty Friedan, Addie Wyatt, and Jean Stapleton lead a march in Chicago for the Equal Rights Amendment, May 1980.

Left: Astronaut Sally K. Ride aboard the earth-orbiting space shuttle Challenger, *1983.*

Below: Women's team sports develop enthusiastic followings.

The Feminine Mystique and Beyond
1945 to 1965

9

In 1945, the belief held sway that women would return from wartime employment to their homes where they would contentedly bear children and keep house. Many Americans expressed a desire to "get back to normal," by which they seemed to mean a return to a happy, industrious lifestyle in an idyllic country. Of course, such a time had never really existed in the nation's history, but a war-weary generation clung to such illusions. Postwar America had definite plans for the nation's women. Newspaper articles, political speeches, sermons, and casual conversations indicated that many Americans assumed that "true" women should, and would, now limit their activities to their homes and leave the endeavors of the "outside" world to men.

This "feminine mystique," as Betty Friedan termed it in 1963, was more or less an updated version of the nineteenth-century cult of domesticity. Eventually, it met with resistance from American women. By the early 1960s, a significant number of them created the contemporary feminist movement. Soon, the nature of woman was no longer a societal given; rather, it provided the grist for open and controversial discussion.

THE BACK-TO-THE-HOME MOVEMENT OF THE LATE 1940S AND 1950S

Sex and Marriage

Initially, it appeared that numerous women accepted with joy the postwar return to domestic life. Because World War II had lasted far longer than World War I, it caused considerable delay in marriage for single women and in childbirth for married women, all of whom now wanted to move forward with their lives. Other women were willing to return home because they had tired of simultaneously running a home and holding paid employment, while still others swallowed propaganda assuring them it was their patriotic duty to bear children to replace Americans killed in the war, make democracy strong, and fuel the postwar economy.

Once domesticated, however, women found their roles less than clearly defined. American society had one foot planted in the postwar world and one in the prewar; transition and confusion thus marked the late 1940s and 1950s. For instance, American society now encouraged American women to act more sensual, but continued to impose taboos on sexual behavior. Sex seemed to appear everywhere, yet the old rules remained in place as well.

One example of this contradictory thinking was *Playboy* magazine, which presented photographs of unclothed women in highly sexual poses, yet faced government censorship and gained only grudging public acceptance. At first, few stores sold *Playboy*, and it never became a coffee-table publication purchasers would display to guests.

Another example of inconsistent attitudes was the new degree of re-spectability that vaudeville striptease artists gained. Gypsy Rose Lee (Rose Lee Hovick) parlayed her earlier vaudeville stardom into a career as a writer and film actress. Lee's 1944 film, *Belle of the Yukon*, and her 1957 book, *Gypsy, A Memoir*, celebrated not only sex but women as sex objects. Still, although Lee proved funny, self-educated, and eminently quotable, her lifestyle failed to capture real public respect as an ideal.

During the late 1940s and early 1950s, sex even invaded the western film, yet always with instructive intent. In 1946, sex provided the motif for *Duel in the Sun*, widely referred to as "Lust in the Dust." In this film, Gregory Peck as Lewt seduced Jennifer Jones as Pearl, who eventually paid with her life for her unbridled sensuality. Sexual women similarly suffered in *The Gunfighter* (1950) and *The Maverick Queen* (1956). Among Latinas in film, light-skinned women appeared as virgins, and dark-skinned women as whores. John Wayne and Gary Cooper carried off the virgins, but the whores were shot. Clearly, sex furnished a new theme, but the message remained prewar: women had the responsibility to act moral and hold amoral men to the "proper" social standards.

From such media, most American women derived similar messages. Before marriage, nice girls could experiment with sex, especially "petting," but did not "go all the way." If they did, they refused to admit it to their friends and certainly to their mothers. In addition, the fear of an unwanted pregnancy further proscribed sexual behavior. Although Planned Parenthood made diaphragms available and drugstore pharmacies sold condoms, neither were easily available to single women. After marriage, women could also be sensual but only in a "wifely" way.

Given such opinions, the declining age of first marriage during the 1940s and 1950s is unsurprising. During the late 1940s, the average age of women at time of first marriage fell to twenty years of age. By 1951, one out of every three women married by age nineteen, and by 1958 more women married between the ages of fifteen and nineteen than in any other age category.

The Baby Boom

Once married, women's sexuality was supposed to lead to childbirth. Such thinking fit the age, for returning veterans from World War II and the Korean War (1950–1953), as well as their wives, wanted children. At the same time, postwar prosperity made possible the financial support of four or more children, while American's growing faith in the nation's future created an optimistic aura that further encouraged childbearing.

Thus, in 1946 a dramatic rise in the birthrate known as the "baby boom" began. During the late 1940s and the 1950s, childbearing occurred most often in the women's late teens and early twenties, with the average woman bearing her last child by age twenty-six. Of course, such rates differed between groups of women and between regions of the country. Women of color and immigrant women generally bore more children and thus continued giving birth through a later age than did native-born Anglo women, while rural women had more children and bore them at later ages than did urban women.

In part, these differences reflected values regarding childbirth. Some women appreciated large families more than others. But the disparities also revealed relative amounts of information regarding birth control, accessibility of contraceptives and other devices, and the money with which to purchase them. Located largely in urban areas, Planned Parenthood remained largely a middle- to upper-class organization during this era.

In 1953, the boom peaked with a record 4.3 million births. Three years later, however, *Look* magazine continued to rejoice that the American woman "marries younger than ever, bears more babies and looks and acts far more feminine than the emancipated girl of the 1920s and even '30s." It also lauded women's ability to raise "bumper crops of children." In addition, American women now strove for "natural" childbirth, for they believed it the most healthy method for their babies and themselves. The Lamaze method of natural childbirth gained great popularity, while the La Leche League, an organization dedicated to helping mothers nurse their babies rather than bottlefeed them, attained great popularity.

Home-bound in Suburbia

Such developments, among others, encouraged a massive exodus to a new form of residential area, the suburb. The configurations of urban areas changed dramatically as primarily Anglo, middle- and upper-class residents left cities to relocate in suburbs ringing their periphery. No longer were cities meant for both family living and work. Instead, they became urban planners' nightmares; poorer people, often people of color, remained as urban residents, while primarily Anglo male workers from the suburbs invaded cities at 8 A.M. and exited at 5 P.M. on weekdays. Meanwhile, women and children remained in the suburbs, either keeping house or attending school. On weekends, urban residents and suburbanites led increasingly different lives.

Because of its physical isolation, suburban living involved a total commitment to home, family, and childcare on the part of women. A huge building boom created one million new homes a year, all demanding decoration, furnishing, and upkeep. In addition, modern architectural styles reinforced what *McCall's* magazine in 1954 termed "togetherness"; suburban homes substituted open arches for kitchen walls, a dining area for a formal dining room, and a family room for the ladies' parlor. During mealtimes, families increasingly huddled around television sets, their TV dinners on individual TV tables. During the summer months, they adjourned to patios behind houses where they barbecued dinners on charcoal grills, watching across open yards as their neighbors did the same.

In this system, women served as the primary family consumers. Because housewives, who now made 75 percent of all family purchases, formed a significant market, Madison Avenue soon excelled in convincing them that domestic consumption offered fulfillment and satisfaction. As one advertising expert pointed out, "the buying of things can provide a sense of identity, purpose, creativity, and self-realization" for women.

Consequently, one set of tasks replaced another in these women's lives. Although technology had freed them from heavy labor, they now had to select, purchase, and operate new "worksaving" gadgets as well as choosing and bringing home food, clothing, and other items for family members' consumption. Consequently, by the end of the 1950s women's household workload increased slightly from fifty-two to fifty-four hours per week.

Consumerism thus proved an important factor in keeping suburban women in their homes, but a variety of experts reinforced the importance of modern-day domesticity at every turn. In 1946, psychoanalyst Helene Deutsch insisted that a truly feminine woman "leaves the initiative to the man, and out of her own needs, renounces originality and experiences her own self through identification." The following year sociologist Marynia Farnham and historian Ferdinand Lundberg published *Modern Woman: The Lost Sex*, which maintained that such contemporary problems as world war and economic depression stemmed from women leaving their homes and families. Clearly antifeminist in tone, this book argued that the "independent woman" was an oxymoron, and that feminism equated with mental illness and neuroses. To these authors, only women suffering from psychological disorders challenged the rightness and inevitability of male dominance.

During the 1950s, a number of other authors elaborated on the domestic theme. In 1952, Ashley Montagu's *Natural Superiority of Women* emphasized the importance of "mother love" to human development and progress. Montagu believed that women's ability to bear and raise children invested them with natural superiority over men. Meanwhile, Dr. Benjamin Spock, whose *Baby and Child Care* reached one million readers annually between 1945 and 1960 (and continues to sell well in considerably revised form), created an image of the ideal mother. This woman neither worked nor left her child for extended periods of time. Should a mother feel the need to seek paid employment, Spock advised her to obtain psychological counseling and to take into account the potential deprivation and delinquency of her abandoned children.

Such popular magazines as *Ladies' Home Journal* carried the experts' messages to additional readers. In 1956, for example, a special issue of *Life Magazine* chose a thirty-two-year-old mother of four as the ideal American woman. *Life* described her as a wife, hostess, volunteer, and "home manager." But, above all, *Life* lauded her as a "conscientious mother" who spent "lots of time with her children, helping with their homework and listening to their stories or problems."

Hollywood films also portrayed women as sweet and innocent homebodies, notably the archetypal "girls-next-door" Debbie Reynolds and Doris Day. Even Marilyn Monroe and Elizabeth Taylor combined their aggressive sexuality with an artlessness and dependence that made them more sex objects than threats. Only by watching closely might a viewer notice that in such television shows as "I Love Lucy" and "Father Knows Best" supposedly scatterbrained women actually manipulated their mates and families to get exactly what they themselves wanted.

Women's fashions reflected a similar "feminine" image. In 1947, Christian Dior's "New Look" replaced the mannish, utilitarian styles of the war years. Dior's creations focused on long, full skirts, defined bustlines, and tiny waists. During the 1950s, the "baby doll" style additionally introduced cinch-belted waists, padded brassieres, and full skirts over crinoline petticoats. Shoes featured pointed toes and heels so high and spindly that they had to be made of steel to avoid breakage.

Women and Activism

In this climate of opinion, many women's organizations declined in strength. During the postwar years, the League of Women Voters and the Consumers' League lost members at an alarming rate, while in 1947 the Women's Trade Union League disbanded. The Woman's Party, the National Federation of Business and Professional Women's Clubs, and the National Federation of Women's Clubs continued to support the Equal Rights Amendment, but when the U.S. Senate passed the resolution in 1950 and again in 1953, these groups were unable to push the bill any farther along its route.

In harmony with the back-to-the-home message, women now directed their efforts more toward local parent-teacher associations, churches, and schools than toward national reform or women's rights. Women spent untold hours engaged in PTA, YMCA, church, and social activities. Politics, however, were no longer regarded as valuable female pursuits. By the early-1950s, women held less than 5 percent of political offices from the federal through the local level. In 1952, the Democratic Party terminated its Women's Division, explaining that the party intended to "integrate" women into its overall structure. Later that year, the Republican party introduced a similar program.

Even though women's organizations did not challenge prevailing ideas, they kept women's reform tradition and interests alive and vital. Such groups involved women in the public service ethos and continued to train women in leadership and related skills. At the same time, school and campus organizations opposing racial segregation, consumerism, and nuclear warfare drew young women into civic reform at an earlier age and in greater numbers than any previous generation.

Trouble in Suburbia

The thousands of guidebooks, pro-home articles, and other domestic propaganda that appeared during the postwar years indicated that women were finding it difficult to fit themselves into the prescribed domestic roles; had domesticity been compelling, women would have needed little encouragement to embrace it. Instead, women felt themselves stranded in the suburbs, cut off from family and kin networks, living far from public transportation, and lacking access to downtown shopping areas. After the initial fascination with car-pooling and a frenetic round of volunteer and social activities evaporated, women found such enterprises less than riveting. Moreover, they spent their days in domestic achievement, only to discover that standards rose with the introduction of each new appliance or soap powder. According to one widespread advertisement, laundry should look "whiter than white" and "brighter than bright." Even cake-mix manufacturers removed the eggs and added several extra steps to the directions so women could believe they provided their families with "somethin' lovin' from the oven."

Women also discovered that while society urged them to perform housework, it usually demeaned the results. The lack of a paycheck put housewives on the bottom rung of an industrial culture that judged people's abilities by their earning power. Soon, many responded to the question "What do you do?" with the response "I'm *just* a housewife."

During the mid-1950s, some college-educated wives and mothers publicly admitted that they felt restive in their domestic roles. As one Barnard graduate put it: "We stagger through our first years of childrearing wondering what our values are in struggling to find some compromise between our intellectual ambition and the reality of everyday living." Some women responded to their disillusionment by continuing to hold paid employment outside their homes even though their family incomes were more than adequate. Others acted out their disaffection so that alcoholism and divorce rates rose alarmingly, while the consumption of tranquilizers jumped from virtually none in 1955 to 1.15 million pounds in 1959.

In addition to these signs, a few dissenting voices tried to warn Americans that trouble existed in suburbia. One critic was French commentator Simone de Beauvoir who in 1949 published *The Second Sex*. When the book appeared in the United States in 1952, it gained a limited audience but effectively alerted those who read it to the prejudice directed toward women. De Beauvoir questioned the practice of viewing men's experience as normal and normative at the same time that women's lives had to be explained and rationalized. She also revealed the richness of womanhood by exploring such female experiences as motherhood, daughterhood, and lesbianism.

The following year, Alfred C. Kinsey also attacked prevailing notions of womanhood in *Sexual Behavior of the Human Female* (1953). Kinsey and his team had interviewed volunteers and then published a report indicating that women were highly sexual beings. Kinsey also characterized American women as both sexually active and highly troubled about their sex lives. Women increasingly engaged in premarital sex and extramarital sex, while they explored—with accompanying guilt—a range of sexual activities from masturbation to oral sex to lesbian relationships. Kinsey further startled Americans by maintaining that, despite long-held beliefs to the contrary, the possibility of a vaginal orgasm was doubtful.

In the same year the Kinsey report appeared, sociologist Mirra Komarovsky argued in *Women in the Modern World: Their Education and Dilemmas* (1953) that women's supposed lack of accomplishments resulted from their cultural conditioning rather than from any inherent inferiority. In interviews with college-educated women, Komarovsky discovered that wives and mothers often felt overwhelmed by the demands of child-rearing, disenchanted with volunteer activities, and envious of their husbands' careers. Yet Komarovsky lacked a solution; she continued to view women as the primary caretakers of home and children, while men played secondary domestic roles as fathers and wage earners.

Similarly, anthropologist Margaret Mead criticized American society's rigid sex expectations in her study, *Male and Female* (1955), but also idealized women's domestic functions. In looking for origins of women's roles, Mead offered conservative interpretations, ideas she would sharply revise during the 1960s. But in 1955, the future course of American women appeared unclear to Mead as well as to most Americans.

Repression of Dissent

Why did more women not speak up? complain? rebel? Because it was extremely unpopular and unwise to criticize anything during the late 1940s and the 1950s. Most people wanted to believe that postwar peace and prosperity had ended the nation's problems and that a female utopia had arrived. At the same time, the so-called Cold War between the United States and the Soviet Union, as well as the Chinese Revolution, spread an umbrella of fear of nuclear war across the nation which inhibited people from speaking out.

In addition, as a result of Senator Joseph McCarthy and the House Un-American Activities Committee (HUAC), Americans developed an overwhelming phobia regarding Communist infiltration in the United States. Always loosely defined, Communists could be almost anyone, including feminists and lesbians. Acting on such fears, the U.S. armed services dismissed lesbians or those rumored as lesbians, while urban police raided lesbian bars.

One Cleveland, Ohio, woman recalled that as a girl she had returned from school every afternoon to watch the McCarthy trials on television and to absorb their clear messages. Her parents, too, preached a doctrine of repression: be quiet, stay out of trouble, marry well, and establish a happy family. Little wonder that she avoided questioning her teachers, or later her college professors. She refrained from dissent at all costs, only daring to speak out when the postwar mania had finally dissipated.

BEYOND SUBURBIA DURING THE LATE 1940s AND 1950s

Employed Women

The widely accepted notion that the "typical" American woman was a simple, cheerful, and financially secure suburban housewife ignored reality in many ways. For one thing, many women who did not have to work wanted to hold paid employment. Thanks to the postwar economy, jobs were plentiful, while swelling consumerism gave women the motivation to earn additional income. Moreover, a significant number of suburban women actually held paid employment outside their homes, working as everything from receptionists and clerks to factory operatives. Ironically, although women earned less in wages than men, it was their paid labor that allowed their families to move to the suburbs, to consume, and to try to meet back-to-the-home standards in their nonworking hours.

Second, numerous other women, especially in urban areas, *had* to work because of economic need. Thousands of women who lived in cities, slums, and ghettoes held paid employment to support, or help support, themselves or their families. Still others who were divorced, separated, or deserted had to sustain themselves and their children without the aid of male partners.

Thus, despite the back-to-the-home mentality, during the 1940s and 1950s the number of employed women grew. As the national economy shifted from industry to service, jobs in such "women's work" areas as education, social services, clerical, secretarial, and health care increased. This proved something of a boon for women who had to work and something of a temptation for those who did not. At an average age of twenty-six a suburban woman watched her last child leave for school; as the school bus departed, she recognized that she had to face many years alone in the house each day unless she sought outside employment.

Even when their husbands earned good salaries, growing numbers of women sought paid employment. They felt they had to justify this and did so by arguing that their families needed extra cars, home improvements, or money for children's college educations. They also tended to move in and out of the labor force. Bored at home and rationalizing that they needed money for something or someone, they took a job. Then, underutilized, underpaid, and bored at work, they returned home. Soon, they repeated the cycle, which made it appear that women workers had short attention spans and high attrition rates.

In 1956, *Look* described these women, who constituted one-third of the nation's labor force, as people who "work casually . . . as a way of filling a hope chest or buying a new home freezer." *Look* added that such women had conceded the top rungs of the job ladder to men.

In response, women escalated their claim that it was now necessary for middle-class families to have two incomes in order to live according to their rising expectations. Yet women gained more than income from working. A *Fortune* poll of the same period discovered that a startling 25 percent of American women would have preferred to have been born male and expressed a desire to perform wage-labor or pursue a career. Instead of regretting the possibility of leaving their homes, they exulted in the prospect of joining the world of employment.

The following year, *Life* magazine addressed what it termed the "American Woman's Dilemma." Women now faced two options: either husband, home, and family or a combination of family and paid work. *Life* puzzled over how this could have happened in a society that urged women to remain docilely at home and discouraged their independence and autonomy.

Certainly, women did not gain much either financially or in career advancement. With the attitude that they worked only to "help their families," women sought such gender-defined jobs as clerical, secretarial, or sales work where they often accepted poor pay and lack of promotion. In turn, such women perpetuated the notion of women as "pin-money" workers and generally failed to gain access to the professional, technical, and managerial fields. Under the circumstances, union hostility against women revived.

Despite these difficulties, during the 1950s the level of female employment grew at a rate four times greater than men's. In 1950, women accounted for 29 percent of the total work force, but by 1959, this figure had jumped to nearly 35 percent. In that year, 40 percent of all women over sixteen held a job, while 30 percent of married women worked.

During the 1950s, increasing numbers of women also worked full-time, continued to work after marriage, and returned to work after their youngest children entered school. The number of working mothers rose 400 percent. By the later 1950s, it was apparent that most women would no longer spend most of their lives taking care of homes and children. In spite of the back-to-the-home movement, the lifetime devoted exclusively to home and family was now an exception rather than a rule for American women.

Throughout these developments, only the Women's Bureau represented the interests of working women. Although the Bureau had its hands more than full with such issues as sex-discrimination complaints, demands for equal-pay legislation, the establishment of day-care facilities, and protective legislation, in 1955 it tackled the problem of reconciling the back-to-the-home movement with the reality of rising numbers of women in the labor force. In that year, the Bureau brought the cause of working women to the American public through the White House Conference on Effective Uses of Woman-power.

At this conference, a Bureau speaker urged acceptance of women in all occupations. She also emphasized that women were "achievement-oriented" individuals who had the right to work. Other speakers advocated an increase in the effectiveness of the nation's "woman power." Although the conference concluded that "the structure and the substance of the lives of most women are fundamentally determined by their functions as wives, mothers, and homemakers," it also marked a subtle shift in governmental policy by insisting on women's ability and right to hold other jobs.

Such changes had both pluses and minuses. On the one hand, women workers tended to perpetuate conditions that would plague later generations of female laborers. For example, women's acceptance of low wages caused the median income of female workers to drop from 63.9 percent of that earned by men in 1955 to 60 percent in 1960. On the other hand, although women workers seldom viewed themselves as reformers or crusaders, they still effected change, simply by changing public notions of whether women's place was at home or at work outside the home. Increasingly, Americans began to view women as a permanent part of the labor force, rather than a temporary resource to be utilized during a time of emergency.

Women Religious

A very different type of "employed" woman who also fell outside the confines of the back-to-the-home movement were women Religious. The postwar years proved critical for them as well. In 1956, the Leadership Conference of Women Religious of the USA (LCWR) formed. Bringing together the chief governing officers of American religious communities involved in ministry activities, the LCWR helped spur and regulate a transitional time in the Catholic church and religious communities. Well before Vatican Council II brought dramatic changes in the lives of Roman Catholics and religious sisters, the LCWR had already begun to consider how their church and their orders might adapt to a changed world.

Rural and Native American Women

Other women who lived largely outside the back-to-the-home philosophy were those on farms and in rural areas throughout the Northeast, the South, and the West. Many suffered from poor health, unemployment, and poverty. Among these were American Indian women, many of whom still lived on reservations. Daily they survived scarcity and despair, and endured such policies as involuntary sterilizations by reservation medical services, forced adoptions of their children by Anglo families, and pressure to accept Christianity and the English language. Native American homosexuality—long accepted by many tribes—also came under attack.

In her 1964 autobiography, Polingaysi Qoyawayma revealed the conditions she had faced as a Hopi woman. On one occasion, for example, reservation officials had forced Hopi girls and women to walk naked through a dipping vat to avert a suspected epidemic. Qoyawayma did not oppose assimilation, but neither did she wish to lose her native culture. Thus, between 1924 and 1954, she taught Hopi children, giving them the prescribed instruction in English as well as slipping in Hopi and Navaho whenever possible.

Other Indian women also took matters into their own hands. Potter Maria Montoya Martinez of the San Ildefonso pueblo in New Mexico developed a technique in which she hand-turned pottery on a disk made from a gourd. Martinez polished the surfaces with a river stone, painted decorations in black on the polished pottery, and fired it in a kiln with cow manure until all the carbon burned away. This process resulted in silvery black pots with designs derived from ancient Indian motifs. Martinez's ability to adapt to the market economy helped revive the pueblo economy and create interest in Southwestern and Indian art. She taught others her method, traveled extensively, received numerous awards, and acted as a mediator who reached across cultures to bring people together.

Meanwhile, Maria Tallchief became the first Native American prima ballerina in the United States. Tallchief, an Osage Indian born in Oklahoma, studied with renowned dancer Bronislava Nijinska. Between 1947 and 1960, Tallchief performed with the New York City Ballet; later she directed the Chicago City Ballet. Like Martinez, Tallchief acted as a cultural broker, demonstrating Native Americans' abilities to the nation and the world.

Latinas

Except for some women of the middle and upper classes, Latinas also lived largely outside the suburban myth during the late 1940s and 1950s. A majority of Latinas worked for wages; those who labored in the California cannery industry toiled in appalling conditions. They provided seasonal labor for low wages—usually a piecework rate—and bore such common pressures as gradual speed-ups on the production line.

Like other groups of women, Latinas fought such practices in innovative ways. Mothers, daughters, sisters, cousins, and aunts sought employment in the same cannery, often persuading employers to hire yet one more family member. Thus, although some of these women saw employment as an avenue to independence, most used it to strengthen family ties. In addition, workers built networks within canneries. Because they were often gender-segregated in women's departments and race-segregated in the lowest jobs, Latinas shared a sense of unity and had the opportunity to communicate frequently.

Employers soon learned to fear Latina workers because of what one termed their "labor militancy." Latinas especially resented the fact that employers seldom promoted them to supervisory positions, even though they comprised 75 percent of the workforce. Consequently, Latina workers accounted for one-half of the membership of the United Cannery, Agricultural, Packing, and Allied Workers of America (UCAPAWA). Here, they served as organizers and strikers, asking particularly for equal wages, maternity leave, and improved working conditions. In so doing, they not only gained self-esteem but had the opportunity to cooperate with women workers of other racial/ethnic groups.

Latinas also improved their lot by applying pressure to male workers. In a 1950 strike in the New Mexico mines, Latino workers mounted a strike against Empire Zinc Company's wage cuts and unsafe conditions. When women asked that improved housing be included in the demands, male strikers found this a low priority. But when the company obtained an injunction forbidding miners from picketing and trucked in strikebreakers, the women took the men's places on the picket line. While men ran households, fed children, and cooked meals, women marched with their babies in their arms, then sang and shouted as police arrested them and packed them into jail cells. These women demonstrated their importance to labor movements, convinced men that women needed improvements, and recognized their own power and usefulness.

In New York City a slightly different pattern occurred. Here, Puerto Rican women also worked in segregated conditions and for inadequate wages as cigar makers, seamstresses, and factory operatives. They too maintained strong family ties and preserved their culture; over 90 percent continued to speak Spanish at home. But, unlike the situation in the Southwest, more Puerto Rican women than other Latinas were craftworkers, supervisors, and sales people, while a smaller proportion toiled in domestic and other service occupations. Still, of all groups of workers, including other Latinos, Puerto Ricans were disproportionately represented below the poverty line. They also had the highest proportion of female-headed households—because of death, desertion, separation, divorce, or choice—than any other group.

One reason this occurred was that skilled and craft unions barred Puerto Rican workers, especially women. Union leaders overlooked or ignored Puerto Ricans' strong tradition of labor activism, leaving them to fend for themselves. As great association builders proficient in adapting the association model from their homeland to New York City, Puerto Ricans responded by caring for their own. For instance, in 1934 Sister Carmelita established the *Casita Maria*, which provided social services during the depression, World War II, and the postwar years. Moreover, such aid and social organizations as the Puerto Rico Civic Club sponsored dances, celebrated holidays and special events, and supplied meeting places for single people.

Also, workers formed trade associations which encompassed far more than the workplace. The Puerto Rican postal workers' union, the *Associación de Empleados Civiles de Correo*, implemented work, civic, and social programs. Under the instrumental leadership of Raquel Rivera Hernández, the *Associación* grew, welcomed Puerto Rican women, and incorporated in 1951. Its goals were clear: "to promote friendship and encourage social and intellectual intercourse among veterans born in Puerto Rico employed in the service of the United States of America." Its members, who had all passed civil service exams, including proficiency in two languages, and many of whom were college graduates, sponsored fundraisers for labor causes, cultural events, and recreational activities.

Besides service groups, individual Puerto Rican women worked to improve their communities and workplace. Julia de Burgos, who in 1940 left Puerto Rico for New York City, soon began to write essays and stories with the encouragement of members of the Circle of Ibero-American Writers and Poets (CEPI). Between 1943 and 1945, Burgos worked for *Pueblos Hispanicos*, writing editorials and news stories and reporting on interviews for the Spanish-language publications. Burgos emphasized Puerto Ricans' need for social reform, especially improvement in the living conditions of working-class Puerto Ricans. Later, Burgos wrote poignant poems, usually feminist in tone. In "A Julia de Burgos" and "Yo Misma Fuí," she revealed the restrictions imposed upon women. Both were included in a posthumous volume of her work, *El Mar y Tú y Otros Poemas* (1954).

Black Women

Nor did the back-to-the-home fantasy have much meaning for black women. Discriminatory housing policies excluded black women from suburban life, keeping them, even those of the middle and upper classes, essentially segregated. Many faced rape and poverty as well, especially in the South and urban ghettoes.

Also, a high proportion of black women held paid employment. Over 40 percent of black mothers with small children worked outside their homes, while approximately one-quarter of them headed their own households. In the North, the majority still tended to hold domestic and service jobs, while in the South they labored as tenant farmers, tobacco strippers, and textile workers. During the postwar years, however, black female workers made some gains in white-collar work. Less than one-fifth of black female workers held such jobs in 1940, but over one-third did so in 1960. Black women workers also made substantial advances in the disparity of income between themselves and white women. In 1940, black women earned only 38 percent of the median wage of white women; in 1960, they earned 70 percent.

Several contemporary black authors of fiction effectively captured the plight of black women and conveyed it to the public. Ann Petry, the author of many short stories and several novels, including *The Street* (1946) and *Country Place* (1947), supplied insights into how the lives of black women differed from those of their white counterparts. In *The Street*, for example, Petry detailed the destruction of Harlem's hardworking, earnest, and honest Lutie Johnson.

Other black women served, like Native American women, as cultural arbitrators between the African American and Anglo cultures. Dancer Josephine Baker, for example, became a sensation on stage and in films, both in the United States and Europe. Because Baker performed a traditional black style which incorporated rhythms with sources ranging from the slave quarters to the ghetto, Anglo critics initially viewed her as exotic and primitive. Baker persevered, however, and legitimized black dance forms. She also sang in six languages and was an effective comedian, yet she gained so little acceptance and confronted so much prejudice in the United States that in 1937 she became a French citizen. Although Baker occasionally toured the United States, she resisted returning on a permanent basis: "They would make me sing mammy songs and I cannot feel mammy songs, so I cannot sing them." On a 1951 tour of the United States, Baker said, "my greatest desire will always be to see my people happier in this country." During the mid-1950s, she launched her "experiment in humanity," adopting twelve orphans of different races to show that people of different cultures could live together harmoniously.

Still other black women proved highly assertive in asking for rights for African Americans. Charlotta Spears Bass, editor of the *California Eagle* and the first black woman to run for vice-president of the United States, used essays and speeches to attack racial stereotypes, the Ku Klux Klan, restrictive housing covenants, and discriminatory hiring practices. During the 1940s, Bass entered local politics, then in 1948 helped found the Progressive Party. When running for the vice-presidency in 1952, Bass used the slogan: "Win or lose, we win by raising the issue."

Other black women also protested racial injustice. After the 1954 decision *Brown v. Board of Education of Topeka* declared unconstitutional "racial discrimination in public education," riots to close schools and prevent integration occurred throughout the South. In response, such women as Rosa Parks, Septima Clark, and Bernice Robinson helped generate a black freedom movement. These and other women leaders had learned their skills and gained their voices in black churches, or had participated in workshops at the Highlander Folk School in Grundy County, Tennessee.

Begun in 1932 to help industrial and rural workers in Appalachia, Highlander soon served as a regional training center for labor organizers and reformers. Beginning in 1944, Highlander shifted its focus to desegregating public schools, thus attracting black activists as well. In 1953, Highlander added to its curriculum summer workshops for white and black leaders and educators. Of her 1955 workshop, Rosa Parks later recalled, "that was the first time I lived in an atmosphere of complete equality with the members of the other race." After her Highlander summer, Parks returned home where she initiated the legendary Montgomery, Alabama, bus boycott.

The following year, 1956, Septima Clark became full-time director of Highlander's workshop program. Clark distributed workbooks which included voter registration and other application forms, as well as information on voting requirements, political parties, taxes, and other civil matters. Meanwhile, Bernice Robinson served as the first teacher in the citizenship program on South Carolina's Sea Island. As she became a civil rights activist and teacher, Robinson's citizenship training spread across the South, including a stint at Highlander.

Asian Women

Asian and Asian American women also had concerns other than the back-to-the-home movement during the late 1940s and 1950s. This era proved a turning point for them; their numbers increased, while their diversity and strength grew.

At the end of World War II, the War Brides Act allowed Asian American men and U.S. citizens to send for war brides, wives, and families as nonquota immigrants. The ensuing migration included Chinese, Japanese, Filipino, and Korean women by the thousands, but they faced numerous difficulties, including learning English, adjusting to American culture, and withstanding prejudice from Anglos and Asians alike.

Also in 1945 the War Relocation Authority (WRA) established a program to relocate Japanese Americans from such detention camps as Tule Lake in California and Heart Mountain in Wyoming. The following year the WRA closed the camps entirely. Despite relocation efforts, former detainees generally suffered property losses and personal devastation. One woman recalled that it took nearly thirty years for her to outgrow "the shame and the guilt and the sense of unworthiness" she felt from the internment experience.

Additional legislation further improved the situation for Asians and Asian Americans. In 1948, President Harry S Truman signed the Evacuation Claims Act to help Japanese Americans reclaim some of their losses, but Japanese Americans recouped only ten cents for each dollar. Then, in 1952 the McCarran-Walter Act abolished racial qualifications for citizenship. Soon the Refugee Relief Acts of 1953 and 1957 allowed refugees of the Chinese civil war and the Korean War to immigrate to America.

The percentage of women among these immigrants grew dramatically. Consequently, the male/female ratio among Chinese changed from 2.9 men to 1 woman in 1940 to 1.8 men per woman in 1950, and to 1.3 per woman in 1960. In that year, 217,000 people of Chinese ancestry lived in the United States and nearly 40 percent of them were women.

Many of these were women who had married Chinese men living in the United States but had never expected to reunite their split families. Despite their status as nonquota immigrants, however, they soon discovered that they had to undergo detention and investigation. Because both the American Civil Liberties Union and Chinese American groups protested, by the late 1950s the U.S. Immigration Service resolved women's rights of entry at the point of departure rather than upon entry.

Most female immigrants went to Asian communities in New York, Boston, Los Angeles, and San Francisco. Here they found a familiar culture, family members, and support networks. Soon Asian communities became more family oriented and balanced in gender, but Chinatowns and Little Tokyos also experienced overcrowding, lack of social services, and job segregation. Women labored as seamstresses and tailors, cannery workers, domestic servants, and farm laborers, as well as working in laundries, restaurants, and ethnic small businesses. Those who were able to enter clerical work, technical, and professional fields continued to earn less than their qualifications deserved and less than most non-Asian workers.

The story of Song Zem Ping is representative of such women. At age thirteen she had married a Chinese man living in the United States. After the war, she could migrate only by posing as a war-bride, which required her to leave her son behind. When she arrived in the United States, she spoke no English and took a job as a seamstress. Although she bore four more children, Song Zem Ping continued to work: "I can still recall the times when I had one foot on the pedal and another one on an improvised rocker, rocking one son to sleep while the other was tied to my back. Many times I would accidentally sew my finger instead of the fabric because one child screamed or because I was falling asleep on the job."

Because Asian women who spoke English and had partially acculturated faced an easier time, churches and women's groups offered English and vocational classes, most of which also taught Asian women how to wear western dress and how to cook American food. In 1947, Rose Chiayin Tsou came to study library science and took up residence in Eugene, Oregon, where she helped found the Eugene Chinese Benevolent Association to help others like her. The following year, Dr. Katharine Hsu came to study pediatrics and also remained, becoming a foremost researcher in children's tuberculosis.

The Cold War of the 1950s largely halted such migration. Americans' unreasoning fear of Communism led to violent attacks on such groups as the Chinese American Youth Club and the Chinese Workers' Mutual Aid Association. Although some Asians and Asian Americans waited quietly for this to pass, others protested. Ruby Chow, a member of the Seattle, Washington, city council, urged Seattle's Chinese Benevolent Association to launch an educational campaign to convince the public "that we are democratic, freedom-loving people" rather than Communists.

Of course, many women of Asian heritage were not migrants but were American-born. They often led split lives, following Asian customs at home and western ways in public. Jade Snow Wong's autobiography *Fifth Chinese Daughter* (1945) revealed the tension in these women's lives; she told her parents "you must give me the freedom to find some answers for myself." Because even the most conservative families gradually recognized the value of education for daughters, more Asian American women began to attend college than ever before. Among Chinese American women, a larger proportion graduated from college than among Anglo women. Also, many young women joined the labor force despite continuing discrimination against them.

A few even surmounted the bonds of prejudice to become stage stars and political leaders. In 1946, Ruth Ann Koesun, the first woman of Asian heritage to become a prima ballerina, joined the American Ballet Theatre where she soloed for the next twenty-three years. Yet other women played an active role in public life. In 1956, March Fong successfully campaigned for a seat on the California School Board.

Still, women's social lives continued to center in their own communities. In California's Chinatowns, for example, women formed such organizations as the Oakland Waku Auxiliary, which sponsored women's sporting events, including basketball, volleyball, and softball. Beginning in 1958, Chinatown boosters also sponsored Miss Chinatown contests, while individual families held debutante balls so their daughters could properly enter Chinese American society.

Other Asian American women, especially those of the middle and upper classes, moved to the suburbs. Here, they often found that they missed the support of their own culture and played marginal roles in their

newly adopted communities. Laura Chin, who grew up in an Anglo sec-
tion of Brooklyn, New York, during the 1950s, remembered: "I felt very
lonely when I grew up. We were simply not like the other people in the
neighborhood." Nancy Bing Chew of Mississippi concurred: "We were
made fun of all the time. . . . We had to meet certain expectations that our
parents wanted of us and at the same time, deal with those who could
not totally understand us."

These women had sacrificed their ethnic identity but could not fully
assimilate into the broader American culture either. Moreover, even
though they no longer had to follow the custom of arranged marriage,
their parents usually continued to encourage them to marry Asian men.
But, because most miscegenation laws had been repealed, approximately
one-fourth of Asian American men married outside their racial-ethnic
group. Understandably, then, Asian American women usually felt either
extremely marginalized or learned to draw upon their mixed heritage as a
source of strength.

EMERGING FEMINISM: THE EARLY 1960S

Competent Women of the 1960s

By 1960, American attitudes toward working women were beginning
to change. Certain realities loomed large: the nation's switch to a service
industry which created more jobs for women; improved technology
which allowed women to handle more jobs and heavier ones; and
women's determination to enter the labor force despite proscriptions to
the contrary.

Rather than encouraging women to stay home, a variety of commentators now discussed ways in which women could combine home and
work. Esther Peterson, head of the Women's Bureau, remarked that
"today's homemaking chores are no great challenge" to competent
women whose "sense of frustration is likely to heighten after children go
to school and there is even less need for her in the home."

Researchers and sociologists, too, began to argue that women should
work because employed women exercised a greater role in family decision
making and fostered more self-reliance in their children. Research showed
that working mothers were also less protective and more confident with
their children than were nonworking women. In 1965, sociologist Robert
0. Blood asserted that "employment emancipates women from domina-
tion by their husbands, and secondarily, raises their daughters from inferiority to their brothers." In Blood's view, "the male-dominated,
female-serviced family is being replaced by a new symmetry."

In the meantime, attitudes toward women in general were undergoing
modification. The sentiment against women's progress, which was
largely a reaction against the disruption of homes and families during the

war years, began to abate after 1960. The discontent of women—especially educated, middle-class women—with the limitations on their lives grew at the same time. The media recognized women's dual role, while the continuing education movement tried to train women who would work sometime during their lives. Finally, social criticism and reform efforts concerning numerous issues, ranging from the environment to relations between Anglos and people of color, were starting to shake traditional American attitudes to their very foundations.

President's Commission on the Status of Women, 1961

During John F. Kennedy's 1960 presidential campaign, approximately six million women worked on his behalf. Young women especially saw him as a messiah. One young woman even alienated her anti-Catholic father by voting for, as her father called the Roman Catholic Kennedy, "the Pope's candidate."

When Kennedy achieved the presidency, he found it impossible to appoint a female cabinet member as he had promised, but he tried to make up for it in another way. Thus, in 1961—several years before a revitalized feminist movement erupted in America—President Kennedy created the President's Commission on the Status of Women. At the urging of Democratic party women and Esther Peterson of the Women's Bureau, Kennedy appointed Eleanor Roosevelt as chairperson.

Two years later, the Commission presented a sixty-page report on its deliberations. This included the Commission's endorsement of improved access to education for women, aid to working mothers, childcare services, equal employment opportunities, equality of rights under the law (preferably under the Fifth and Fourteenth Amendments rather than under the controversial ERA), and a wider role for women in government. The report also asked for continuing governmental action on behalf of women, a recommendation that led President Kennedy to establish the Interdepartmental Committee on the Status of Women and the Citizens' Advisory Council on the Status of Women.

Although the commission's findings were fairly conservative, they had widespread impact. The deliberations of the commission helped initiate a national debate on women's issues, while every state formed commissions on the status of women. Furthermore, the government committed itself to a more comprehensive policy of reform for women rather than simply appointing a few to office as the Truman and Eisenhower administrations had done.

The Equal Pay Act of 1963, recommended by the Commission on the Status of Women, further demonstrated this commitment. This act attacked a long-term problem, traceable back to the early years of industrial revolution in the United States. Such factors as occupational segregation and substandard wages for women of color had contributed significantly, but employment bars against married women and part-time hours for women had also depressed female wages. The Equal Pay Act, the first major federal legislation concerning women's employment since the Progressive era, required that employers pay the same wages to women and men who performed jobs requiring equal skill and effort.

The Equal Pay Act soon proved less effective than hoped, however. The U.S. Labor Department attempted to enforce the provisions by making routine checks and taking specific complaints, but the act's wording was unclear as to what constituted equal skill. Also, the law did not apply at all to women who performed specialized "women's work" at lesser pay.

Women and Civil Rights

Feminism was not the only reform cause on the horizon during the early 1960s; the civil rights movement was coalescing as well in a crusade that seemed inevitable. Demographic and other changes had led to growing numbers of African Americans, Latinos, and Asian Americans among the U.S. population. Participation in World War II had not only shown these groups how others lived but made clearer to them the restrictions they had been tolerating and the importance of their own contributions to American life, in and outside of the military. Consequently, they increasingly objected to limits on their political, civic, and social rights.

Of course, women had long participated in the gradual democratization of liberty in the United States. They increased their involvement in matters of civil rights during World War II and after. For instance, in 1944 Helen Gahagan Douglas, a Democrat from California's fourteenth district, gained a seat in Congress where she ably fought legislation undermining civil liberties. Also in 1944, Lillian Smith's novel *Strange Fruit* attacked racial segregation. Smith, a Southern Anglo woman, told the story of a tragic love affair between a black woman and white man in a small Georgia town. Then, in 1949 Smith's *Killers of the Dream* revealed Georgians' determination to preserve segregation and white supremacy. Outspoken on public issues, Smith was in other ways an enigma. She seldom spoke of her lesbianism and generally failed to recognize that sexism restricted the nation's women. It would take the full-blown civil rights movement of the 1960s and 1970s to define the issue and raise the awareness of millions of American women.

The civil rights movement erupted on two fronts simultaneously: among Latinos and among African Americans. Of course, Latinas had a long history of activism regarding both employment and social ills. In multipurpose organizations they had worked for political, economic, social, and cultural improvements. And for years they had watched their people suffer not only exclusion from Anglo-dominated labor unions, but discriminatory poll taxes, literacy tests for voting, voter residency requirements, and gerrymandering that reduced their influence.

The emerging Latino civil rights movement garnered little exposure in the national media, however, for it was concentrated among Puerto Ricans in New York City and Chicanos in the Southwest. Despite low visibility, during the postwar years both groups became more politically oriented. In Texas, for example, the League of United Latin American Citizens (founded in 1929) encouraged the formation of new groups. During the 1950s, the League worked to desegregate movie theaters, restaurants, and other public facilities.

One woman, Dolores Huerta, exercised particular influence on the Latino civil rights battle. In 1960, Huerta supported Kennedy and participated in the *Viva Kennedy* campaign. She also assisted the newly formed Community Service Organization (CSO) in registering voters, then went to Sacramento to lobby the California legislature for CSO programs, asking especially for the right to register voters door-to-door, for drivers' license examinations given in Spanish, and for disability insurance for migrant farm workers. In 1962, Huerta helped Cesar Chavez organize the National Farm Workers Association (NFWA), and recruited women as members.

The nation first became aware of Mexican American militancy during the 1960s as a result of NFWA activities. The movement to help Mexican Americans in the Southwest was known as *la causa*; it attracted strong support from both men and women. In late 1962, Chavez retained Jesse Lopez de la Cruz as a volunteer organizer. De la Cruz especially hoped to strengthen workers' confidence by offering a credit union, a consumer cooperative, and counseling for problems regarding citizenship, voting, unfair rents, and discrimination in schools.

Meanwhile, a student movement emerged, including *La Raza Unida Party* and the Crusade for Justice, which involved middle- and upper-class college and university students. Soon such other groups as United Mexican American Students and the Mexican American Youth Organization developed. Typically, these groups protested housing and health care discrimination, police brutality, substandard education, and unemployment. Although women initially filled traditional "helper" roles in the movement, they soon began to demand their own voice and influence.

African Americans felt restless and discontented as well. Many commentators date the beginning of the black civil rights movement to 1 December 1955 when Rosa Parks refused to give up her bus seat to a white passenger and was subsequently arrested, jailed, and fined. When other blacks rallied around Parks, the Montgomery, Alabama, bus boycott ensued. Women, who constituted 56 percent of the black population in Montgomery and used buses to reach their domestic service jobs, staged a thirteen-month boycott during which they walked as much as twelve miles. "I'm walking for my children and grand-children," one elderly woman said.

As the first black female playwright to have a play produced on Broadway, Lorraine Hansberry also set precedents. During its first Broadway season in 1958–1959, *A Raisin the Sun* told the story of a proud black family struggling against the prejudice of whites who tried to bar them from their neighborhood. *A Raisin in the Sun* not only won the New York Drama Critics' Circle Award as best play of the season but contributed to the public consciousness of the emerging civil rights movement, which the author personally supported. Hansberry often maintained that black Americans lived "in a hostile circumstance in the United States" and thus had "a great deal to be angry about."

Then, in 1960, disquiet erupted throughout the South. In that year, four students "sat-in" at a Woolworth's lunch counter in Greensboro, North Carolina. Their arrest inspired similar actions all over the South, as well as Freedom Rides to desegregate interstate transportation. Thousands of Americans exchanged apathy for concern. Although young African Americans of the 1950s had long been taught not to express themselves, they began to find their voice. They were inspired and joined by the 1960s youth who believed in John F. Kennedy and his promise to change the nation. Like him, the youth wanted to participate in civic affairs. They listened to, and repeated among themselves, his famous summons: "Ask not what your country can do for you. Ask what you can do for your country."

When, however, in 1961, President Kennedy dispatched to Vietnam four hundred Special Forces soldiers and one hundred military advisers, then authorized clandestine warfare against North Vietnam, women and men marched and carried placards protesting the nation's involvement in the Southeast Asian Country. At the same time, others picketed to demand civil rights, meaning governmental assurance of equal opportunities regardless of race, gender, or ethnic background.

Throughout these events, the nation's women lacked a well-articulated feminist consciousness. Black women especially believed they had to deal with racial problems before gender issues. By the early 1960s, black women found themselves increasingly burdened with a plethora of social problems, including marital instability. The number of female-headed households increased; by 1967 the black illegitimacy rate had climbed to 29 percent from 17 percent in 1940. During the 1960s, 58 percent of black women held paid employment outside their homes.

To help themselves and their families, black women remained active in churches. Ultimately, involvement in church programs not only trained women, but positioned them as activists at a crucial moment in their history. Fannie Lou Hamer, for example, went from singing gospel hymns to organizing voter registration drives beginning in 1962.

Other black women also participated in civil rights associations, social service organizations, and the last Highlander summer workshop (1961).

Although the Tennessee state court revoked Highlander's charter in that year, the school had done its job; it had produced people who would lead the waves of sit-ins, Freedom Rides, and other protests throughout the South during the 1960s.

Still, despite women's widespread participation in such groups as the Southern Christian Leadership Conference (SCLC) and the Student Non-violent Coordinating Committee (SNCC), their roles remained more traditional than not. Leader Stokely Carmichael even commented that "the only position for women in our movement is prone." He and others seemed to have overlooked Ella Baker's efforts to help Martin Luther King found and administer SCLC, and board of directors' member Septima Clark's assistance to southern blacks in challenging the denial of voting rights and her later help in organizing SNCC.

Carmichael and others also failed to recognize that women had acquired a language that described oppression and advocated revolt, learned the strategy and techniques of organization, and begun to see themselves collectively as objects of discrimination. Because of their independence, black women especially experienced frustration when the civil rights movement offered them a heightened sense of self-worth on the one hand, and, on the other, forced them into traditional sex roles. Typically, these women's male colleagues expected them to make coffee and provide other services, rather than write pamphlets, make speeches, and march in protest.

When Cynthia Washington, an engineering student who became a member of SNCC in 1963, rose to leadership positions and became director of her own freedom project in Mississippi, she observed the limitations placed on other women workers, especially Anglo women, and listened to their complaints. Then, in 1964, the first formal analysis of sexism in the civil rights movement appeared. In it white activist Casey Hayden charged SNCC with rampant paternalism: "Assumptions of male superiority are as widespread and deep rooted and every much as crippling to the woman as the assumptions of white supremacy are to the Negro." Other indictments followed, providing further catalysts for the emergence of vehement feminism among disgruntled women.

During the "freedom summers" of 1964 and 1965, 650 northern Anglo women went south to work on behalf of civil rights. They confronted a movement that defined oppression and equality in terms of race and class rather than gender. Working within the Congress on Racial Equality (CORE), the SCLC, and the SNCC, they soon came to resent sexist definitions of their roles in the movement. Sexual stereotyping, rather than their interests and abilities, determined their job assignments. They were seldom asked to participate in policy decisions and they were often the recipients of unwelcome sexual advances.

In 1965, white freedom-fighters Mary King and Casey Hayden left the civil rights movement. They addressed a memorandum to black women workers which expressed the hope that "perhaps we can start to talk with each other more openly than in the past and create a community of support for each other so we can deal with ourselves and others with integrity and can therefore keep working."

Perhaps King and Hayden left too soon, for 1965 proved a turning point. In that year, the U.S. Congress approved the Voting Rights Act of 1965 which ensured black men's *and* women's right to vote, and thus spurred both the black power movement and feminism.

Betty Friedan and the Feminine Mystique, 1963

It appears that the black civil rights movement developed before feminism, but it is more likely that civil rights was simply more violent and therefore more visible. Although civil rights helped raise women's awareness, politicize them, and legitimize their actions and claims, feminism also emerged on its own during the early 1960s.

In 1961, writer Tillie Olsen set the tone. Her first novella, *Tell Me a Riddle*, demonstrated that women writers had limited their expression because of restrictive conditions in their lives. Olsen, who maintained that when artists' voices are silenced women go unheard, won the O. Henry Award in 1961.

Other women took a different tack by using public deification of women's importance as mothers to demand change. Founded by Dagmar Wilson, Women Strike for Peace (WSP) vehemently opposed nuclear weapons, especially Strontium 90. In 1961, WSP called for a one-day peace demonstration to protest radioactive fall-out from nuclear testing in the Soviet Union. Over fifty thousand women participated in the strike, which generated the organization of local peace groups in sixty towns, and cities. Fully 61 percent of these group's members were full-time homemakers. The following year, HUAC accused WSP members of being Communists. In reply, Wilson stated that WSP was concerned with mother love and protecting children rather than influencing politics: "I would like to say that unless everybody in the whole world joins us in the fight, then God help us."

Then, in 1963, a seminal book coalesced the contemporary feminist movement. As a young woman, Betty Friedan had graduated from Smith College and received a fellowship to the University of California at Berkeley to study psychology. But, like many women of her era, she withdrew from the program, married, and alternated work with marriage and childbearing. When her second pregnancy led to her being fired, Friedan retreated into a suburban home on New York's Long Island. When, during the late 1950s, Friedan sent a questionnaire to other Smith College graduates it revealed a discontent which she subsequently labeled "the problem that has no name."

In 1963, Friedan reported on her findings in *The Feminine Mystique*. She described "the problem that has no name" as "a strange stirring, a sense of dissatisfaction, a yearning that women suffered in the middle of the twentieth century in the United States." Friedan added that a vague discontent gnawed at wives and mothers who supposedly lived "happy" and "fulfilled" lives. Moreover, they felt guilty and ill at ease about their feelings. "What kind of a woman was she if she did not feel this mysterious fulfillment waxing the kitchen floor?" Friedan asked. "She was so ashamed to admit her dissatisfaction that she never knew how many other women shared it." Friedan concluded that women had to add other pursuits to "occupation housewife" and the "comfortable concentration camp" of the home as soon as possible.

Friedan also attacked Freud, especially his theories regarding "penis envy," and his tendency to stereotype women according to gender expectations. Friedan pointed out that Freud drew upon men to establish norms, then argued that women wanted to act and feel like men. But there was more to women's sexuality and abilities, Friedan argued, than penis envy and motherhood.

Affirmative Action

One early result of the contemporary feminist movement's pressure was affirmative action programs. In 1964, the U.S. Congress passed Title VII of the Civil Rights Act. The Civil Rights Act prohibited racial discrimination on many fronts, while Title VII in particular prohibited discrimination on account of race or sex by employers, employment agencies, and labor unions, and created an Equal Employment Opportunity Commission (EEOC) to enforce these provisions. A few years later, Senator Everett Dirksen of Illinois commented that Title VII was Congress's attempt to "remake the social pattern of this country." Certainly, women activists quickly urged the new EEOC to take seriously the ban on gender discrimination.

The Office of Federal Contract Compliance (OFCC) enforced these regulations through fifteen departments and compliance agencies which conducted periodic reviews. Enforcement proved less than adequate, however, because the OFCC had a small staff and limited funding, sanctioned few employers, and received widespread criticism when it exercised what many Americans viewed as preferential treatment on behalf of people of color and women.

Backlash and Antifeminism

Opponents to feminist goals argued that women must continue to be domestic and maternal if the American family were to survive. Although the high divorce rate did not rise significantly again until after 1963, many Americans feared the demise of the American family. When antifeminists raised the issue of "family," however, they usually meant the traditional patriarchal family which was indeed disappearing. Generally, antifeminists attracted an audience composed of political and religious fundamentalists. Such women as Phyllis Schlafly and Mirabelle Morgan built careers upon urging women, especially white middle- and upper-class women, to return to their homes. They also borrowed such feminist techniques as speeches, petitions, and lobbying to advance what they described as profamily messages. They especially pointed to the high divorce rate and the growth of displaced homemakers as evidence that American women must resume their maternal "destiny" and subordination within the family.

WOMEN'S LIVES: THE EARLY 1960s

Consumerism

Based upon a relentless search for innovative fashions, novelty items, and new technology during the early 1960s, consumerism reached a new peak and spurred the economy. Manufacturers tried to anticipate women's needs and create domestic products that women did not even know they wanted. Next, Madison Avenue launched an elaborate and expensive advertising campaign to encourage women to buy an increasing number of items.

Despite women consumers' important contributions to the economy, advertising often used patronizing and sexist themes to attract them. Madison Avenue viewed women as easily manipulated and gullible consumers who would buy anything, and often women did. But in other cases, they boycotted goods. One woman who grew up during the 1950s explained that her mother avoided fad-fashions and refused to buy polyester pantsuits.

Sex

During the early 1960s, the so-called sexual revolution was well underway. As the diaphragm and the birth-control pill became widely and easily available, recreational sex also became more possible without crisis pregnancies. Thus, Americans heard a great deal about the "new morality" and free love.

In the ensuing quest for "better" sex, experts rejected the vagina as a source of orgasm, identifying instead the clitoris as its center. They also recommended masturbation as either a substitute for sex or a supplement to it, while they recognized that women could gain sexual pleasure with either men or women.

Lesbianism thus emerged as a public issue. In 1955, eight San Francisco women had founded the first lesbian organization, the Daughters of Bilitis (DOB). Named after the erotic poem "Songs of Bilitis," DOB sounded like a traditional woman's club, yet offered a code name to attract lesbians. By 1960, DOB membership included 110 women with chapters in Los Angeles, Chicago, and New York. The association issued a bimonthly newsletter called the *Ladder*, which emphasized lesbian rights and culture. It also used public education to achieve civil rights and an improved image for lesbians, as well as providing speakers for radio and television, high schools and colleges, and other programs. During the early 1960s, additional lesbian groups appeared. Usually more assertive and explicitly lesbian-feminist in nature, they provided an important antecedent for the subsequent gay rights movement and to a lesser extent the feminist movement.

Many Americans could not easily accept lesbianism, for it posed a difficult issue for western culture. In the United States, culture proscribed behavior according to the gender a person was born with. In cases of children born with amorphous genitalia, culture assigned them one gender or the other for their upbringing.

Other cultures, however, made very different choices. In some "low" cultures, infanticide settled the problem; while in some "high" cultures, such as the caste system of India, special rank and rules of behavior accrued to amorphous children. Some Native American cultures even accepted or revered those who were different physically, or practiced cross-gender dressing, or established homosexual relationships. But, because western, Christian culture inveighed against such practices, American society expected children to be clearly either girls or boys, and to follow the prescribed rules for each. This made it difficult for Americans to accept lesbianism, much less to find a place for it in existing American beliefs and customs.

Courtship, Marriage, and Divorce

During the early 1960s, dating essentially disappeared. Single people pursued activities in groups, while sex became casual and "living together" increased. Marriage rates rose, but beginning in 1964 birth rates began to decline.

In 1965, a landmark case established Americans' right to practice birth control. When officials of the Planned Parenthood League of Connecticut were arrested and fined for defying state laws that banned birth-control devices and prohibited the distribution of birth-control information, a major judicial decision soon followed. In the case of *Griswold v. Connecticut*, the U.S. Supreme Court declared unconstitutional Connecticut's birth-control laws and established citizens' right of privacy in matters of marital intimacy. Justice William O. Douglas set an important precedent when he found for the protected nature of the "intimate relation of husband and wife."

Meanwhile, Americans resumed their penchant to divorce. The divorce rate had settled on a plateau between 1955 and 1963, then continued its ascent toward a world record. Divorce continued to be higher in urban areas than in rural, while the western United States had the highest divorce rate, the South rose to second position, and the Northeast dropped to third place. African Americans suffered the highest rate of di-

voice of all groups, but divorce among such populations as Roman
Catholic Chicanos was increasing. Divorce also rose among women employed outside the home and those with children. Few realized that the
divorce rate, while serious, also suffered inflation by such factors as
people who now obtained multiple divorces, people who sought divorces
rather than deserting as their forbearers had, couples who lived longer
and whose long-term marriages thus ended through divorce rather than
the death of one spouse, and more thorough reporting of divorce statistics. Nor did they recognize that the American family had entered a transitional phase that would lead to the development of new and disparate
family forms.

Clearly, women now demanded more from marriage than had their
mothers and grandmothers, while they faced new difficulties combining
jobs with home, husband, children, and consumerism. As a result, authors of such so-called guidebooks as *The Complete Guide to Divorce* and
other self-help literature sharply indicted employed women as destroyers
of the American family. In 1963, the author of *The Complete Guide* charged
that the high divorce rate resulted from "the emancipation of women—
economic, legal, sexual, and intellectual."

Popular Culture

Fads characterized the early 1960s. The relaxed "hippie" culture spread
over the nation, along with marijuana smoking, hitchhiking, communal
living, and music of the counterculture. In the matter of attire, both
young women and men adopted jeans, work-shirts, combat boots, long
hair, and beads. When young men began to look like women by wearing
sandals and long hair, it raised the ire of conservatives. Undaunted,
youths simply replied that Jesus had favored both sandals and long hair.

In this era of protest and transition, films and other forms of popular
culture sent mixed messages to women. For the most part, popular
women's magazines continued to underwrite the feminine mystique by
depicting suburban housewives and their supposedly ideal lifestyles. One
of the few dissenting voices was that of Helen Gurley Brown, editor of
Cosmopolitan. Brown led *Cosmo*, as she liked to call it, to a new frankness
that supported the sexual revolution as well as women's increasing participation in the workplace.

Images of women in magazine and newspaper cartoons were also
mixed. Stereotypes included the wild spender, the emotional female, the
gabby woman, the reckless woman driver, and women who were un-
aware of, or unable to grasp, politics and current events. Cranky mothers-
in-law and sexy, air-headed secretaries were favorite targets. In one
cartoon, a boss remarked to his secretary as she left the office on a Friday
afternoon: "Nice going, Miss Hamblin. You certainly put in a full day's
work this week!" Yet at the same time, Blondie continued to boss
Dagwood and Superwoman romped through "masculine" adventures.

In film, a similar contradiction existed. Although Marilyn Monroe entered a mental hospital in 1961, and the following year committed suicide, her sex-kitten image and films lived on. American men continued to view Monroe as a dream lover. Norman Mailer, for example, described Monroe as "the sweet angel of sex. . . . a very Stradivarius of sex, so gorgeous, forgiving, humorous, compliant and tender that even the most mediocre musician could relax his lack of art in the dissolving magic of her violin."

Meanwhile, other Hollywood women avoided the Monroe myth. Katharine Hepburn continued to be one of the most admired and independent movie stars ever, earning Best Actress Academy Awards for *Morning Glory* (1933), *Guess Who's Coming to Dinner* (1967), *The Lion in Winter* (1968), and *On Golden Pond* (1981), as well as receiving eight more Academy Award nominations. On screen, Hepburn played strong women who were inevitably irascible and smart. Off screen, she provided a role model for American women who chafed at the prescriptions of traditional female roles.

Similarly, Ida Lupino supplied a strong prototype. When she tired of playing women in crisis in modern melodramas, Lupino formed in 1949 an independent production company called The Filmmakers. Lupino soon became a feminist filmmaker who wrote, acted in, directed, and produced such films as *Hard, Fast, and Beautiful* (1951), *The Bigamist* (1953), and *The Hitchhiker* (1953). In these, Lupino presented a searing analysis of women as consumers, and as people torn by divisive allegiances to marriage, family, and career. Given the fact that Americans were just beginning to consider new ideas regarding women, it is little wonder that Lupino's cynical characters generally alienated critics, except for feminist and European reviewers.

Hollywood also vacillated between characterizing women of color as sexy or strong. Much like Monroe's usual characters, Nancy Kwan played a clever, but submissive prostitute in *The World of Suzie Wong* (1960). In the meantime, comic books of the era portrayed the diabolical Dragon Lady in the "Terry and the Pirates" and the "Steve Canyon" series.

In other cases, however, women of color rose above their roles to appear assertive and smart. For *Carmen Jones* (1954), Dorothy Dandridge became the first black woman to earn an Academy Award nomination as Best Actress. As Bess in *Porgy and Bess* (1959), she won the Golden Globe Award for best actress in a musical. Although Dandridge tried to develop independence and autonomy in her professional and personal lives, she usually found her acting parts and private actions circumscribed by both her gender and her race. One of her last films was *Malaga* (1962), in which, once again, she played a love scene with a white man who was not allowed to kiss her for fear of offending theater audiences. Such racism also kept her out of films. In one especially ironic instance, she was sought out for the major role of black temptress Cleopatra, but the director's choice was overruled in favor of Elizabeth Taylor. Dandridge died in 1965 from an overdose of an antidepressant.

In popular music, the contradictions appeared as well. On the one hand, such singers as Barbra Streisand followed the Broadway and musical theater traditions, generally appearing feminine and sensual, even in such gutsy roles as Fanny Brice and Yentl. In Los Angeles, the Hollywood Paladium featured such talented and "womanly" singers as Celia Cruz and Nita Cruz. On the other, rock star Janis Joplin gained fame for her flamboyant, frenetic performances as well as her self-destructive lifestyle, while Aretha Franklin and Diana Ross developed the more mellow music of "soul."

Professional Women

During the early 1960s, American women increasingly obtained higher education. As they applied for medical and law schools, they challenged and defeated the customary quotas on women students. They also earned a growing number of Ph.D.'s, especially in the humanities, but still fell short of gaining full professorships and administrative posts.

Overall, between 1940 and 1960 the number of professional women increased by 41 percent. Because most Americans still viewed the only professions suitable for women as extensions of their traditional domestic duties, women remained clustered in teaching and nursing. Such professional segregation underwrote lower pay and fewer opportunities for promotion to top-level positions.

Women were also still expected to leave their jobs when they married. One young college graduate seeking employment in 1960 recalled that the school superintendent who interviewed her first checked clandestinely with her student-teaching supervisor regarding her marriage plans. Reassured that she was not engaged, he hired her. But she left within two years anyway—to attend graduate school where she earned an M.A. and a Ph.D.

This portrayal of the conflicting forces on women's lives is not meant to suggest that women achieved little or nothing during the postwar years. In fact, despite the back-to-the-home movement and the contradictory messages of the early 1960s, women excelled in many fields.

Maria Goeppert Mayer, for example, became the first woman to receive the Nobel Prize for theoretical physics. Her *Elementary Theory of Nuclear Shell Structure*, published with Hans D. Jensen, in 1955, and her other work in nuclear physics gained her the Nobel Prize in 1963 and helped the United States enter the nuclear age.

Another leading figure was Hannah Arendt, a German Jew who migrated to the United States in 1940 and later became a significant postwar intellectual. Between 1949 and 1952, Arendt served as the research director for the Jewish Cultural Reconstruction and later its executive secretary, helping to reassemble Jewish writings the Nazis had dispersed.

Arendt then entered academia and became the first woman appointed as full professor at Princeton University. By the late 1950s and early 1960s, Arendt achieved renown for such writings as *On Revolution* (1958), *The Human Condition* (1958), and *On Violence* (1962), which argued that revolution and war constituted the primary forces of the era.

Similarly, Rose Hum Lee, a Chinese American woman from Montana, became the first woman to chair a department at an American university. Lee, a University of Chicago Ph.D., an authority on Chinese American culture, and an author of children's books, chaired the sociology department at Roosevelt University in Chicago. She also produced pioneering work on social structures and the assimilation of Chinese Americans, pacifists, and Quakers into American society.

Women in the Military
Women also now found opportunities in the U.S. armed forces. Beginning in 1948, when President Harry S Truman had signed the Women's Armed Forces Integration Act making the women's corps a permanent part of the armed forces, women had begun to pursue military careers. Subsequently, women served during the Korean Conflict and the Vietnam War. Although the numbers of women who served during Korea remain unclear, during the Vietnam years some 260,000 women served in the U.S. military, with 11,000 stationed in Vietnam and thousands more located in neighboring countries. Of these, 92 percent were nurses, eight of whom died as a result of combat. The other 8 percent of women worked in administration, communications, and personnel positions.

Literary Women
Poet Gwendolyn Brooks, the winner of a Pulitzer Prize in 1950, proved herself a major poet and writer of the twentieth century. Living and writing in her home area of South-side Chicago, Brooks presented brave, hopeful women who endured the difficulties of being black in postwar America. In one of her best-known works, *The Bean Eaters* (1960), Brooks celebrated the everyday life of the black community. By the mid-1960s, she addressed herself to such issues as black pride and power, as well as inspiring young black writers.

A Latino Renaissance also emerged during the early 1960s. Latina writers now included working- and middle-class women, rather than only the upper-class ladies of earlier generations. They also demonstrated growing pride in their combined Indian and Spanish ancestry and explored such contemporary problems as urban living. Among these writers were Angela de Hoyos, Estela Portillo, and Bernice Zamora.

Reform-minded Women
During the early 1960s, women's longstanding penchant for social and cultural reform revived. For instance, singer Joan Baez used music, writ-

ing, and speaking to protest various forms of oppression and violence. Baez played a significant role in the rediscovery of folk music that characterized the early 1960s, but utilized such music in a political way. Active in civil rights and the protest against U.S. involvement in Vietnam, Baez built her reputation on such songs as *Where Are You Now, My Son?* and *Carry It On*.

During these years, New York attorney Bella Abzug also worked in the political realm but in a different way. Abzug, who had defended the accused during the McCarthy anti-Communist trials, gave legal advice to civil rights workers and assisted the passage of civil rights legislation in 1964. During the 1960s, Abzug also lobbied for the Women's Strike for Peace, supported nuclear disarmament, and aided the passage of the Voting Rights Act of 1965. Colorful and outspoken, Abzug often called men to task for their deeds and urged women onward.

Yet other women rediscovered the cause of children's rights. Although child labor and child neglect had long interested women reformers, during the 1960s women tried to emphasize physical abuse. Although the medical profession defined the battered child, the media generally skirted the issue, and it largely remained an unmentionable phenomenon. In 1965, Project Head Start brought to national attention another kind of abuse—the lack of services and education suffered by poor children. Begun as a summer program in President Lyndon B. Johnson's "War on Poverty," Project Head Start offered health, social, and psychological services for children and their families, as well an enriched preschool experience for impoverished children.

Sports-minded Women

From playing paddle tennis on the streets of Harlem, Althea Gibson progressed to being the first black player in the American Lawn Tennis Association championships. In 1957 and 1958, Gibson won at Wimbledon and Forest Hills respectively, and was named Woman Athlete of the Year in both years. In 1960, Gibson won the world professional tennis championship, thus opening a previously Anglo-dominated sport to poor women and women of color.

Such groups as the Unified Golf Association worked for further integration in women's sports. The Olympic games proved especially receptive to integration; athletes of many racial and ethnic backgrounds not only competed but won gold and silver medals.

Environment-minded Women

The early 1960s also witnessed the growth of environmental concerns. Antonia Caetana de Paiva Pereira Maury, an astronomer of Portuguese and British background, not only contributed to stellar spectroscopy, but also trained herself as a naturalist and ornithologist who especially fought for California's endangered redwood forests.

Perhaps best-known was Rachel Carson, an aquatic biologist with the U.S. Fish and Wildlife Service until 1952 and later an environmental writer. Carson wrote *The Sea Wind* (1941) and *The Sea Around Us* (1951) before she gained national attention with *The Silent Spring* (1962), which helped unify the emerging environmental movement much as Friedan's *Feminine Mystique* had ignited the feminist movement. Carson drew international attention to the destructive effects of pesticides on the environment, warning that if preventive measures were not undertaken a "strange stillness" or a "silent spring" would fall over the land.

Immigration and Resettlement

Clearly, American women had developed an awareness of the existence and pain of discriminatory actions and attitudes. Still, even though many fought prejudice on public and political levels, racial and ethnic hostility remained entrenched in daily lives. Such major cities as Cleveland, Chicago, Denver, Los Angeles, New York, and Seattle continued to foster segregated streets and sections where only poor, Native American, Latino, African American, or Asian American people lived. In Cleveland, one downtown street was considered "black," while a parallel street was "white."

In 1965, the Naturalization Act formalized such divisions between groups by establishing a yearly maximum of 20,000 immigrants from every country. Its provisions gave preference to split-families, skilled workers and professionals, and refugee resettlement. Although the Act kept the American population in racial and ethnic "balance," it also led to a more diversified immigration which included Chinese, Koreans, Filipinos, and Asian Indians, and to more female immigrants. Over half of the migrants were women, one-fourth of whom married outside their race. A significant number of these women came from urban backgrounds where they had worked as teachers, nurses, doctors, dentists, and attorneys. In the United States, however, they faced language problems and discriminatory licensing examinations that kept them from practicing their professions and intensified the ordeal of resettlement.

During the postwar years, numerous forces challenged the back-to-the-home movement. Gradually, just as the dream of pervasive cheerfulness and prosperity proved illusory, so did the belief in a sweet, docile, model American woman evaporate. Instead, Americans found it necessary to cope with the modern world and with the modern woman.

By the early 1960s, increasing numbers of women began to argue that they had a right to participate in both the private and public worlds. In so doing, they literally created the contemporary feminist movement. Rather than narrowly focusing on improved education, the vote, or other specific rights as they had in the past, for the first time American women called into question the basic nature of American gender expectations, constructs, and beliefs.

Suggestions for Further Reading

Ackerman, Lillian A. "Marital Instability and Juvenile Delinquency Among the Nez Perces," *American Anthropologist* 73 (June 1971): 595–603.

Asian American Studies Center and Chinese Historical Society of Southern California, eds. *Linking Our Lives: Chinese American Women of Los Angeles*. Los Angeles: Chinese Historical Society of Southern California, 1984.

Bem, Sandra Lipsitz. *The Lenses of Gender: Transforming the Debate on Sexual Inequality*. New Haven, CT: Yale University Press, 1993.

Berkin, Carol R., and Mary Beth Norton, eds. *Women of America: A History*. Boston: Houghton Mifflin Company, 1979. Part IV.

Berry, Mary Frances. *The Politics of Parenthood: Child Care, Women's Rights and the Myth of the Good Mother*. New York: Penguin USA, 1994.

Breines, Wini. *Young, White, and Miserable: Growing Up Female in the Fifties*. Boston: Beacon Press, 1992.

Camacho, Roseanne V. "Race, Region, and Gender in a Reassessment of Lillian Smith," 157–76, *Southern Women: Histories and Identities*, edited by Virginia Bernhard, Betty Brandon, Elizabeth Fox-Genovese, and Theda Perdue. Columbia: University of Missouri Press, 1992.

Caraway, Nancie. *Segregated Sisterhood: Racism and the Politics of American Feminism*. Knoxville: University of Tennessee Press, 1991.

Chato, Genevieve, and Christine Conte. "The Legal Rights of American Indian Women," 229–46, in *Western Women: Their Land, Their Lives*, edited by Lillian Schlissel, Vicki L. Ruiz, and Janice Monk. Albuquerque: University of New Mexico Press, 1988.

Chafe, William H. *The American Woman: Her Changing Social, Economic, and Political Roles, 1920–1970*. New York: Oxford University Press, 1972.

Cott, Nancy F. *The Grounding of Modern Feminism*. New Haven, CT: Yale University Press, 1987.

Crawford, Vicki L., Jacqueline Anne Rouse, and Barbara Woods, eds. *Women in the Civil Rights Movement: Trailblazers and Torchbearers, 1941–1965*. Bloomington: Indiana University Press, 1993.

Davis, Madeline D., and Elizabeth Lapovsky Kennedy. "Oral History and the Study of Sexuality in the Lesbian Community: Buffalo, New York, 1940–1960," 450–62, in *Unequal Sisters: A Multicultural Reader in U.S. Women's History*, edited by Vicki L. Ruiz and Ellen Carol DuBois. 2d ed. New York: Routledge, 1994.

Davis, Ronald L. *The Glamour Factory: Inside Hollywood's Big Studio System*. Dallas: Southern Methodist University Press, 1993.

D'Emilio, John, and Estelle B. Freedman. *Intimate Matters: A History of Sexuality in America*. New York: Harper & Row, 1988.

Deslippe, Dennis. "'We Had an Awful Time with Our Women': Iowa's United Packinghouse Workers of America, 1945–75," *Journal of Women's History* 5 (Spring 1993): 10–32.

Dunne, Sara. "Women as Children in American Comedy: Baby Snooks' Daughters," *Journal of American Culture* 16 (Summer 1993): 31–35.

Epstein, Cynthia Fuchs. "Positive Effects of the Multiple Negative: Explaining the Success of Black Professional Women," *American Journal of Sociology* 78 (January 1973): 912–35.

———. *Deceptive Distinctions: Sex, Gender, and the Social Order*. New Haven, CT: Yale University Press, 1988.

Evans, Sara. "Women's Consciousness and the Southern Black Movement," *Southern Exposure* 4 (Winter 1977): 10–14.

————. *Personal Politics: The Roots of Women's Liberation in the Civil Rights Movement and the New Left*. New York: Alfred A. Knopf, 1979.

————. *Born for Liberty: A History of Women in America*. New York: Free Press, 1989. Chapters 11–12.

Fleming, Cynthia Griggs. "Black Women Activists and the Student Nonviolent Coordinating Committee: The Case of Ruby Doris Smith Robinson," *Journal of Women's History* 4 (Winter 1993): 64–82.

Foote, Cheryl J. "Changing Images of Women in the Western Film," *Journal of the West* 22 (October 1983): 64–71.

Friedman, Jean E., William G. Shade, and Mary Jane Capozzoli, eds. *Our American Sisters: Women in American Life and Thought*. 4th ed. Lexington, MA: D.C. Heath and Company, 1987. Part IV, 19–21.

Gabin, Nancy. "Women Workers and the UAW in the Post-World War II Period: 1945–1954." *Labor History* 21 (Winter 1979–80): 5–30.

García, Richard A. "Dolores Huerta: Woman Organizer, Symbol," *California History* 72 (Spring 1993): 56–71.

Gill, Gerald R. "'WIN OR LOSE-WE WIN': The 1952 Vice-Presidential Campaign of Charlotta A. Bass," 109–88, in *The Afro-American Woman: Struggles and Images*, edited by Sharon Harley and Rosalyn M. Terborg-Penn. Port Washington, NY: Kennikat Press, 1978.

Goldin, Claudia. *Understanding the Gender Gap: An Economic History of American Women*. New York: Oxford University Press, 1990.

Harrison, Cynthia E. *On Account of Sex: The Politics of Women's Issues, 1945–1968*. Berkeley: University of California Press, 1988.

Hartmann, Susan M. *From Margin to Mainstream: American Women and Politics Since 1960*. New York: Alfred Knopf, 1989.

Hewitt, Nancy A., ed. *Women, Families, and Communities: Readings in American History*. Vol. II. Glenview, IL: Scott, Foresman, 1990. Part 6.

Hine, Darlene Clark. "Rape and the Inner Lives of Southern Black Women: Thoughts on the Culture of Dissemblance," 177–90, in *Southern Women*, edited by Bernhard, et al. Columbia: University of Missouri Press, 1992.

Hoff, Joan. "The Unfinished Revolution: Changing Legal Status of U.S. Women," *Signs* 13 (Autumn 1987): 7–36.

————. *Unequal Before the Law: A Legal History of U.S. Women*. New York: New York University Press, 1991.

Jamieson, Kathleen. "Multiple Jeopardy: The Evolution of a Native Women's Movement," *Canadian Ethnic Studies* 13 (1981): 130–43.

Kennedy, Elizabeth Lapovsky, and Madeline D. Davis. *Boots of Leather, Slippers of Gold: The History of a Lesbian Community*. New York: Routledge, 1993.

Kerber, Linda K., and Jane DeHart Mathews, eds. *Women's America: Refocusing the Past*. 2d ed. New York: Oxford University Press, 1987. Part III.

Kim, Bok-Lim C. "Asian Wives of U.S. Servicemen: Women in Shadows," *Amerasia Journal* 4 (March 1977): 91–115.

Lamphere, Louise, Patricia Zavella, Felipe Gonzalez, with Peter Evans. *Sunbelt Working Mothers: Reconciling Family and Factory*. Ithaca: Cornell University Press, 1993.

Loveland, Anne. *Lillian Smith: A Southerner Confronting the South, A Biography*. Baton Rouge: Louisiana State University Press, 1986.

Matthews, Glenna. *"Just a Housewife": The Rise and Fall of Domesticity in America*. New York: Oxford University Press, 1987.

May, Elaine Tyler. *Homeward Bound: American Families in the Cold War Era*. New York: Basic Books, 1988.

Meyerowitz, Joanne. "Beyond the Feminine Mystique: A Reassessment of Postwar Mass Culture, 1946–1958," *Journal of American History* 79 (March 1993): 1455–82.

Miller, Sally M. "California Immigrants: Case Studies In Continuity and Change in Societal and Familial Roles," *Journal of the West* 33 (July 1993): 25–34.

Morantz, Regina Markell. "The Scientist as Sex Crusader: Alfred C. Kinsey and American Culture," 145–66, in *Procreation or Pleasure? Sexual Attitudes in American History*, edited by Thomas L. Altherr. Malabar, FL: Robert E. Kreiger Publishing Company, 1983.

Movshovitz, Howard. "The Still Point: Women in the Westerns of John Ford," *Frontiers* 7 (1984): 68–72.

Parezo, Nancy J., Kelley A. Hays, and Barbara F. Slivac. "The Mind's Road: Southwestern and Indian Women's Art," in *The Desert Is No Lady: Southwestern Landscapes in Women's Writing and Art*, edited by Vera Norwood and Janice Monk. New Haven, CT: Yale University Press, 1987.

Quiñonez, CDP, and Mary Daniel Turner, SNDdeN. *The Transformation of American Catholic Sisters*. Philadelphia: Temple University Press, 1992.

Rebolledo, Tey Diana. "Tradition and Mythology: Signatures of Landscape in Chicana Literature," 96–124, in *The Desert Is No Lady: Southwestern Landscapes in Women's Writing and Art*, edited by Vera Norwood and Janice Monk. New Haven, CT: Yale University Press, 1987.

Robinson, Jo Ann. *The Montgomery Bus Boycott and the Women Who Started It*. Knoxville: University of Tennessee Press, 1987.

Romo, Ricardo. "Southern California and the Origins of Latino Civil-Rights Activism," *Western Legal History* 3 (Summer/Fall 1990): 379–406.

Rosenberg, Rosalind. *Divided Lives: American Women in the Twentieth Century*. New York: Hill and Wang, 1992.

Rothschild, Mary Aickin. "White Women Volunteers in the Freedom Summers: Their Life and Work in a Movement for Social Change," *Feminist Studies* 5 (Fall 1979): 466–95.

Ruiz, Vicki L. *Cannery Women, Cannery Lives: Mexican Women, Unionization, and the California Food Processing Industry, 1930–1950*. Albuquerque: University of New Mexico Press, 1987.

Rupp, Leila J. "The Survival of American Feminism: The Women's Movement in the Postwar Period," 33–65, in *Reshaping America: Society and Institutions, 1945–1960*, edited by Robert H. Bremer and Gary W. Reichard. Columbus: Ohio State University Press, 1982.

Rupp, Leila J., and Verta Taylor. *Survival in the Doldrums: The American Women's Rights Movement, 1945 to the 1960s*. New York: Oxford University Press, 1987.

Ryan, Mary P. *Womanhood in America: From Colonial Times to the Present*. New York: New Viewpoints, 1979. Chapters 6–7.

Sawyer, Mary R. "Black Religion and Social Change: Women in Leadership Roles," *Journal of Religious Thought* 47 (Winter/Spring 1990–91): 16–29.

Scobie, Ingrid Winther. *Center Stage: Helen Gahagan Douglas, A Life*. New York: Oxford University Press, 1992.

Segura, Denise. "Chicana and Mexican Immigrant Women at Work," *Gender and Society* 3 (March 1989): 37–52.

Segura, Denise, and Beatriz Pesquera, "Beyond Indifference and Apathy: The Chicana Movement and Chicana Feminist Discourse," *Aztlan* 19 (Fall 1988–1990): 69–92.

Sklar, Kathryn Kish, and Thomas Dublin eds. *Women and Power in American History: A Reader*. Vol. II. Englewood Cliffs, NJ: Prentice-Hall, 1991. Parts 16–20.

Smith, Patricia Clark with Paula Gunn Allen. "Earthy Relations, Carnal Knowledge: Southwestern American Indian Women Writers and Landscape," 146–73, in *The Desert Is No Lady: Southwestern Landscapes in Women's Writing and Art*, edited by Vera Norwood and Janice Monk. New Haven, CT: Yale University Press, 1987.

Solinger, Rickie. *Wake Up Little Susie: Single Pregnancy and Race before Roe v. Wade*. New York: Routledge, 1992.

Stoller, Marianne. "'Peregrinas' with Many Visions: Hispanic Women Artists of New Mexico, Southern Colorado, and Texas," 125–145, in *The Desert Is No Lady: Southwestern*

Landscapes in Women's Writing and Art, edited by Vera Norwood and Janice Monk. New Haven, CT: Yale University Press, 1987.

Swerdlow, Amy. "Ladies' Day at the Capitol: Women Strike for Peace Versus HUAC," 479–96, in *Unequal Sisters: A Multicultural Reader in U.S. Women's History*, edited by Vicki Ruiz and Ellen Carol Dubois. 2d ed. New York: Routledge, 1994.

———. *Women Strike for Peace: Traditional Motherhood and Radical Politics in the 1960s*. Chicago: University of Chicago Press, 1993.

Szasz, Margaret Connell, ed. *Between Indian and White Worlds: The Cultural Broker*. Norman: University of Oklahoma Press, 1994.

Taylor, Sandra C. "Leaving the Concentration Camps: Japanese Americans and Resettlement in the Intermountain West," *Pacific Historical Review* 60 (May 1991): 169–94.

Weigand, Kate. "The Red Menace, the Feminine Mystique, and the Ohio Un-American Activities Commission: Gender and Anti-Communism in Ohio, 1951–1954," *Journal of Women's History* 3 (Winter 1992): 70–94.

Weiss, Nancy Pottishman. "Mother, the Invention of Necessity: Dr. Benjamin Spock's *Baby and Child Care*," *American Quarterly* 24 (Winter 1977): 519–46.

Williams, Teresa K. "Marriage between Japanese Women and U.S. Servicemen Since World War II," *Amerasia Journal* 17 (1991): 135–54.

Woloch, Nancy. *Women and the American Experience*. New York: Alfred A. Knopf, 1984. Chapters 19–20.

Zavella, Patricia. "The Impact of 'Sun Belt Industrialization' on Chicanas," 291–304, in *The Women's West*, edited by Susan Armitage and Elizabeth Jameson. Norman: University of Oklahoma Press, 1987.

Contemporary American Women
1965 to the Present

10

The emerging feminist movement launched a controversy about contemporary American women to which Americans could not easily respond. Some people grasped at the past, hoping that traditional American values would provide ballast in an increasingly stormy sea. Meanwhile, others sailed ahead in anticipation that rough water would eventually give way to a better port than the one left behind. Thus, between 1965 and the present, the United States has attempted to navigate, without an agreed-upon direction and destination, the deep questions and issues related to gender.

THE CONTEMPORARY FEMINIST MOVEMENT, 1965–1985

National Organization for Women, 1966

Formal organization of the contemporary feminist movement came in 1966 during the Third National Conference of State Commissions on the Status of Women. Tired of ponderous discussion concerning women's issues that often lacked concrete results, twenty-eight women met in Betty Friedan's hotel room in Washington, D.C., to contribute ideas and five dollars each to the founding of the National Organization for Women (NOW). At an organizational meeting several months later, three hundred women and men adopted bylaws, elected officers, and named Friedan president.

This assembly also issued a statement of purpose that attacked "the traditional assumption that a woman has to choose between marriage and motherhood on the one hand and serious participation in industry or the professions on the other." NOW intended to bring women into "full participation in the mainstream of American society NOW, exercising all the privileges and responsibilities thereof in truly equal partnership with men."

NOW leaders developed other arguments as well. They criticized sex role socialization and gender expectations which claimed that women were naturally passive, emotional, and nurturing. Instead, NOW maintained that so-called female traits were learned rather than biologically given. NOW also assumed that equality with men provided the best possible goal, but other feminists would soon resist what they considered "being coopted" into a system created and dominated by men.

To achieve its ends, NOW advocated such reforms as legal abortion, maternity leaves, tax deductions for childcare expenses, day-care centers, reform of the welfare system, job-training programs for women, and, beginning in 1967, the passage of the Equal Rights Amendment (ERA). NOW pressed its case through literature, speeches, public protests, lobbying, and litigation, as well as encouraging "rap" groups and consciousness-raising (c-r) sessions among women.

Soon other newly organized women's groups joined NOW in its reform efforts. These included the Women's Equity Action League (WEAL), founded in 1968, which specialized in women's economic issues, conducted research, sponsored education projects, supported litigation, and lobbied Congress. The Professional Women's Caucus (PWC) followed in 1970 and the National Women's Political Caucus (NWPC) in 1971. The latter especially encouraged women's participation in politics, including urging women to run for office, serve as convention delegates, act as lobbyists and voters, and take part in campaigns.

Feminist Publications

Soon, a number of publications spread the feminist message. Four dynamic and controversial books urging feminist reforms appeared in 1970. In *Sexual Politics*, Kate Millett indicted American society as a patriarchy and asked for immediate revision. Similarly, in the *Dialectic of Sex: The Case for Feminist Revolution*, Shulamith Firestone envisioned a nation in which class and gender would play no role. Robin Morgan's *Sisterhood Is Powerful* and Germaine Greer's *Female Eunuch* also presented feminist polemics. Greer, a native of Melbourne, Australia, who earned a Ph.D. in Renaissance literature from Cambridge University in 1968, especially exercised tremendous influence on the contemporary women's movement. Greer argued that because "female sexuality had been masked and deformed" by sexism, women now had to "take possession" of their bodies and seize "their power."

The foremost feminist publication of the popular press was *Ms.* magazine, founded in 1971 by Gloria Steinem and the Women's Action Alliance. *Ms.* was the nation's first explicitly feminist magazine, as well as the first national publication created and controlled by women for women. In its attempt to raise women's consciousness, *Ms.* aimed at both professional women and traditional homemakers. In its pages, *Ms.* revealed career and lifestyle choices to its readers, ran articles on women's history, and published the work of women writers and poets.

Abortion and Gynecology

Women's control of their own bodies loomed as a major feminist issue. For the first time, women posed searching questions to their obstetricians and gynecologists and requested doctors to refer to women patients as something other than "girls." Too, women increasingly demanded that doctors pay more attention to the whole woman rather than attempt to isolate problems such as birth control, sexual dysfunction, hormones, menopause, and aging.

As part of this movement to take charge of their bodies, a growing number of women demanded the right to abortion. In 1965, all fifty states prohibited abortion and allowed therapeutic abortions only in life-threatening situations. Feminists argued that abortion should also be allowed in cases of rape, incest, and known fetal deformity. Although a number of states liberalized their laws somewhat, many did not, and even most liberalized laws required parental or spousal consent. As in the past, whatever the law in each state, wealthy women were able to go to other countries for abortions, while other women attempted illegal and self-induced abortions that often resulted in injury or death.

In response, feminists sought the right to abortion on demand, insisting that women should be able to make their own personal decisions rather than the medical community or government. When state governments hesitated to offer abortion on demand, feminists mounted during the early 1970s a series of legal attacks on restrictive laws. Consequently, the 1973 U.S. Supreme Court decision *Roe v. Wade* overturned state laws that prohibited abortion during the first twelve weeks of pregnancy, as well as between twelve weeks and viability (when a fetus can survive outside the womb) in life-threatening cases. Subsequent rulings struck down laws requiring parental or spousal consent except in cases involving unemancipated minors.

In the meantime, in 1971, the Boston Women's Health Collective, Inc., published the revolutionary *Our Bodies, Ourselves*. This medical handbook attempted to educate women about health care, including abortion, birth control, menopause, pregnancy, rape, and venereal disease. It also raised questions regarding the customary medical treatment of women and urged the establishment of female clinics. *Our Bodies, Ourselves* became a best-seller and helped create the climate in which many women's health clinics and rape crisis centers began to appear throughout the United States.

An antiabortion movement also developed in the wake of *Roe v. Wade*. The National Conference of Catholic Bishops created the National Right to Life Committee, which had eleven million members by 1980. These and other antiabortion advocates protested that abortion constituted murder of unborn children. Most also opposed surrogate motherhood, in which an artificially inseminated woman bore a child for another woman for a fee.

Advertising and the Media

Feminists also assaulted advertising and media images of the "happy housewife." They especially took issue with fantasy women who found personal fulfillment in waxing floors and cleaning toilet bowls. Noting that such models discouraged women from thinking and speaking out, they urged more women to become writers, editors, publishers, producers, and directors. In turn, the increase of women in such positions led to the establishment of the Women's Institute for Freedom of the Press in Washington, D.C., which encouraged further alterations in the American mass media system. More specifically, the Institute insisted that all people should have equal access to the means of communication in the United States.

Androgyny

Androgyny, a concept in which people are free to express both "female" and "male" characteristics, originated with the Greek comic playwrights, notably Aristophanes, who maintained that Zeus created people with two faces, one female and one male. When these dual-sided beings seized too much power, Zeus cut each into two, condemning them to seek their other halves through love and sexual relationships.

Writer Virginia Woolf was probably the first to introduce and support the concept in the modern United States. Woolf argued for androgyny in *A Room of One's Own*, first published in 1929 and most recently reprinted in 1991. During the 1960s, most feminists also advocated androgyny, although a few opposed it. Adrienne Rich, overtly feminist and lesbian in her work, maintained in *The Dream of a Common Language* (1978) that women could stand strong, gentle, and persistent on their own, without manifesting such supposedly male qualities as violence and competitiveness.

Role Models

Women also began to look for role models. One woman who became a role model was Coretta Scott King. In 1953 she had married Martin Luther King, Jr., and in 1971 earned a Ph.D. in music. Coretta Scott King, who frequently gave concerts to benefit the Southern Christian Leadership Conference (SCLC), was voted in 1968 Woman of the Year and Most

Admired Woman by U.S. college students. King later contributed her energy and expertise to both SCLC and the Martin Luther King, Jr. Memorial Center in Atlanta.

During these years, a French-born author named Anaïs Nin attained status as something of a cult figure among feminists. In diary form, she explored her struggle as a female author trying to carve out a professional and personal life for herself in America of the 1960s. The resulting six-volume *Diary of Anaïs Nin* (1966) soon ranked as one the world's premier women's autobiographies.

Jane Fonda provided yet another type of model for women. As a vitriolic opponent of U.S. involvement in Vietnam (1961 to 1972), Fonda organized the Indo-China Peace Campaign (IPC), a film company that produced *Coming Home* (1978) and *The China Syndrome* (1979), the first of which criticized the war in Southeast Asia and the second of which dealt with the possibility of a nuclear meltdown at a U.S. power plant. In a later film, *Nine to Five* (1980), Fonda satirized sexist practices and low pay among clerical workers.

Women's Studies

In colleges and universities, scholars began to teach courses concerning women, including women's history, literature, psychology, and sociology. By 1972, American colleges and universities offered more than 600 such courses. Two years later, 500 schools gave over 2,000 women-oriented courses; by 1982, they had grown to 30,000 courses.

The founding of such journals as *Women's Studies* and *Signs* further recognized the significance of women's issues, along with a proliferation of women's studies programs, meaning interdisciplinary programs analyzing women's experiences from a feminist perspective. In 1969, San Diego State University established the first women's studies bachelor's degree program. In 1974, 39 programs existed; by 1984 this had jumped to 444. In 1979, the National Women's Studies Association (NWSA) organized, while individual disciplines formed their own women's groups. To work for reform in the practice and teaching of history, women historians founded such groups as the Coordinating Committee for Women in the Historical Profession and Women Historians of the Midwest.

Other impetus for reform came from scholars in literature and linguistics who questioned the dominant Anglo, male canon in literature and patriarchal usages in the English language. As a result, feminist literary criticism began to use gender as a basic category of literary analysis and to restore women's writings to the canon. Literary scholars also experimented with deconstruction, the theory of textual analysis that questions whether language can represent reality. In this case, scholars attempted to dismantle language to remove its gender bias, then reconstruct it in a bias-free way so that women's topics could be studied with words not defined from patriarchal and "woman-as-other" perspectives. Similarly, linguists added a feminist perspective to lexicography.

Math anxiety among women constituted yet another concern. Although some outstanding women mathematicians had existed in the United States, ordinary women usually viewed mathematics as a male preserve. In 1971, the Association for Women in Mathematics (AWM) organized to promote equal treatment of women in mathematics training and careers. The AWM established a speakers' bureau, distributed information, and initiated programs intended to eradicate math anxiety among young women.

International Women's Year Conference, 1977

In 1977, the feminist movement demonstrated its growing strength and maturity at the International Women's Year Conference in Houston, Texas. Congressperson Bella Abzug served as primary organizer of the conference, as well as the presiding officer of its commissioners.

At the conference, two thousand delegates and twenty thousand observers gathered to devise a plan for the liberation of womankind. The delegates—who represented Native Americans, Latinas, Anglos, African Americans, Asian Americans, all women, in other words—presented their views and outlined their needs. The wants of rich and poor, young and old, worker and full-time housewife, heterosexual and homosexual were also considered. Betty Friedan, who had once called lesbians the "lavender menace," now defended their right to their sexual preference and civil rights. The National Plan of Action, presented by conference leaders to President Jimmy Carter on 22 March 1978, included twenty-six planks regarding child abuse, childcare, disabled women, education, employment, the ERA, health, homemakers, insurance, older women, rape, reproductive rights, rural women, poverty, and women of color. Although few suggestions received implementation, the conference and its report inspired women, men, and government leaders, and generated spirited public discussion.

Antifeminism

Of course, these varied attempts at feminist reform did not go unopposed. The Equal Rights Amendment provided especially explosive fodder. In 1972, attorney Phyllis Schlafly of Illinois organized a group called STOP ERA. Schlafly declared that the "ERA offers absolutely no benefit to women, no new right, no new opportunity that we do not have now." At least partly due to Schlafly's efforts, the ERA fell three states short of achieving ratification before an extended deadline ran out in 1982.

Abortion also generated controversy, even after the 1973 Supreme Court decision supporting women's right to choose abortion, and became a litmus test for the appointment of federal and Supreme Court justices. As a consequence of vehement opposition to abortion, courts began to backtrack somewhat. In 1980, *Harris v. McRae* upheld the Hyde Amendment limiting federal Medicaid funds for abortion to cases involving rape, incest, and life-threatening situations. The following year, a U.S. Congressional committee considered a Human Life Amendment, which stated that human life begins at conception. This would have struck down women's right to choose abortion, but the committee never forwarded the provision to the full Congress for a vote.

Other setbacks to feminist reform came from several presidents. One curb to the feminist momentum of the 1970s was President Richard M. Nixon's 1972 veto of the Comprehensive Child Development bill. This act would have provided nationwide day-care centers for employed mothers, a move that Nixon believed to be a "communal approach to child-rearing" that had "family-weakening implications." A similar presidential roadblock appeared with the inauguration of President Ronald Reagan in 1981 and again in 1985. The Reagan administration proved hesitant to enforce affirmative action laws and anxious to cut such social welfare programs as Aid to Dependent Children. Reagan also consistently opposed the right to choose abortion, the ERA, and the concept of "comparable worth" in determining women's wages.

FEMINISM AMONG GROUPS OF WOMEN, 1965–1985

Native American Women

Confined largely to reservations or urban ghettoes, Native American women faced particularly strong prejudice in housing, education, and employment. They tolerated policies geared toward nuclear families, which ignored the extended kinship systems still maintained by numerous Native Americans.

During the 1960s, the reemergence of the movement for Indian self-determination brought a few gains to Native Americans in general, including more control over Indian schools and some public recognition of the degrading stereotyping of American Indians in the media. In 1974, a Wisconsin Menominee woman named Ada Deer explained that her people overturned the government's termination policy; they preferred to control their holdings themselves rather than put them in the hands of private developers.

By the late 1970s and early 1980s, the American Indian Movement (AIM) brought national attention to the desperate conditions of such reservations as Rose Bud and Pine Ridge in South Dakota. Social problems, including alcoholism and unemployment, were also widely discussed. Gradually, Bureau of Indian Affairs' schools began to give preference to

Native American teachers and even diversified their curriculums. In turn, this resulted in more Indian women attending colleges and professional schools.

Still, Indian women felt overlooked. Thus, they built upon their long-term tendency to develop endurance while seeking liberation. In 1978, under the leadership of Lorelei Means and Madonna Gilbert, Native American women formed Women of All Red Nations (WARN) to oppose enforced sterilization, political imprisonment, decline of Indian family life, forced adoptions, loss of land, and destruction of Indian culture.

Also in 1978, the U.S. Supreme Court and the Congress granted Indian women further gains. In *Santa Clara Pueblo v. Martínez*, the court ruled that men and women must receive identical tribal rights. Both the American Indian Religious Freedom Act and the Indian Child Welfare Act reinforced this principal.

With such catalysts, Indian women continued to fight their underrepresentation in tribal governments and lack of legal protection. This resulted in the 1984 establishment of the Navajo Office for Women, which offered to women counseling, childcare, family planning, and job placement. The following year, the Indigenous Women's Network met in Yelm, Washington, where it supported WARN's programs. It especially demonstrated the ability of Indian women to build networks among themselves, which even reached into academia and urged universities to offer additional Indian studies courses and programs.

Thousands more Native American activist women spurned organizations, working on their own instead, especially for increased civil rights. By the early 1980s, among the Oglala between one-fourth to one-third as many women as men ran for tribal office. In 1981, for the first time one of the six Oglala candidates for tribal president was female.

Native American women also continued to act as cultural mediators. In education, Beatrice Medicine researched and wrote about Indian women. In politics, Wilma Mankiller served as chief of the Cherokee Nation. And in literature, such writers as Paula Gunn Allen, Leslie Marmon Silko, and Louise Erdrich carried Indian culture and concerns to a larger public. Although Indian "literature" had long depended on oral tradition, especially songs and stories that contained the history and traditions of various tribes, these Native American writers now successfully turned to the written word. In 1977, Silko won both the prestigious National Book Award and the MacArthur Award for her novel, *Ceremony*, while Erdrich received several awards for *Love Medicine* (1984) and *The Beet Queen* (1986). Paula Gunn Allen received wide recognition both for her poetry and her novel, *The Woman Who Owned the Shadows* (1983). Yet other outstanding Native American writers include Joy Harjo, Carol Lee Sanchez, and Mary Tall Mountain.

Latinas

Latinas also raised a variety of issues, ranging from feminism to an articulation of their myriad identities. In the Southwest, Chicanos had the longest history of all Latino groups, their own distinct culture, and thus their own particular problems. Here, Chicana feminism grew, at least in part, out of a long tradition of labor protest. In 1966, when UFW grape-pickers struck in Delano, California, the event garnered widespread media coverage. Most Americans knew about the men and women workers who marched 230 miles to Sacramento to lodge protests, their ranks swelling as they went.

The following year, Jessie Lopez de la Cruz became the first female farm-workers' union organizer. In this UFW position, de la Cruz utilized feminist terms in arguing for more female members: "Women can no longer be taken for granted . . . it's way past the time when our husbands could say, 'You stay home!'" She then became a Chicana spokesperson and a member of the California Commission on the Status of Women.

Increasingly, employed Latinas attacked their numerous problems. In 1969, for example, the U.S. Equal Employment Opportunity Commission reported that the majority of factory workers labored in agriculture, food, textile, and apparel. Of these, approximately 85 to 92 percent worked as laborers, and the rest as operatives. Thousands of additional Latinas toiled as domestic help in such cities as El Paso and Los Angeles. Most were underpaid and lacked maternity leave, which meant they had to start over on the seniority ladder and accept beginning pay upon their return from childbirth.

Between 1972 to 1974, Texas Latinas demonstrated their growing willingness to organize and even to picket. In the Farah Strike in El Paso, women brought their children to the picket lines. Julia Guilar, a Farah worker, explained that, "because we were women, we were staying behind. Now we just bring our children to our meetings, and we bring them to picket lines."

In the meantime, numerous Latinas experienced growing disillusionment with *el movimiento*, which called for an end to discrimination against Latinos but failed to recognize the need for entirely reconstructed male-female relationships. Although men disparaged them as "women's libbers" and warned that Anglos wanted women to adopt feminism to defeat *el movimiento*, Latina feminists remained convinced that they had to generate their own liberation rather than waiting for Latino men to do so.

Thus, in Southwestern urban areas, including Los Angeles and Houston, Latinas began to raise both Latino and feminist issues, including asking for representation of Spanish-heritage peoples on school boards, town councils, and police forces; bilingual education in the schools they attended; and access to food stamps. In 1971, more than six hundred women participated in the First National Chicana Conference in Houston, Texas.

Students too questioned women's traditional place. By the 1970s, students formed their own groups, *Las Chicanas* and *Hijas de Cuauhtemoc*. Among other things, they demanded Chicano studies programs, faculty, and scholarships, especially dealing with Chicana's experiences. Although some women resisted, by 1972 awareness of the issues had clearly spread.

In the Northeast, Latina protest took a slightly different direction. Here, Puerto Ricans and Cuban Americans were more recent arrivals who brought their own cultural and historical backgrounds and, in turn, had their own needs and concerns. Generally, Latina feminists in New York City remained separate from Anglo feminists, arguing that Latinas could not gain freedom until Latinos did so. These Latinas' rebellion grew out of community organizations more than labor unions and included fewer student organizations, but like Latinas in the Southwest they wanted to destroy triple oppression—racism, sexism, and poverty.

New York Latinas also appeared less bound by tradition and history. One New York woman who urged her friends and coworkers to speak up informed them that times had changed: "It's not like when I was a little kid and my grandmother used to say, 'You have to especially respect the Anglos.' We can stand up! We can talk back!" She added that the time had come also for women to reject their customary deference to men.

By the early 1970s, statistics showed that although Latinas nationwide remained family oriented, they now delayed childbirth, limited family size, and divorced more than had previous generations. Also, in their poetry, essays, and stories, Latina writers self-consciously worked to create a literature. In 1973, Estela Portillo edited the first major collection of Latina writing, while Bernice Zamora helped open the way for other Latina writers such as Lorna Dee Cervantes, Sandra Cisneros, Patricia Mora, Mary Helen Ponce, and Evangelina Vigil.

Many Latinas who followed explored such issues as assimilation, lesbianism, and family loyalty. In 1983, poet Elena Avila wrote these poignant lines in "Coming Home": "Mama! Mama! I've been so cold without you/ The big city does not hold me like you do Mama." Such authors also directed complaints at *macho* attitudes of Spanish-heritage men and the short-sightedness of women who overlooked or ignored feminist issues. The authors pointed out that in the past lack of education and even illiteracy had silenced Latina voices, and that traditional literature and art deified women as maternal figures, strong yet limited. Even epic *corridos* incorporated few women; in *Teatro Campesino* productions of *los corridos*, women disappeared further by disguising themselves to play men's parts. Where were the *soldaderas* (soldiers), the new writers asked, who fought in the Mexican Revolution of 1910, or other women of strength and cunning?

Soon, Latinas reaped some benefits from their efforts. They fought their way into Women's Studies and Chicano Studies programs on both coasts. No longer did Latina actors have to hide their true heritage in fear of typecasting of the kind Rita Moreno had experienced. In sports, Rosemary Casals excelled in tennis. In popular music, Vicki Carr and Linda Ronstadt made their marks; Ronstadt won a Grammy Award in 1988 for her *Canciones di mi padre*, recorded in Los Angeles.

African American Women

African American women also developed their own strain of feminism to meet their particular situations. Unlike many Anglo women, black women were often paid laborers and enjoyed a degree of equality within the black family structure. Thus, black women already possessed some of the autonomy that white feminists demanded. Such issues as domesticity, the feminine mystique, and inequality in the family were far more meaningful to white women than to black.

Moreover, because black women tended to see racism as a more direct cause of their subordination than sexism, they often viewed the feminist movement with disdain or even distrust. The failure of Anglo feminists to reach out to black women and understand their problems exacerbated this situation. In 1970, Dara Abuakari (also known as Virginia E. Y Collins), vice-president of a group called the Republic of New Africa, explained to the white women's liberation leaders that:

> The black woman is not undergoing the same kind of oppression that white women have gone through in the homes. The black woman is independent. The struggle of black women and white women is not the same. White women have to look at their problem and it is their husbands. He is the oppressor, because he is the system. It's a white male system.

In that same year, Renee Ferguson of the *Washington Post* similarly emphasized that although "the women's liberation movement touches some sensitive nerves among black women . . . they are not always the nerves the movement seems to touch among so many whites." To Ferguson, "the first priority of virtually all black people is the elimination of racial prejudice in America." Ferguson added that once that occurred then perhaps black women would turn to "the elimination of oppression because of sex."

Given the differences in black and white women's needs, why did a black feminist movement eventually develop? It happened, at least in part, because a number of black women concluded that they too could gain from some of the reforms that the white feminist movement advocated. The right to have abortions, childcare centers, equal pay, equal access to employment, and the destruction of degrading stereotypes were some of the changes that would benefit all women. In 1964, attorney and poet Pauli Murray pointed out that black and white women shared "a common burden because of traditional discriminations based upon sex."

Similarly, Dr. Anna Hedgeman of Harlem and Dorothy Height, president of the National Council of Negro Women, noted that such problems as job discrimination, false stereotypes, and sexual exploitation transcended race.

In addition, a growing number of black women became more responsive to feminist issues as they encountered blatant sexism outside their own communities. As they increasingly pursued college educations, entered white-collar jobs and professions, and attempted to enlarge their political participation, they faced gender discrimination. In politics, for example, far fewer black women than men held political office. In 1974, 337 black women obtained office as opposed to 2,293 black men.

As a consequence, in 1973 a group called Black Women Organized for Action (BWOA) established itself in San Francisco. Later that year, the first conference of the National Black Feminist Organization (NBFO) met in New York. Although these organizations recognized the distance between black and white women's issues, they also asserted the critical importance of such mutual goals as day care, abortion, equal pay, and maternity leaves, adding that perhaps some of these were of even greater importance to black women due to their poverty.

In 1977, a black feminist group in Boston known as the Combahee River Collective explained that they battled "interlocking" systems of oppression: racial, sexual, heterosexual, and class. During the late 1970s and early 1980s, the Collective worked to organize women-of-color workers, picketed hospitals that cut back on already inadequate health care, and helped organize rape-crisis and childcare centers.

Asian American Women

Much like Latinas, Asian American women struggled to establish their diverse identities: Asian Indians, Burmese, Cambodian, mainland Chinese, Filipino, Hong Kong Chinese, Japanese, Korean, Laotian, Malaysian, Singaporean, Taiwanese, and Vietnamese. They, too, wanted such reforms as affirmative action for both women and people of color. And they increasingly asserted themselves in civil rights matters. In 1975, for example, a group of Chinese American women in Boston boycotted public schools and demanded racial/ethnic/feminist reforms.

But women of Asian heritage had their own particular issues as well. One of these related to their communities, where they fought such traditions as having to perform all the housework even though employed outside their homes, avoid speaking and leading groups, and refrain from seeking further education and political involvement. Another special cause was their desire to practice their own professions. When in 1976 Dr. W. W. Tom migrated from China to the United States, language barriers kept her from practicing medicine; instead she took a job as an electronics assembler. Also, women wanted to join American society on their own terms, that is, as Asian American women rather than pseudo-Anglos.

Moreover, Asian American women viewed their wage parity and employment opportunities as a major priority. In 1980, U.S census data indicated that of the 1.9 million Asian American women living in the United States, 60 percent were married, 71 percent had high school educations, 20 percent had college degrees, and 57 percent were in the labor force. Employed women earned a median annual income of $6,685, which was higher than the median income for U.S. female workers but lower than that earned by men. Two-fifths of these women worked in clerical, sales, and technical jobs; one-fourth in managerial and professional positions; and one-fifth in such unskilled and semiskilled jobs as factory work and domestic service.

To achieve their ends, Asian American women occasionally joined Anglo-dominated groups, where they often provided leadership and supported assimilation programs. They worked primarily, however, through educational, ethnic, religious, and political organizations in their own communities. In 1980, the first National Asian Pacific American Women's Conference on Educational Equity met in Washington, D.C.

Individual women wielded influence as well. Television reporter Connie Chung and writer Maxine Hong Kingston carried a different image of Asian American women to the larger population. The efforts of such television producers as Chris Choy, Loni Ding, and Felicia Lowe also helped eliminate destructive stereotypes. Then, in 1981, Hong Kingston won the National Book Award for *China Men*. Two years later, Kitty Tsui became one of the first Asian American women to declare her lesbianism in *The Words of a Woman Who Breathes Fire*. Others scaled political barriers. Lillian Sing sat on the Municipal Court bench in San Francisco, while Lily Lee Chen served as mayor of Monterey Park, California.

Lesbians

Nineteenth- and early twentieth-century lesbians had hesitated to declare their sexual preference or work for legal reform, but by the mid-1960s lesbians seemed more willing to speak out. A growing number opposed heterosexism, such as the assumption that all women are heterosexual. In its extreme form, heterosexism also views lesbianism as perverted behavior, and thus vilifies lesbians.

Many lesbians believed that feminist leaders manifested heterosexism. They maintained that feminists failed to realize that women's oppression resulted from sexual oppression, and that women must have the freedom to form bonds with other women and resist their shared oppression.

Lesbians also viewed their sexual preference as an act of resistance against the dominant heterosexual culture. More specifically, they challenged homophobia, the fear of homosexuality that led to laws prohibiting lesbians from legally marrying their partners, and thus denying them spousal rights in permanent relationships, including insurance and social security benefits. Homophobia also caused lesbians to lose jobs, denied them equal access to housing, banned them from adopting children, and caused their exclusion as a couple from social events. Numerous lesbians charged that such homophobic attitudes were little more than patriarchal and political ideologies holding the current structure in place.

One especially articulate lesbian spokesperson was Rita Mae Brown. As a student at New York University, in 1967 Brown helped found the first Student Homophile League. When NOW leaders rejected Brown's assistance because of her outspoken lesbian sentiment and aggressive stance, she turned her energies during the late 1960s and early 1970s to supporting an organized group called Radicalesbians. Soon, Brown espoused lesbian separatism and advocated an exclusively female culture. In 1970, Radicalesbians published an influential statement of lesbian-feminist philosophies and beliefs titled "The Woman-Identified Woman." This defined a lesbian as "the rage of all women condensed to the point of explosion."

Next, Brown helped form the first lesbian separatist group, the Furies, a collective in Washington, D.C. In 1972 and 1973, the Furies published a newspaper advocating lesbian separatism, while Brown began writing full-time. In 1973, Brown's semiautobiographical novel, *Rubyfruit Jungle*, became the first not only to reveal lesbian life, but to do so in positive terms. Brown thus introduced a new subgenre, the lesbian-comic novel. In the same year, the American Psychiatric Association stated that homosexuality did *not* constitute deviant behavior. Subsequently, Brown continued to use her writing, especially *Plain Brown Rapper* (1977) and *Southern Discomfort* (1982), to bring the topic of lesbianism into the open.

Poet Adrienne Rich also contributed the on-going definition of lesbian issues. In 1980, Rich established lesbianism as a category of discussion and analysis in literature. She also questioned the influence of "compulsory heterosexuality" as a force affecting all American women, as well as defining scholarship regarding women. Perhaps Rich's most important contribution was illuminating the heterosexist inclination of most scholarship.

Hearing-impaired and Disabled Women

Women with one or more disabilities had long worked to improve their situations, yet gained little recognition for their achievements. As early as 1880, when Bridget Highes became one of the first hearing-impaired women Religious, she persuaded the archbishop to found a school for deaf children in Pennsylvania. Later, in 1928 Nellie Zabel Willhite of Hill City, South Dakota, became the first hearing-impaired pilot in the

United States. Then, in 1953 swimmer Gertrude Ederle became the first hearing-impaired person to win a place in the Helms Foundation Hall of Fame.

Civil rights and feminism helped empower such women. Hearing-impaired women and women who faced physical and mental challenges pursued myriad programs and causes, including demanding a wider recognition of American Sign Language as a valid language in its own right. In 1972, a San Francisco television station offered a daily news program with signers for the hearing impaired. Other women asked for better access to schools, businesses, and public buildings, as well as less discrimination in employment. They also provided role models for other disabled women and offered a new image to the public.

Consequently, Americans increasingly accepted and supported disabled individuals. During the 1970s, the National Theatre of the Deaf and the Gallaudet College Dancers entertained enthusiastic audiences, while in 1980 Phyllis French won the Tony Award for her leading role in the Broadway play *Children of a Lesser God*.

Women in Religion

Religiously oriented women showed new strength and assertiveness as well. In 1970, an ecumenical Center for Women and Religion organized in Berkeley, California. Ten theological institutions associated with the Graduate Theological Union sponsored the Center, which attracted an international membership. It intended to help end sexism and promote justice through religion and religious values. To that end, the Center offered theological curriculums based upon feminist structures and processes, and sponsored conferences, forums, and publications. In addition, Womanchurch, an ecumenical gathering of women who hold their own services, organized and gradually established chapters throughout the United States.

In more traditional churches, women struggled for increased participation. One well-known instance was the ordination of women as Episcopalian priests. Another was the rise of such women as Tammy Faye Baker in televangelism. Especially among Lutherans and Roman Catholics, women took yet another tack, participating in the Sanctuary Movement, which transported Central Americans who were illegally in the United States across the border to safe houses in Mexico and Canada.

Meanwhile, Mary Daly, a radical feminist and theologian, published her first controversial book, *The Church and the Second Sex* (1968), which attacked church policies that banned women from full participation. This polemic almost cost Daly her tenure at Boston College, a Catholic school where she had begun teaching in 1966. After *God the Father* appeared in 1978, Daly began a trilogy presenting a radical feminist argument for women's need to liberate themselves from patriarchy and all its related institutions, including consciousness, language, and myths. This resulted in *Gyn/Ecology* (1978), *Pure Lust* (1984), and *Outer Course* (1987).

The American Jewish community responded more slowly and cautiously to the feminist impetus. Yet, after 1971, when groups of Jewish women began to synthesize American feminism and American Judaism, some significant modifications occurred. A partial reconciliation between feminism and Judaism resulted in greater female participation in communal prayer, limited acceptance of innovative liturgy and life-cycle rituals, and the entry of women into positions of communal authority and status. These changes encouraged Jewish women to criticize Jewish religious texts, propose changes in Jewish pedagogy, and pursue such professions as the rabbinate, customarily reserved for men.

Golda Meir proved a wonderful role model not only for Jewish women but all women. Meir, born in Kiev, Russia, migrated to the United States in 1906 with her family. As she grew up in Milwaukee, Meir increasingly participated in the local Zionist movement. After college, Meir worked for the socialist labor Zionist group Poale Zion. In 1917, Meir and her husband migrated to Palestine, where she worked her way up the ladder of the Israeli labor organization. Between 1931 to 1934, Meir lived in the United States and served as secretary of the Pioneer Women's Organization. After she returned to Palestine, Meir took a seat in 1948 as the only woman in Israel's first legislature. Meir later worked for such goals as peace, better ties with the United States, and labor reforms through a variety of positions, including minister of labor, delegate to the United Nations, minister of foreign affairs, and from 1969 to 1974, Israeli prime minister.

Socialist and Communist Women

Socialist feminists took a different approach to the problems of American women. They advocated radical feminism, meaning they wished to eliminate male dominance from American society and, rather than simply gain equality with men, institute a leaderless participatory democracy. They were the first to use consciousness-raising techniques to educate women and to enhance their awareness of feminist issues. They also utilized demonstrations and protests that frequently alienated more middle-of-the road feminists.

The best-known of these women was Angela Davis. Davis, who was born in Birmingham, Alabama, later graduated from Brandeis University where she had studied Marxist philosophy with Herbert Marcuse. After graduation, Davis continued to study with Marcuse and entered the civil rights movement, especially SNCC and the Black Panthers. In June, 1968, Davis joined the Communist Party. During the fall of 1969, Davis began teaching at the University of California at Los Angeles, but because conservative governor Ronald Reagan had helped pass a state law prohibiting California universities from hiring known Communists, Davis was fired.

She was rehired and then fired again for making "inflammatory" remarks supporting three black prisoners accused of killing a white guard.

Reportedly, Davis then bought a gun for one of the prisoners, fled from California, and wound up on the FBI's list of the "ten most wanted fugitives." In 1970, Davis was arrested and endured a twenty-month trial; two years later, courts declared her innocent of all charges. In 1974, she published *Angela Davis: An Autobiography* to help people understand "why so many of us have no alternative but to offer our lives—our bodies, our knowledge, our will—to the cause of our oppressed people." Davis resumed her aborted academic career, teaching philosophy and women's studies at San Francisco State University and publishing in 1981 a scholarly study titled *Women, Race, and Class*.

Rural Women

The lot of rural women generally underwent less modification than that of the above groups. In the rural South, both black and white women continued to labor in their homes as well as work in the fields for long hours for wages that kept them living below the poverty level. A study of tobacco farms indicated that a significant number of women continued to contribute their unpaid labor as sisters, wives, and daughters. According to one researcher, this family system of survival functioned "under the leadership of the male head" and "blended patriarchal forms with the market economy."

Because of the growing economic pressures on family farms during the 1970s and 1980s, many farm women across the nation also "helped out" by working off the farm or running the farm while the men of the family held outside jobs. A study of Kentucky farm women in 1980 revealed that 38 percent worked off the farm. Another researcher noted that farm women "not only . . . have to fill in for their part-time farming husbands on the land, but they themselves are increasingly entering the non-farm labor force."

The lives of women migrant farm workers were also fraught with difficulties. Largely Chicana, these women endured shocking working conditions, poor wages, wretched housing, patriarchal family structures, and lack of opportunities to improve their situations. Elizabeth Loza Newby described the anguish that she felt when, in 1966, her migrant worker father shunned her because she had decided to pursue the education that was her only escape from the migrant life and an arranged marriage. Other Chicana women, including a number of women Religious, joined together to protest the terrible conditions and lack of opportunities suffered by workers in *colonias* outside such cities as El Paso.

By the 1980s, rural women had begun to develop their own brand of feminism. For instance, although 1978 census figures had indicated that 5 percent of all farmers were female, in 1981 a Department of Agriculture survey showed that 55 percent of all farm women considered themselves the main operators. These results suggest that growing numbers of women were demanding recognition as farmers, and challenging such widespread discrimination as banks refusing to loan them money, male farmers excluding them from information-sharing sessions, and tractor manufacturers ignoring their need for smaller-scale equipment.

Assessing Gains and Losses, 1965–1985

The Second Wave

Between 1965 and 1985, customary gender expectations and social constructs increasingly became more of an unrealized myth than a functional model for American women. But how many of these alterations can be directly attributed to the feminist movement itself is unclear. In all probability, the feminist movement was both a cause and an effect of the changing social climate. Certainly, the feminist movement forced Americans to recognize the existence of gender discrimination, confront its high cost to the nation, and grapple with implementing the necessary changes.

Women's awareness rose quickly. Although a Gallup poll in 1962 revealed that less than one out of three women felt discriminated against, eight years later 50 percent of women questioned said that they had experienced discrimination. In 1974, two out of three said they had suffered discrimination. In 1979, another study showed that between 1962 and 1977 the beliefs of women of all classes and ages had undergone a significant shift toward egalitarianism. Even though they might not count themselves as members of the feminist movement, the majority of American women espoused feminist positions regarding day care, abortion, and equal access to job and professional opportunities.

Yet another study indicated that during the 1970s many American men also dramatically revised their attitudes toward women. Some of these even translated their new attitudes into action. In 1978, officials in Indianapolis, Indiana, appointed two women to police patrol duty. During the late 1970s and early 1980s, other police forces hired significant numbers of women, and gradually the term "policeman" turned into "police officer."

Federal Regulations

The federal government proved especially influential in urging feminist reform and in initiating the process of adjusting policies and laws. For instance, in 1967 President Lyndon B. Johnson issued an executive order prohibiting gender discrimination by federal contractors. The growing number of female judges sitting on national, state, and local court benches also contributed to such alterations.

Congress proved active as well. In 1972, Congress added Title IX to the Education Amendments Act, forbidding discrimination against students and employees in hiring and funding by federally assisted educational programs. Also in 1972, Congress finally approved the Equal Rights Amendment, which stated that "Equality of Rights shall not be denied or abridged by the United States or by any state on account of sex." When Congress sent the ERA to the states for ratification, the civil rights sentiment of the time made ratification appear highly likely within the seven-year deadline. Law schools even introduced special courses to train future lawyers in Equal Rights law. But by 1973, when thirty states had ratified and only eight more were needed, opposition to the ERA was increasingly organized and widespread. Congress eventually extended the ERA ratification deadline to 30 June 1982, but a nation experiencing economic instability and a rebirth of political conservatism ultimately failed to ratify the amendment.

During the 1970s and 1980s, Congress enacted a virtual barrage of additional equity laws, including the Women's Equity Act, which supported various training programs for women. It also nationalized and publicized Women's History Month, which had begun in 1977 when Sonoma County, California, schools denoted March as Women's History Month in hopes of raising interest in women's history and integrating it into school curriculums. In 1980, the National Women's History Project organized in Santa Rosa, California, to supply information on International Women's Day and Women's History Month, and in 1981 the U.S. Congress adopted a national Women's History Week proclamation. Congress later enlarged it to Women's History Month, now celebrated every March in the United States.

Women in Paid Employment

Women in the workforce especially experienced widespread changes. By 1980, over half of all married women worked, and approximately three out of five women with children held jobs. By 1985, more than three out of five women worked. No longer considered a temporary or marginal labor force, women workers began to receive a number of benefits, including maternity leave, day care, and training programs.

Not all problems reached resolution, however. The majority of women continued to experience segregation into clerical, sales, and office jobs at low wages. In 1985, they earned between fifty-five to fifty-seven cents for every dollar men made. Furthermore, women's work frequently called for generally unappreciated skills and offered little opportunity for advancement. Moreover, contrary to popular belief, rather than improving the position of women in the labor market, changes in technology from the typewriter to the computer frequently contributed to their subordination.

Equal pay also remained problematic. Because the Equal Pay Act of 1963 amended the Fair Labor Standards Act of 1938, the U.S. Labor Department was responsible for its enforcement. Officials conducted routine checks for violations and investigated complaints with only limited success, largely due to imprecision in the wording of the act itself. During the 1970s, women began to bring comparable-worth suits, later called sex-equity suits, which demanded equal pay for work of like value. By 1985, such complainants had obtained favorable judgments in six states but continued to face stubborn resistance from the New Right and other conservative factions.

Women also demonstrated a growing willingness to participate in labor organizations. Cesar Chavez and Dolores Huerta's National Farm Workers Association (NFWA) not only captured the nation's attention with its nationwide grape boycott, but during the strike the NFWA became the United Farm Workers (UFW). Later, in 1974 Dolores Huerta became UFW's first elected vice-president. As both vice-president and chief negotiator, Huerta said that women and men welcomed her efforts. She explained that "they will appreciate anybody who will come in and help them."

By 1977, UFW represented some 30,000 workers. Women now served in administrative positions and on the picket lines, proving themselves as the mainstay of the UFW and its nonviolent approach. Jessie Lopez de la Cruz, for example, was the first woman to organize workers in the field, while Helen Chavez headed the Credit Union and Marie Sabadado directed the Robert F. Kennedy Farm Workers Medical Plan.

In overall union membership nationwide between 1956 and 1976, women workers, many of whom were teachers and public employees, accounted for nearly half of the growth in membership. Meanwhile, in 1974, 3,500 union women launched a new organization, the Coalition of Labor Union Women (CLUW). This group committed itself to increasing affirmative action on the job, pressing for passage of legislation affecting female laborers, supporting women's involvement in politics, and bringing unorganized women into unions. Shortly thereafter, between 1976 and 1978, Department of Labor statistics indicated that women trade union members increased by 455,000, bringing women to approximately 28 percent of union membership.

Union leaders began to understand that their willingness to consider the needs of growing numbers of women in the workforce could affect not only the unions' effectiveness but their very survival. In 1980, the new president of the AFL-CIO announced his intention to bring women into top leadership positions. During the 1980s, unions also began to reach out to nonunion women workers, to introduce coverage of women's issues and activities into their newsletters and other publications, and to include women's causes in their lobbying efforts.

The place of black women in the labor force altered as well. Black women workers moved in great numbers into areas customarily dominated by white female workers. In 1965, only 24 percent of employed black women were white-collar workers, but that figure rose to 46 percent in 1981. Black women also abandoned domestic service in significant numbers, leaving immigrants from Puerto Rico, Mexico, other areas of Latin America, and elsewhere to replace them. Although in 1965, 30 percent of all working black women were in domestic service, this figure had dropped by 1977 to 9 percent.

In addition, black women entered the organized labor movement. In 1970, black garment-worker Lillian Rice complained that unions were of little use to black workers because they discriminated against people of color. This situation improved, however, during the 1970s. Trade union activist Lillian Roberts is an outstanding example of the change. A hospital employee in Chicago, Roberts was hired by the hospital workers' union—the American Federation of State, County, and Municipal Employees (AFSCME)—and served with distinction. By the end of the 1970s, she achieved the position of associate director of District Council 37 for the organization in New York. She later became Labor Commissioner for the state.

Education and the Professions

Between 1965 and 1985, education experienced widespread modifications as well. Special programs designed to eradicate women's "fear of success" and "math anxiety" now attempted to offset the negative effects of gender stereotyping in female students. Women's athletics expanded and, in some respects, became more equitable with men's athletics. The number of female college students rose noticeably, while in 1975 Congress mandated that U.S. military academies accept women. The following year the United States Military Academy at West Point, New York, and the Annapolis Naval Academy began to admit women; the first classes graduated in 1980. By 1985, affirmative action programs were in place in a large number of the nation's schools, colleges, and universities.

Consequently, the number of women in the professions increased. Women entered law schools at a growing rate; in 1962 women constituted 3.6 percent of law students but by 1972 accounted for 12 percent. Thus, between 1971 and 1981, the percentage of female lawyers and judges jumped from 4 to 14. By 1984, women constituted one-third of law school graduates. In medicine, women filled a wide variety of roles, including nurse, nurse midwife, nurse practitioner, physician, and surgeon. Between 1962 and 1972, the percentage of women medical students rose from 9 to 22. Women also attended graduate schools in growing numbers. After 1970, the number of women obtaining doctorates grew more than 1 percent each year; by 1985, women earned nearly 30 percent of all Ph.D. degrees granted.

At the same time, librarians began to challenge the customary image of librarianship as a woman's profession. Female members of the American Library Association publicized discriminatory practices against women, especially in matters of pay equity and career opportunities. Women of color also fought for additional access to library training programs and jobs, thus intensifying the long tradition of offering library services to communities of color that had begun during the 1920s.

Overall, however, women of color participated in these gains at a lower rate than did Anglo women. Teaching, nursing, and the social sciences continued to attract women of color, and they also began to enter law and medicine in growing numbers. Still, even though they benefited from affirmative action and economic opportunity programs, the number of women of color in the professions remained relatively small compared to Anglo women.

Women in the Media and Film

Largely as a result of legal pressure, women became notable in every type of media job ranging from reporter to disc jockey, but black women especially made a breakthrough. Black correspondent Phillippa Duke Schuyler covered the Vietnam War, Dorothy Gilliam served as the first black woman columnist for the *Washington Post*, and black radio broadcaster Yvonne Daniels earned the title "First Lady of Chicago Radio."

Television producers quickly pushed Anglo women into highly visible positions as news-show reporters and anchors. Barbara Walters, for example, became an outstanding and highly paid television journalist. The number of women of color in such positions grew more slowly, but Connie Chung gained an early reputation as a respected journalist and carried a new image of Asian women to the viewing public. Later, Ethel L. Payne spent ten weeks in Vietnam and became the first African American woman in broadcasting when she reported on CBS News. PBS's Charlayne Hunter-Gault, the first black woman reporter on a daily news program, won an Emmy; and Oprah Winfrey won three Emmy awards as talk-show host and producer of the "Oprah Winfrey Show."

The media and Hollywood's propensity to present sexual stereotypes also came under widespread attack, and gradually the number of women's roles and themes increased. In 1985, the television show "Cagney and Lacy," which featured two female detectives, received high ratings. At the same time, black women played leading roles in such television series as "The Cosby Show," "Head of the Class," "21 Jump Street," and "I'll Fly Away." In the film *Norma Rae*, Sally Field portrayed a gutsy labor organizer in southern cotton mills; in *Yentl* Barbra Streisand raised serious questions about Jewish women's roles; in *Silkwood* Meryl Streep protested nuclear plant policies; in *Country* Jessica Lange demonstrated the strength of women in times of economic crisis; and Cicily Tyson in *Sounder* and Whoopi Goldberg in *The Color Purple* revealed the strength of black women and the talents of black women as actors.

Women in Sports

After 1965, the sports world also exhibited some marked changes relating to women. In Olympic competition, track and field stars Wilma Rudolph and Wyomia Tyus dramatically lowered women's record times, while figure-skaters Peggy Fleming and Dorothy Hamill won medals. In basketball, the Women's Professional Basketball League formed in 1978. In golf, Nancy Lopez won purses whose amounts approached those of male golfers; and retired tennis great Althea Gibson continued to smash the color barrier by playing professional golf from 1963 to 1967. In horse racing, jockeys Mary Bacon and Robyn Smith not only rode against male jockeys but frequently won. And automobile race car driver Janet Guthrie drove in the renowned Indianapolis 500.

In tennis, Billie Jean King established women's tennis as a major sport. After becoming in 1961 the youngest player to win at Wimbledon, King won twenty more titles in the next twelve years. In 1972, *Sports Illustrated* named King Sportswoman of the Year. In 1973, King helped found the Women's Tennis Association, which acted as a union and fought to improve women's wages. Also in 1973, King startled Americans by defeating male challenger Bobby Riggs. Although King increasingly spoke out on such issues as abortion and lesbianism, she continued to reap titles and in 1980 was inducted into the Women's Sports Hall of Fame. Others who carried on King's work were Chris Evert and Martina Navratilova.

Women in the Arts

Impressive numbers of women produced works ranging from folk art to surrealism. The work of black folk artists Minnie Evans, Ethel Mohamed, Inez Nathaniel, and Queena Stovall gained a wide audience. Other folk artists included Theodora Hamblett and Gertrude Rogers, who had begun painting late in their lives but were soon known for their autobiographical scenes, and Malcah Zeldis, who in her late thirties began painting historical events, Jewish religious themes, and personal memories. An accompanying resurgence of interest in quilting also occurred, leading in turn to the formation of quilting clubs and conferences.

Of special note was Judy Chicago's massive work, *The Dinner Party*. Chicago, a West Coast minimalist sculptor during the 1960s, founded or helped found the first feminist art programs of Womanhouse, the Woman's Building, and the Feminist Studio Workshop. In 1973, Chicago started *The Dinner Party*, which eventually encompassed four hundred artists who drew upon such traditional women's crafts as china painting, embroidery, and weaving to create thirty-nine place settings, each celebrating an outstanding woman. For early feminist Mary Wollstonecraft, artists embroidered scenes from her life in stempwork, a type of raised needlework done in England during the seventeenth century.

When *The Dinner Party* opened in 1979 at the San Francisco Museum of Modern Art, it attracted 100,000 viewers. Subsequently, it toured the United States, but because of its outspoken feminist and lesbian themes it was seldom exhibited in major museums. In 1980, Chicago began another massive undertaking, *The Birth Project*, which expressed the experience of childbirth among different generations and cultures of women.

Women in Music

In the field of music, women also demonstrated creativity and productivity. Anna Lockwood's 1976 composition, *World Rhythms*, combined natural sounds from rivers, earthquakes, and human breathing with the tones of a gong. Joyce Mekiet gained critical acclaim for her experiments with unusual ways of combining the human voice and traditional instruments. Another frequently performed composer was classical musician Barbara Kolb, who wrote many pieces for chamber ensembles.

Meanwhile, other classical women musicians, performers, and conductors also gained stature. In 1966, the New York Philharmonic hired its first woman performer, and by 1983 Beverly Sills was artistic director of the New York City Opera Company. Among the best-known opera singers were Marion Anderson, Marilyn Horne, Roberta Peters, and Leontyne Price. Price, a black woman from Laurel, Mississippi, first sang in a church choir and later studied at the Julliard School of Music in New York. In 1966, Price celebrated the Metropolitan Opera's move to Lincoln Hall by performing Samuel Barber's *Anthony and Cleopatra,* which Barber had written for her. Ten years later, the Metropolitan Opera Company hired its first woman conductor, Sarah Caldwell.

In popular music, jazz pianist Marian McPartland and black jazz singers Ella Fitzgerald, Sarah Vaughan, and Nancy Wilson enjoyed great popularity. Vaughan and Fitzgerald developed expertise in "scatting," a form of singing that uses improvised nonsense sounds instead of words, while Wilson inspired such popular singers as Aretha Franklin, Diana Ross, and Natalie Cole. Such Anglo singers as Helen Reddy, Janis Joplin, and Bette Midler were a few of the many other outstanding female vocalists.

Meanwhile, Madonna challenged both gender stereotypes and media norms through her concerts and videos. Beginning in 1982, Madonna grabbed public attention with such hits as "Everybody," "Borderline," and "Into the Groove." Perhaps most important, her 1984 hit, "Like a Virgin," attacked long-standing conventions regarding American women.

Women in the Literary Arts

Women writers of the time were also prolific and imaginative. Maya Angelou, who had served as northern coordinator for the Reverend Dr. Martin Luther King's Southern Christian Leadership Conference, wrote poems, essays, and a series of autobiographical works. Perhaps Angelou's most famous work was *I Know Why the Caged Bird Sings* (1970), which described her childhood in the rural community of Stamps, Arkansas, including her rape at eight years of age. At sixteen, Angelou moved to California where the San Francisco Streetcar Company hired her as its first black woman fare collector.

Audre Lorde, a black lesbian feminist poet and essayist, further analyzed sexual and social justice issues. In such works as *Between Ourselves* (1976), *The Black Unicorn* (1978), and *Sister/Outsider* (1984), Lorde attacked the suppression of certain voices in literature, including those of women of color and lesbians.

Black writer Toni Morrison also attracted favorable attention with such works as *Sula* (1975) and critical acclaim with *Song of Solomon* (1978), while black feminist writer Alice Walker explored relationships among women and within families in *The Color Purple* (1982). In 1983, Walker received the Pulitzer Prize for this poignant exploration of the lives of black women in the rural South. Similarly, Gloria Naylor focused on the black female experience and attacked greed, racism, sexism, and homophobia in such works as *The Women of Brewster Place* (1982) and *Linden Hills* (1985).

To this rich outpouring, Maxine Hong Kingston added her autobiographical *The Woman Warrior* (1975), which explored a Chinese American girl's struggle to surmount Chinese traditionalism and American prejudice. In 1976, Kingston won the National Book Critics Circle Award for nonfiction.

Nicholasa Mohr, an artist, novelist, and essayist, was the first Puerto Rican woman living in the mainland United States to write in English about her ethnic origins. Born of Island migrants in New York City, Mohr recalled that she and her family felt like "strangers in their own country" due to differences in culture, language, and race between them and other Americans. In *El Bronx Remembered* (1973), *Nueva York* (1977), and *Felita* (1979), Mohr documented her people's problems, including those of rural people transported to an industrial society, an abundance of female-headed welfare households, segregation into low-skill jobs, and widespread religious discrimination. But Mohr also captured the joyous side of Puerto Rican life, including the pervasiveness of family unity, neighborhood solidarity, and vibrant religious celebrations and feast days.

Anglo women also enriched this feminist literature. Novelists Sylvia Plath, Erica Jong, and Marilyn French, among others, used fiction to build the case against male chauvinism. Plath poignantly described limitations upon women in *The Bell Jar* (1971), while Jong especially wrote novels exploring freedom in sex and relationships. Jong's ribald *Fear of Flying* (1974) introduced uniquely female fantasies in a lusty yet intellectual eroticism. French, in *The Women's Room* (1977), explored the issue of identity. She portrayed the angst of a displaced homemaker who entered a graduate program at Harvard University and eventually "found" herself. In a wide variety of works, Joan Didion and Joyce Carol Oates dealt with topics relating to the struggle of women to understand modern society.

Women in Politics

Women also became more visible in the political realm. Between 1969 and 1981, the number of female state legislators grew from 301 to 908. Between 1975 and 1981, the overall number of female elected officials increased from 5,765 to 14,225.

Democrats demonstrated an especially strong record. The era of President Lyndon B. Johnson and "Lady Bird" Johnson proved good years for women. Johnson appointed more women to office than any president before or since, with the exception of Bill Clinton. In 1968, Democrat Shirley Chisholm became the first black woman elected to the U.S. House of Representatives. Chisholm served until 1982 as representative of the Twelfth District of Brooklyn, New York, where during the late 1960s thirteen thousand more women than men lived, and three times as many black women as men registered to vote. In 1972, Chisholm also introduced feminist issues on the national level when she ran unsuccessfully with Sissy (Frances) Farenthold of Texas for the Democratic nomination.

In that same year, Representative Barbara Jordan, a black Democrat from Texas, delivered the nominating speech at the Democratic convention, while Representative Martha Griffith, a Democrat from Michigan, distinguished herself fighting for the ERA. During the Watergate scandals, Representative Elizabeth Holtzman, a Democrat from New York, proved to be a forceful interrogator as part of the House Judiciary Committee's investigative team, and Jordan voted for the articles of impeachment against President Richard M. Nixon. Jordan, who described Nixon's resignation as a "cleansing experience" for American politics, continued to work for civil rights, the environment, and the underprivileged. Among other key legislation she sponsored during her three terms, Jordan initiated the extension of Social Security coverage to full-time homemakers.

Similarly, the years of President Jimmy Carter and Rosalynn Carter brought women to the peak of their influence in the Democratic party thus far. Carter appointed two women to his cabinet—Patricia Harris as Secretary of Housing and Urban Development and Juanita Kreps as Secretary of Commerce—while overall, 12 percent of Carter's appointees were women. On the local level, in 1978, Diane Feinstein became mayor of San Francisco, and in 1979, Jane Byrne gained election as Chicago's first woman mayor. In 1981, Kathy Whitmire successfully campaigned for the mayor's position in Houston, Texas.

The Republican Party established a more checkered record regarding women. Certainly, the Republicans achieved a significant feat in 1978 when Nancy Kassebaum of Kansas became the first woman elected to the U.S. Senate who was not the widow of a member of Congress. Then, in 1981, President Ronald Reagan appointed Sandra Day O'Connor as the first woman justice on the U.S. Supreme Court. Two years later, Reagan named Elizabeth Dole as Secretary of Transportation and Margaret Heckler as Secretary of Health and Human Services but appointed few women to lower judicial and administrative positions.

Meanwhile, the so-called gender gap began to have some effect as women gradually recognized that they frequently had different political interests than those of men. For instance, in 1982, 5 percent less women than men voted for conservative candidates. In subsequent elections, female voters demonstrated less support than men for President Reagan's policies, including his opposition to the ERA and his military and economic decisions. Women also gave more support than men to such issues as abortion, childcare, and the ERA. Although they did not comprise a voting bloc, by the mid-1980s women composed approximately 53 percent of the voting population and registered to vote in greater numbers than did men.

The year 1984 proved especially crucial for women in politics when New York congressperson Geraldine Ferraro became the Democratic Party's candidate for the vice-presidency of the United States. Ferraro, an attorney admitted to the New York bar in 1961, left her private practice in 1974 to serve as assistant district attorney for Queens County, New York, where she handled cases of child abuse, domestic violence, and rape. In 1978, Ferraro gained a seat in the U.S. House of Representatives and ran successfully for two additional terms. In the House, Ferraro usually voted with liberal Democrats on most issues, including abortion, despite her own membership in the Roman Catholic church. In 1984, Walter Mondale chose Ferraro as his running mate in what turned out to be an unsuccessful campaign. The fact that she campaigned with forebearance, intelligence, and style throughout the rigors of her bid for national office established Ferraro as a memorable role model for women in politics.

Women and the Family

The family was one of the most dramatic areas of change for women. During the 1950s, 70 percent of American families were composed of a father who worked and a mother who stayed at home to care for the children. By 1980, only 15 percent of families were so constituted. Moreover, with the assistance of the birth-control pill, the average family size had fallen to 1.6 children. At the same time, roughly 50 percent of marriages ended in divorce and 23 percent of adults chose to live in single-person households.

As a consequence, the definition of family expanded to accommodate two employed adults; spouses who lived in separate households; a single-parent household; a "reconstituted" family made up of two remarried adults and their children from previous marriages; "skip-generation" families which included a grandparent and grandchild but not the child's parent; a group of unmarried people representing several generations living together; or an unmarried person living alone. Dual-career marriage, single-parent family, commuter marriage, supermom, singlehood, and latchkey child all became common terms.

Americans also seemed more than willing to expand their sexual lives. Now marriage manuals and other self-help literature offered explicit sexual advice. Alex Comfort's *The Joy of Sex* (1972) became a long-term best-seller. It supported oral sex, which was still against the law in many states; advocated the use of masturbation, which feminists had urged; and endorsed homosexuality.

Americans also continued to experiment with gender roles and to reshape gender expectations. A 1980 Gallup poll revealed widespread support for women's reproductive freedom and their right to hold political office, while a 1983 survey indicated that the majority of respondents believed that wives and husbands should share not only household chores and childcare but financial and other decision-making as well.

Feminization of Poverty

On the deficit side of the ledger, an especially unfortunate development was the "feminization" of poverty, which in turn increased the number of homeless women and children in the United States. The rise in number of female-headed households combined with segregation of women into low-paying jobs to create a huge group of American women who lived near or under the poverty level.

Women's growing poverty was partly a negative side effect of no-fault divorce. Initially implemented in California in 1970 when then-governor Ronald Reagan signed it into law, no-fault divorce gave women who opposed their husbands' wish to divorce them little legal recourse. Against their wills, millions of women who had never worked and thus lacked job skills moved into the category of "displaced homemakers," a term coined during the early 1970s. In addition, because most states now did not require grounds to divorce a spouse, a woman's ability to charge her adulterous husband with fault and thus obtain a favorable settlement to support herself and her children was seriously diluted. In 1973, Congress at least responded with the Comprehensive Employment and Training Act (CETA), which made grants to local agencies that would train displaced homemakers and help them find jobs.

The growth of female poverty also resulted from an unprecedented rise in female-headed households due to separation, desertion, mutually agreed upon divorce, widowhood, and pregnancy without marriage. Although in 1890 women headed only fourteen of every one hundred households, in 1970 women headed twenty-one out of every hundred and in 1980 twenty-six out of every hundred. Ten years later, two-thirds of female-headed families received child welfare, while over 80 percent of welfare recipients were female. Moreover, two-thirds of those living in poverty were women.

This growth of female poverty especially affected black women. By 1980, 55 percent of black children were born outside marriage, 85 percent of black teenage mothers were unmarried, and 47 percent of black families had female heads. Lacking skills and still discriminated against in employment, most of these women turned for assistance to welfare or to such organizations as the National Council of Negro Women.

Other women of color also headed households. Innocencia Flores, a Puerto Rican woman living in Harlem, is one example. A mother of four separated from her husband and living on relief, Flores waged a daily battle with rats, junkies, the indifference of landlords, and the frequent incompetence of exhausted and overloaded welfare caseworkers.

Eating Disorders

Another problem—and another entry in the deficit column—that resulted from the growing pressures on women were eating disorders, including anorexia nervosa, bulimia, and obesity. Although none of these ailments were new to the United States, they rose rapidly during the late 1960s, the 1970s, and early 1980s; anorexia and bulimia especially afflicted daughters of educated and successful parents. Paradoxically, such women had more societal options available than ever before yet appeared more stressed than ever.

Anorexia is a psycho-sociological disease of self-imposed starvation; bulimia is marked by a binge-purge cycle, in which a person eats huge amounts of food and then purges through vomiting or using laxatives; and obesity results chiefly from compulsive overeating. Dr. Hilde Bruch of the Baylor College of Medicine in Houston, Texas, identified three causal factors for eating disorders: increasing emphasis on thinness in the United States, the pressure on women to achieve in both their personal and professional lives, and societal pressures to experiment with sex at an early age. By the mid-1980s, 80 percent of ten-year-old girls had been on a diet or were currently dieting, a statistic that called into question social and cultural values for women.

SINCE 1985

A Turning Point?

The nation stood at a crossroads in 1985. When Geraldine Ferraro accepted the Democratic National Convention's vice-presidential nomination in 1984 she had said, "By choosing a woman to run for our nation's second highest office, you send a powerful signal to all Americans. There are no doors we cannot unlock." But, in 1985 Ferraro and presidential candidate Walter Mondale failed to overcome the widespread popularity of incumbent president Ronald Reagan.

Many of those who had helped initiate the contemporary feminist movement no longer felt confident that they would see solutions and closure in their lifetimes. Apparently, even though some Americans felt ready to elevate a woman to a leadership position, others resented the demands of feminists and reformers. In 1985, for example, one male public figure commented: "So cry not for the Ferraro candidacy. Nobody lost by it. The women were in the kitchen when the thing started, and they're in the kitchen where they belong at the end of it."

The year 1985 was crucial in other ways as well. It marked the eruption of violence against abortion clinics, an obvious demand for a return to past policies. At the same time, a national poll revealed a growing willingness on the part of both women and men to destroy the traditional double standard and erect new social roles and expectations in its place. This flexibility extended to issues concerning other categories of people as well, including racial and ethnic groups, veterans, and the physically and mentally challenged.

Influence of Feminism

The contemporary feminist movement can fairly take credit for creating pervasive revisions in American attitudes and policies. The second wave of feminism, which began in the 1960s, had considerably more impact than had the first wave, including the intervening small ripples, because of four distinguishing characteristics.

First, the second wave of feminism established an encompassing movement that included women of myriad social classes, races, and ethnicities. Rather than drawing mainly upon middle- and upper-class Anglo women as Elizabeth Cady Stanton and Susan B. Anthony had done, contemporary feminism paid increasing attention to such special groups as women of color, lesbians, and older women. It also elicited the support of such women's organizations as the Girl Scouts of America, the League of Women Voters, and the YWCA.

Second, unlike the Stanton-Anthony brand of feminism, contemporary leaders refused to focus upon specific solutions. Instead, the second wave questioned underlying assumptions regarding women and their roles, for the first time holding everything up to examination and disputing its fairness. Beginning with young women in the civil rights movement, feminists challenged the inevitability of patriarchy and the "rightness" of it.

Women emerged from the civil rights experience with a dedication to egalitarianism and the need to change the quality of human relationships. In turn, they questioned all gender expectations and constructs. While earlier feminist movements had accepted and built on the societal beliefs that women were moral, virtuous, and natural social housekeepers, contemporary feminists demanded new strategies.

Third, the second wave analyzed the effect of culture on the development of gender roles and behavior —that is, the effect of societal rules that generate learned behavior. Up to point of birth, human development is largely genetic, with chromosomes and hormones determining gender attributes. At birth, however, culture largely takes over. During its first three years, a child learns well how she or he is expected to behave. In feminists' eyes, traditional societal rules provided girls with invidious and crippling lifelong roles.

Fortunately for feminists the public was generally receptive to such ideas because many Americans now had an expanded grasp of comparative cultures. The work of such anthropologists as Ruth Benedict and Margaret Mead had demonstrated that various cultures made different decisions about such matters as gender. Technology, too, especially the print media and television, daily brought other cultures into people's homes, while improved transportation also made other cultures a reality to many Americans.

Feminists pointed out that various cultures had historically defined gender roles according to the demands of such factors as climate, available resources, physical strength, and fertility rates. This led to systems in which, on the one hand, men usually performed heavy, dangerous labor away from their home base because they were both physically strong and expendable to childcare; and in which, on the other hand, women did lighter jobs because they were physically smaller and weaker and needed to stay closer to home so that they would be accessible to children.

Throughout history, however, different groups defined "heavy" and "light" work, and "far" and "near" labor sites differently. Among numerous Native American groups, women farmed and traded, ranging far from home with their babies secure in cradle-boards on their backs. Among Anglos, however, men frequently farmed and traded. Clearly, then, no universal and inviolable gender laws existed.

Moreover, feminists added, in the United States, technology had further changed the definitions of labor. Women could now perform formerly "heavy" jobs with the assistance of machinery, better regulate birth by means of pills, and, with infant formulas and bottle-feeding, leave infants in someone else's care. Why then, feminists asked, should gender expectations and social constructs not be revised to suit the current situation?

Fourth, American women increasingly wielded new kinds of power, which feminists were quick to use. Among demographic changes, women now outnumbered men in the United States, and female college students outnumbered males. Employed women were freer than ever before of economic dependence on men, which allowed them to take advantage of the increasing ease of divorce when their marital expectations were not met. As primary consumers, women greatly influenced the economy, even to the point of purchasing approximately 75 percent of such men's products as underwear. They also selected more liberating lines of products and styles for themselves, including jeans, comfortable shoes, short haircuts, and minimal make-up. Moreover, because women outlived men, as widows they often controlled the fortunes men had earned.

Impact of Other Modifications in American Society

Despite the extensive influence of contemporary feminism, it would be inaccurate, of course, to assign it full credit for recent changes. Certainly, the questioning of rules and authority received a major boost from the civil rights movement and anti-Vietnam protests.

In addition, U.S. prosperity, and, ironically, lack of it, created jobs for women, or at least allowed them to work. Even when the economy contracted, women felt they had to continue to work to keep up standards—thus, the dual-income couple. Meanwhile, improved technology made it possible for women to perform numerous jobs, including those that had once demanded physical prowess. Women could also control family spacing through technology and ease childcare with such products as disposable diapers.

A complex of other factors also influenced change. For instance, because the United States democratized education and professional training, advanced jobs and professions were increasingly open to women. And because women live longer today, they have more years of "empty-nest" time in which to pursue graduate degrees or other credentials and careers.

Opposition to Change

Of course, change generated opposition. People naturally feared that chaos might result when the old rules altered or disappeared entirely. Also, people with deep religious convictions believed that certain concepts were innate, natural, and God-given. The Roman Catholic church, for example, maintained that abortion constitutes murder and concerns a decision that belongs only to God. Viewing itself as countercultural, the church resisted the development of a society in which individuals have the choice to give birth or abort, take drugs or not, live or elect suicide.

Such opposition led to a reexamination of numerous issues. The anti-abortion, or Right-to-Life, movement led in 1989 to *Webster v. Reproductive Health Services*, in which the U.S. Supreme Court allowed states to limit a woman's access to legal abortion. Meanwhile, a range of feminist writers including Camille Paglia on the one hand, and Susan Faludi and Naomi Wolf on the other, debated the cause and effects of the "backlash" against the women's movement.

Change Triumphant

Despite such opposition, a majority of Americans seemed to stand behind change. As a case in point, during the 1980s the U.S. Department of Justice went to court to oppose the use of numerical objectives in Affirmative Action programs. In 1988, Congress approved the Civil Rights Restoration Act, which required institutional compliance with antidiscrimination laws by institutions accepting federal assistance. When President Ronald Reagan vetoed the bill, Congress overrode his veto.

In the U.S. armed forces, women gained increasing influence as well. A new, light weapon—the M-16 rifle—made women's participation at the front more feasible, while the Supreme Court ordered the gender integration of the Citadel in Charleston, South Carolina. In 1990, when President George Bush called for American troops to fight in the Gulf War, women formed part of the battlefield troop movement. Military officials also demonstrated a growing commitment to resolve the problems of military women, including the possibility of rape by the enemy, sexual relations and pregnancy among soldiers, and the need for women to leave small children behind.

Military women also earned leadership positions. In 1989, Christine Baker became the first woman to head the Corps of Cadets at West Point. Baker, a twenty-one-year-old cadet, received the U.S. Military Academy's highest cadet honor. Selected on academic achievement, athletic ability, and military expertise, Baker led West Point's brigade of 4,400 cadets, composed of about 10 percent women.

Then, in 1993 on Veterans Day, the U.S. government dedicated a Vietnam Women's Memorial in Washington, D.C. The bronze statue depicts three women nurses wearing combat fatigues, one holding a wounded soldier, another kneeling in shock over the horror of the war, and a third looking upward for a Medevac helicopter. Directly across from the Vietnam Veterans Memorial, the Vietnam Women's Memorial fulfills the dreams and efforts of the project's founder, nurse Diane Carlson Evenas.

Similarly, another significant modification has occurred in the government's attitude toward historical sites. Although presidents, generals, forts, and battlefields once dominated the nation's statues and historic sites, the National Park Service has more recently created such sites as the Women's Rights National Historical Park in Seneca Falls, New York, which interprets the first women's rights convention of 1848 to visitors. Also located there is the National Women's Hall of Fame, first organized in 1968 to honor outstanding American women.

The number of women-related sites continues to grow. In Richmond, Virginia, the Maggie I. Walker National Historical Site preserves the home and neighborhood of a leader in Richmond's black community, who was also the first woman bank president in the United States. Others include the Eleanor Roosevelt National Historic Site in Hyde Park, New York; the Clara Barton National Historic Site in Glen Echo, Maryland; the

Whitman Mission National Historic Site near Walla Walla, Washington (the 1836 mission of Narcissa and Marcus Whitman); and the Lowell National Historical Park in Lowell, Massachusetts.

Women have also gained greater recognition in the art world. This change includes the National Museum of Women in the Arts, which was organized in Washington, D.C., in 1981. When it opened in 1987 it included permanent collections ranging from Renaissance work to contemporary art, a library, and a research center. Today, the National Museum exhibits Native American pottery, Georgian silver, paintings, sculpture, and photographs, and special showings of women's work.

Contemporary literature also demonstrates far more change than continuity. Recent black women writers have explored the meaning of the black past, especially the role of the blues and jazz. Such works as Xam Cartiér's *Muse-Echo Blues* (1991) establish connections between women's present situation and the historical conditions of African Americans as revealed in their music.

Other black women writers have drawn upon slavery. In 1988, Toni Morrison won the Pulitzer Prize for her exquisite novel *Beloved*, which explores the legacy of slavery through intricate and poetic shifts of consciousness. In 1993, Morrison became the first black American to win the Nobel Prize in literature. The Swedish Academy described Morrison's work as "unusually finely wrought and cohesive, yet at the same time rich in variation." In response to the prize announcement, Morrison explained that her work attempted to remedy "huge silences in literature, things that had never been articulated, printed or imagined, and they were the silences about black girls, black women."

Coping with Change

Because after 1985 American society entered a transitional phase—which always incurs difficulties and disruptions—such groups as feminist organizations, governmental agencies, researchers and scholars, social workers, sociologists, and private individuals suggested various strategies for dealing with the far-reaching alterations in American society. Consequently, workshops and other public programs which assisted individuals in their adjustment to the changing world proliferated, while a large self-help literature existed, with many titles enjoying best-seller status.

Among the ideas considered and worked on were enhanced affirmative action programs, continued strategies for passage of the ERA, litigation equalizing wages of female and male workers, job training programs, paid maternity leaves, a remodeling of outdated notions of femininity and masculinity, crisis intervention programs, nonsexist education, and equal political representation for all individuals. The federal government remained both active and insistent. For instance, Congress attempted to partially address the problems of accelerating divorce with the Family

Support Act of 1988, which dictated the development of a system in which employers would withhold child-support payments from paychecks. When the provision went into effect on 1 January 1994, some states had already complied, while others struggled to catch up. Also, after the hearings for confirmation of Clarence Thomas to the Supreme Court, in which Anita Hill spoke vividly of sexual harassment, the government intensified its attack on such harassment of women.

Local officials also participated in further change. For instance, they developed a growing recognition of and sensitivity to the seriousness of rape, or sexual assault, as feminists preferred to call forced sex. By the 1980s, reformed rape laws, female police officers, rape counseling, and rape-crisis centers existed in most towns and cities. Courts also began to define marital rape, meaning sexual intercourse against a spouse's will. Research indicated that spousal rape caused more trauma than rape between strangers because the raped spouse had not only trusted the other spouse but was usually subject to multiple offenses. By 1989, thirty-eight states had marital rape laws, and by 1993 all fifty declared marital rape a crime. During the following year, 1994, Lorena Bobbitt's violent reaction to her husband's alleged mistreatment of her accelerated public discussion of private sex to a notorious and often tawdry level.

Individuals also continued to contribute their ideas about dealing with major changes. Once shrouded in myth and a subject for jokes, menopausal women have gained new dignity, at least partly through Gail Sheehy's *The Silent Passage: Menopause* (1991). Sheehy's book pointed out that while the menopause usually occurs between ages 45 and 50, women's life expectancy is 75 and rising. Thus, women have some twenty-five years after menopause to enjoy life, work, and sex.

Other women have spoken on behalf of the deteriorating environment and new eco-feminism. In 1990, Winona LaDuke of the Anishinabe tribe in northern Minnesota called for reciprocity with the environment. LaDuke explained that when her people gathered wild rice or hunted they always tried to give something back to the environment: "we're an integral part of the ecosystem in our areas . . . reciprocity is an essential part of our value system, which is very contrary to the industrial value system and the industrial society in the United States." Other native women have implemented or inspired experiments with organic food cooperatives, tree planting, and alternative healing methods.

This is not meant to suggest that after 1985 all contemporary women-related problems neared solution. On the contrary, single motherhood among women ages 18 to 44 continued to rise. In 1982, 15 percent of mothers were unwed, but, in 1992, 24 percent of mothers were unwed. In that period, the rate of single motherhood rose from 17.2 to 32.5 percent among women with four years of high school, and from 5.5 to 11.3 percent among women with one or more years of college. The rate increased from 10 to 17 percent among Anglo women, from 16 to 27 percent among Latinas, and from 49 to 67 percent among African American women.

Another critical problem was AIDS, or Acquired Immune Deficiency Syndrome, which is a fatal disease contracted by transmission of bodily fluids through sexual relations or infected needles. By the spring of 1987, 2,207 women had been identified as AIDS victims. Two years later, this figure jumped to 7,821 women. Women became the fastest-growing AIDS population in the United States, and more women were known to contract AIDS through sexual contact than through infected needles. Although the federal government was slow to recognize the threat AIDS poses to women and their children, President Bill Clinton funded additional research, established AIDS care and research as a national priority, and focused attention on women's health care through such events as Breast Cancer Awareness Month.

Persistence of Regionalism

After 1985, American culture homogenized to an unprecedented degree. But it is unclear how that homogenization affected American women. Scholars have yet to conduct the comparative research and studies that will reveal whether women of various regions are more different from each other than they are similar.

Certainly, both differences and similarities continued to exist. As one example, in the northeastern United States, women divorced at a lower rate than in the South and the West. Still, as in the South and the West, northern women of color frequently clustered in urban ghettoes and confronted racism on a daily basis.

In the South, women divorced at the second-highest rate among the three regions. Yet, as in the North and West, southern women of color also battled racism. Moreover, Latinas who lived primarily in Florida shared with their Puerto Rican sisters in New York a concern regarding whether Spanish would become an accepted language in schools and workplaces.

In the West, women divorced at the highest rate of American women, and thus of all women in the world. Here, racism also abounded, yet far more Latinas lived in the West than in the North and South, while Native American women also formed a fast-growing group. In the early 1990s, Indian women experienced the highest rate of infant mortality of all races, while the rate of fetal alcohol syndrome was three to six times higher than the national average. In 1988, Suzanne Harjo, a Cheyenne, testified before the U.S. Civil Rights Commission that Indians suffered high unemployment, alcoholism, and increased teenage suicide resulting from being "mocked, dehumanized, cartooned, stereotyped."

The nation has recognized the persistence of social class, racial, and gender problems. Perhaps it now needs to recognize, and attack, issues peculiar to the women of each region.

In a sense, this story of American women has gone full circle—from native women at the beginning and back to native women at the end. In reality, however, there is little unity to the story of American women. Patterns appear. Continuity vies with change, and resistance with innovation, but the story is openended and unfinished. What qualities will characterize the future? The answer will be determined not just by American women but by all Americans.

Suggestions for Further Reading

Ammer, Christine. *Unsung: A History of Women in American Music.* Westport, Ct: Greenwood Press, 1980.

Anzaldua, Gloria. *Borderlands/La Frontera: The New Mestiza.* San Francisco: Spinsters/Aunt Lute Book Co., 1987.

Arendell, Terry J. "Women and the Economics of Divorce in the Contemporary United States," *Signs* 13 (Autumn 1987): 121–35.

Attebury, Lt. Col. Mary Ann, USAFR. "Women and Their Wartime Roles," *Minerva: Quarterly Report on Women and the Military* 8 (Spring 1990): 11–28.

Baehr, Nina. "Women Making a Choice: The Long Quest for Reproductive Rights," *Radical America* 22 (1989): 44–48.

Baer, Judith A. *Women in American Law: The Struggle toward Equality from the New Deal to the Present.* New York: Holmes & Meier, 1991.

Banner, Lois W. *Women in Modern America: A Brief History.* New York: Harcourt Brace Jovanovich, Inc., 1984.

Bataille, Gretchen M., and Charles L. P. Silet, eds. *The Pretend Indians: Images of Native Americans in the Movies.* Ames: Iowa State University Press, 1980.

Berch, Bettina. *The Endless Day: The Political Economy of Women and Work.* New York: Harcourt Brace Jovanovich, Inc., 1982.

Berry, Mary Frances. *The Politics of Parenthood: Child Care, Women's Rights, and the Myth of the Good Mother.* New York: Viking Press, 1993.

Binion, Gayle. "Toward a Feminist Regrounding of Constitutional Law," *Social Science Quarterly* 72 (June 1991): 207–20.

Blum, Linda M. "Mothers, Babies, and Breastfeeding in Late Capitalist America: The Shifting Contexts of Feminist Theory," *Feminist Studies* 19 (Summer 1993): 291–311.

Booher, Alice A. "American Military Women: Prisoners of War," *Minerva: Quarterly Report on Women and the Military* 11 (Spring 1993). 17–22.

Burt-Way, Barbara J., and Rita Mae Kelly. "Gender and Sustaining Political Ambition: A Study of Arizona Elected Officials," *Western Political Quarterly* 45 (March 1992): 11–25.

Calderón, Roberto, and Emilio Zamora, Jr. *Chicana Voices: Intersections of Class, Race, and Gender.* Austin: Center for Mexican American Studies, University of Texas at Austin, 1986.

Campbell, D'Ann. "Combatting the Gender Gulf," *Temple Political and Civil Rights Law Review* 2 (Fall 1992): 63–91.

Cantarow, Ellen. "Jessie López de la Cruz," 94–151, in *Moving the Mountain: Women Working for Social Change*, edited by Ellen Cantarow. Old Westbury, NY: Feminist Press, 1980.

Caraway, Nancie E. "The Challenge and Theory of Feminist Identity Politics: Working on Racism," *Frontiers* 12 (1991): 109–29.

———. *Segregated Sisterhood: Racism and the Politics of American Feminism.* Knoxville: University of Tennessee Press, 1991.

Casal, Lourdes, and Yolanda Prieto. "Black Cubans in the United States: Basic Demographic Information," 314–55, in *Female Immigrants to the United States: Caribbean, Latin American, and African Experiences*, edited by Delores M. Mortimer and Roy S. Bryce-LaPorte. Washington, DC: Research Institute on Immigration and Ethnic Studies, Smithsonian Institution, 1981.

Chan, Sucheng, Douglas Henry Daniels, Mario T. García, and Terry P. Wilson, eds. *Peoples of Color in the American West.* Lexington, MA: D.C. Heath, 1994.

Christian, Barbara. *Black Women Novelists: The Development of a Tradition, 1892–1976.* Westport, CT: Greenwood Press, 1980.

Cohen, Steve Martin. "American Jewish Feminism: A Study in Conflicts and Compromises," *American Behavioral Scientist* 23 (March/April 1980): 519–58.

Cook, Elizabeth Adell. "Feminist Consciousness and Candidate Preference among American Women, 1972–1988," *Political Behavior* 15 (September 1993): 227–46.

Córdova, Teresa, et al. *Chicana Voices: Intersections of Class, Race, and Gender.* Albuquerque: University of New Mexico Press, 1990.

Coyle, Laurie, Gail Hershatter, and Emily Honig. "Women at Farah: An Unfinished Story," 117–43, in *Mexican Women in the United States: Struggles Past and Present*, edited by Magdalena Mora and Adelaida R. del Castillo. Los Angeles: Chicano Studies Research Center, University of California, Los Angeles, 1980.

de Alba, Alicia Gaspar. "*Tortillerismo*: Work by Chicana Lesbians," *Signs* 18 (Summer 1993): 956–63.

Degler, Carl N. *At Odds: Women and the Family in America from the Revolution to the Present.* New York: Oxford University Press, 1980.

del Castillo, Adelaida R., ed. *Between Borders: Essays on Mexicana/Chicana History.* Encino, CA: Floricanto Press, 1990.

delli Capini, Michael X., and Esther R. Fuchs. "The Year of the Woman? Candidates, Voter, and the 1992 Elections," *Political Science Quarterly* 108 (Spring 1993): 29–36.

Dill, Bonnie Thornton. "The Dialectics of Black Womanhood," *Signs* 4 (Spring 1979): 543–55.

Echols, Alice. *Daring to be Bad: Radical Feminism in America.* Minneapolis: University of Minnesota Press, 1989.

Epstein, Cynthia Fuchs. "Ten Years Later: Perspectives on the Woman's Movement," *Dissent* 22 (Spring 1975): 169–76.

Epstein, Lee, and Joseph F. Kobylka, *The Supreme Court and Legal Change: Abortion and the Death Penalty.* Chapel Hill: University of North Carolina Press, 1992.

Estep, Rhoda. "Women's Roles in Crime as Depicted by Television and Newspapers," *Journal of Popular Culture* 16 (Winter 1982): 151–56.

Evans, Sara M. *Born for Liberty: A History of Women in America.* New York: Free Press, 1989. Chapter 13.

Ferree, Myra Marx. "A Woman for President? Changing Responses: 1958–1972," *Public Opinion Quarterly* 38 (Fall 1974): 390–99.

———. "Employment Without Liberation: Cuban Women in the United States," *Social Science Quarterly* 60 (January 1979): 35–50.

Foner, Philip S. *Women and the American Labor Movement: From World War I to the Present.* New York: Free Press, 1980.

Fout, John C., and Maura Shaw Tantillo. *American Sexual Politics: Sex, Gender, and Race since the Civil War.* Chicago: University of Chicago Press, 1993.

Fox-Genovese, Elizabeth. *Feminism Without Illusions: A Critique of Individualism.* Chapel Hill: University of North Carolina Press, 1991.

Franzen, Trisha. "Differences and Identities: Feminism and the Albuquerque Lesbian Community," *Signs* 18 (Summer 1993): 891–906.

Friedman, Jean E., William G. Shade, and Mary Jane Capozzoli, eds. *Our American Sisters: Women in American Life and Thought.* 4th ed. Lexington, MA: D.C. Heath and Company, 1987. Part IV, 22–25.

García, Alma M. "The Development of Chicana Feminist Discourse, 1970–1980," *Gender and Society* 3 (1989): 217–38.

García, María Cristina. "Adapting to Exile: Cuban Women in the United States, 1959–1973," *Latino Studies Journal* (Spring 1991): 17–33.

Golden, Stephanie. *The Women Outside: Meanings and Myths of Homelessness.* Berkeley: University of California Press, 1992.

Goldin, Claudia. "Female Labor Force Participation: The Origin of Black and White Differences, 1870 and 1880," *Journal of Economic History* 37 (March 1977): 87–108.

Green, Rayna, ed. *That's What She Said: Contemporary Poetry and Fiction by Native American Women.* Bloomington: Indiana University Press, 1984.

Groneman, Carol, and Mary Beth Norton, eds. *"To Toil the Livelong Day": America's Women at Work, 1780–1980.* Ithaca: Cornell University Press, 1987.

Harrison, Cynthia E. "A 'New Frontier' for Women: The Public Policy of the Kennedy Administration," *Journal of American History* 67 (December 1980): 630–46.

Herbert, Mellisa S. "From Crinoline to Camouflage: Initial Entry Training and the Marginalization of Women in the Military," *Minerva: Quarterly Report on Women and the Military* 11 (Spring 1993): 41–57.

Hernández, Patricia. "Lives of Chicana Activists: The Chicano Student Movement," 17–26, in *Mexican Women in the United States: Struggle Past and Present*, edited by Magdalena Mora and Adelaida R. del Castillo. Los Angeles: Chicano Studies Research Center, University of California, Los Angleles, 1980.

Herrera-Sobek, María, ed. *Chicana Creativity and Criticism: Charting New Frontiers in American Literature.* Houston: Arte Público Press, University of Houston, 1988.

——. *The Mexican Corrido: A Feminist Analysis.* Bloomington: Indiana University Press, 1990.

Hondagneu-Sotelo, Pierrette, "New Perspectives on Latina Women," *Feminist Studies* 19 (Spring 1993): 193–207.

Howe, Louise Kapp. *Pink Collar Workers: Inside the World of Women's Work.* New York: G. P. Putnam's Sons, 1977.

Huyck, Heather. "Beyond John Wayne: Using Historic Sites to Interpret Women's History," 303–30, in *Western Women: Their Land, Their Lives*, edited by Lillian Schlissel, Vicki L. Ruiz, and Janice Monk. Albuquerque: University of New Mexico Press, 1988.

Katzenstein, Mary Fainsod. "Feminism and the Meaning of the Vote," *Signs* 10 (Autumn 1984): 4–26.

Kennedy, Elizabeth Lapovsky, and Madeline D. Davis. *Boots of Leather, Slippers of Gold: The History of a Lesbian Community.* New York: Penguin USA, 1993.

Kennedy, Susan Estabrook. *If All We Did Was to Weep at Home: A History of White Working-class Women in America.* Bloomington: Indiana University Press, 1979.

Kessler-Harris, Alice. *Out to Work: A History of Wage-Earning Women in the United States.* New York: Oxford University Press, 1982.

——. *A Woman's Wage: Historical Meanings and Social Consequences.* Lexington: University Press of Kentucky, 1990.

Kibria, Nazli. "Power, Patriarchy, and Gender Conflict in the Vietnamese Immigrant Community," *Gender & Society* 4 (1990): 9–24.

Kidwell, Clara Sue. "Indian Women as Cultural Mediators," *Ethnohistory* 39 (1992): 97–107.

Kidwell, Claudia Brush, and Valerie Steele. *Men and Women: Dressing the Part.* (History of fashion.) Washington, DC: Smithsonian Institution Press, 1989.

Kim, Elaine H., with Janie Otani. *With Silk Wings: Asian American Women at Work.* San Francisco: Asian Women of California, 1983.

King-Kok, Cheung. *Articulate Silences: Hisaye Yamamoto, Maxine Hong Kingston, Joy Kogawa.* Ithaca, NY: Cornell University Press, 1993.

Klein, Ethel. *Gender Politics.* Cambridge, MA: Harvard University Press, 1984.

Knack, Martha E. "Contemporary Southern Paiute Women and the Measurement of Women's Economic and Political Status," *Ethnology* 2 (1989): 233–48.

Kobrin, Frances E. "The Fall in Household Size and the Rise of the Primary Individual in the United States," *Demography* 13 (February 1976): 127–38.

Kubitschek, Missy Dehn. *Claiming the Heritage: Afro-American Women Novelists and History*. Jackson: University Press of Mississippi, 1991.

Lamphere, Louise. "Bringing the Family to Work: Women's Culture on the Shop Floor," *Feminist Studies* 11 (Fall 1985): 518–40.

Lamphere, Louise, Patricia Zavella, and Felipe Gonzales. *Sunbelt Working Mothers: Reconciling Family and Factory*. Ithaca, NY: Cornell University Press, 1993.

Lerner, Gerda. *The Majority Finds Its Past: Placing Women in History*. New York: Oxford University Press, 1979. Chapters 3, 4, and 9.

Lewis, Diane K. "A Response to Inequality: Black Women, Racism, and Sexism," *Signs* 3 (Winter 1977): 339–61.

Litoff, Judy Barrett. *American Midwives: 1860 to the Present*. Westport, Ct: Greenwood Press, 1978.

Loza, Steven. *Barrio Rhythm: Mexican American Music in Los Angeles*. Urbana: University of Illinois Press, 1993.

Lynch, Robert N. "Women in Northern Paiute Politics," *Signs* 11 (1986): 352–66.

Margolis, Maxine L. *Mothers and Such: Views of American Women and Why They Changed*. Berkeley: University of California Press, 1984.

McKay, Nellie Y. "Black Women's Literary Scholarship: Reclaiming an Intellectual Tradition," *Sage* 6 (Summer 1989): 89–91.

Melosh, Barbara. *"The Physicians' Hand": Work, Culture, and Conflict in American Nursing*. Philadelphia: Temple University Press, 1982.

———, ed. *Gender and American History since 1890*. New York: Routledge, 1993.

Melville, Margarita, ed. *Twice a Minority*. St. Louis, MO: C. V. Mosby, 1980.

Miller, Page Putnam, ed. *Reclaiming the Past: Landmarks of Women's History*. Bloomington: Indiana University Press, 1992.

———. "Women's History Landmark Project: Policy and Research," *The Public Historian* 15 (Fall 1993): 82–88.

Mills, Kay. *The Little Light of Mine: The Life of Fannie Lou Hamer*. New York: Dutton, 1993.

Mirandé, Alfredo, and Evangelina Enríquez. *La Chicana: The Mexican-American Woman*. Chicago: University of Chicago Press, 1979.

Mora, Magdalena, and Adelaida R. del Castillo, eds. *Mexican Women in the United States: Struggles Past and Present*. Occasional Paper No. 2, Chicano Studies Research Center Publications, University of California: Los Angeles, 1980.

Moraga, Cherríe, and Gloria Anzaldúa. *The Bridge Called My Back: Writings by Radical Women of Color*. New York: Kitchen Table, Women of Color Press, 1981.

Musick, Judith S. *Young, Poor, and Pregnant: The Psychology of Teenage Motherhood*. New Haven, CT: Yale University Press, 1993.

Powers, Marla N. *Oglala Women: Myth, Ritual, and Reality*. Chicago: University of Chicago Press, 1986.

Prieto, Yolanda. "Cuban Women in the U.S. Labor Force: Perspectives on the Nature of Change," *Cuban Studies* 17 (1987): 73–91.

———. "Cuban Women in New Jersey: Gender Relations and Change," 185–202, in *Seeking Common Ground: Multidisciplinary Studies of Immigrant Women in the United States*, edited by Donna Gabaccia. Westport, CT: Greenwood Press, 1992.

Rebolledo, Tey Diana, Erlinda Gonzales-Berry, and Teresa Márquez, eds. *Las Muyeres Hablan: An Anthology of Nuevo Mexicana Writers*. Albuquerque: El Norte Publications, 1988.

Richmond, Marie La Liberté. *Immigrant Adaptation and Family Structure Among Cubans in Miami, Florida*. New York: Arno Press, 1980.

Robinson, Donald Allen. "Two Movements in Pursuit of Equal Employment Opportunity," *Signs* 4 (Spring 1979): 413–33.

Rogow, Faith. *"Gone to Another Meeting": The National Council of Jewish Women, 1893–1993*. Tuscaloosa: University of Alabama Press, 1993.

Romero, Mary. *Maid in the U.S.A.* New York: Routledge, 1992.

Rowbotham, Sheila. *The Past Is Before Us: Feminism in Action Since the 1960s*. Winchester, MA: Pandora Press, 1989.

Ruiz, Vicki, ed. *"Las Obreras*: The Politics of Work and Family," Special Edition, *Aztlan* 20 (Spring/Fall 1991).

Ruiz, Vicki L., and Susan Tiano, eds. *Women on the U.S.-Mexico Border: Responses to Change*. Boulder, CO: Westview Press, 1991.

Ryan, Barbara. *Feminism and the Women's Movement: Dynamics of Change in Social Movement, Ideology, and Activism*. New York: Routledge, 1992.

Sánchez, Marta. *Chicana Poetry: A Critical Approach to an Emerging Literature*. Berkeley: University of California Press, 1985.

Sánchez, Rosaura, and Rosa Martinez Cruz. *Essays on La Mujer*. Los Angeles: University of California Chicano Studies Center Publications, 1977.

Sanders, Marlene, and Marcia Rock. *Waiting for Prime Time: The Women of Television News*. Urbana: University of Illinois Press, 1994.

Scott, Anne Firor. *Making the Invisible Woman Visible*. Urbana: University of Illinois Press, 1984.

Scott, Joan Wallach. "The Mechanization of Women's Work," *Scientific American* 247 (September 1982): 166–87.

Senese, Guy. "Promise and Practice: Important Developments in Wartime and Post-War Indian Education Policy, 1940–1975," *Journal of Thought* 19 (Fall 1984): 11–30.

Singleton, Carrie Jane. "Race and Gender in Feminist Theory," *Sage* 6 (Summer 1989): 12–17.

Smith, M. Dwayne, and Ellen S. Kuchta. "Trends in Violent Crime Against Women, 1973–1989," *Social Science Quarterly* 74 (March 1993): 28–45.

Sommer, Laurie Kay. "Inventing Latinismo: The Creation of 'Hispanic' Panethnicity in the United States," *Journal of American Folklore* 104 (Winter 1991): 32–53.

Stoddard, Ellwyn R. "Female Participation in the U.S. Military: Gender Trends by Branch, Rank, and Racial Categories," *Minerva: Quarterly Report on Women and the Military* 11 (Spring 1993): 23–40.

Strasser, Susan. *Never Done: A History of American Housework*. New York: Pantheon Books, 1981.

Taylor, William B., and Franklin Pease, eds. *Violence, Resistance, and Survival in the Americas: Native Americans and the Legacy of Conquest*. Washington, DC: Smithsonian Institution Press, 1993.

Thornton, Arland, and Deborah Freedman. "Changes in the Sex Role Attitudes of Women, 1962–1977: Evidence from a Panel Study," *American Sociological Review* 44 (October 1979): 831–42.

Tucker, Sherrie. "'Where the Blues and the Truth Lay Hiding': Rememory of Jazz in Black Women's Fiction," *Frontiers* 13 (1993): 26–44.

Wallace, Michele. *Black Macho and the Myth of the Superwoman*. New York: Dial Press, 1979.

Wandersee, Winifred D. *On the Move: American Women in the 1970s*. New York: Twayne Publishers, 1988.

Wells, Robert V. "Demographic Change and the Life Cycle of American Families," *Journal of Interdisciplinary History* 2 (Autumn 1971): 273–82.

Wertheimer, Barbara Mayer. *We Were There: The Story of Working Women in America*. New York: Pantheon Books, 1977.

Ybarra, Lea. "When Wives Work: The Impact on the Chicano Family," *Journal of Marriage and Family* 44 (February 1982): 169–78.

Zavella, Patricia. "'Abnormal Intimacy': The Varying Work Networks of Chicana Cannery Workers," *Feminist Studies* 11 (Fall 1985): 541–57.

———. "Reflections on Diversity among Chicanas," *Frontiers* 12 (1991): 73–85.

CONCLUSION
Looking Toward the Future

Unlike members of numerous other cultures, Americans have usually believed that change equates with progress, that progress is always positive, and that the United States achieves progress in a linear fashion. Customarily, American history has reinforced these notions, teaching that the colonists who migrated to the shores of North America launched a democratic experiment, and that subsequent generations enlarged the tradition, reaping power and prosperity as their rewards.

In the 1990s, however, most Americans realize that the historical trajectory is far more complicated: change can move a nation forward or backward, progress can be destructive as well as constructive, and continuity can exert at least as powerful a force as change. Thus, change has consisted of cycles, which often lack clear direction and include conflict, dissension, and uncertainty. At the same time, only some people enjoyed the rewards of power and prosperity, while others paid the costs, enduring loss, poverty, and relative powerlessness.

The survey of American women's history presented here has revealed similar patterns. Between 1607 and the mid-1800s, for example, expectations of American women altered in many ways, yet their overall configuration stayed much the same. Between the mid-nineteenth century and the early 1900s, customary gender expectations and social constructs came under attack from every side but continued to resist destruction.

During this latter period, numerous people argued for the expansion of women's participation in American society. Both female and male reformers exerted pressure on all levels of society to become more egalitarian. Through voluntary associations, these people worked for social and gender reforms. Those who advocated woman suffrage argued particularly for women's right to the ballot. Yet when the United States finally granted the right of suffrage to its female citizens in 1920, it became clear that the vote was not a panacea. Years earlier, Elizabeth Cady Stanton had dismissed the right to vote as "not even half a loaf . . . only a crust, a crumb." Following the achievement of suffrage, women's rights advocates realized that Stanton had been prophetic; the right of suffrage barely scratched the surface of necessary reform.

Then, during the Great Depression and World War II, additional forces encouraged close scrutiny of the efficacy of the customary model of American womanhood. Economic collapse, war, industrialization, urbanization, and energetic reform movements led to a general rethinking of women's roles and responsibilities. Were women to be limited only to wife- and motherhood? Or were there other roles that they might happily and effectively play in addition to these? Was the nation squandering a crucial resource in restricting women to customary, domestic lifestyles?

At the same time, however, the national determination to see American women as domestic, docile, cheerful, simple, and submissive beings enjoyed periods of rejuvenation, especially during the Great Depression and the back-to-the-home movement that followed the conclusion of World War II. Apparently, many Americans felt reluctant to surrender the traditional view of women as properly relegated to, and fulfilled by, the world of home and family.

Throughout each of these eras, women of color and such others as employed, lesbian, and single women received less attention and assistance than so-called mainstream women. Thus, in the 1960s, the need for a renewed feminist movement seemed apparent to women from a wide variety of backgrounds. The resulting contemporary feminist movement of the 1960s appealed to people of all races, classes, and types; and it proved the largest ever in membership and the most widely based in constituencies, platforms, and programs.

In following years, American society experienced basic and pervasive modifications in the structure of American institutions, the fabric of American culture, and Americans' interpersonal relations. Still, the traditional pattern persevered. By the 1980s, backlash and resistance developed. The struggle between the model of womanhood and the reality of women's lives exhibited more complexity than ever before, while women of color and other groups of women often endured isolation.

Thus, the current perplexing and often strife-ridden situation is part of a process that is seldom linear but more typically uneven and diverse. Even though the current climate may be uncertain, it does offer American women and men many opportunities to participate in fashioning their future and that of American society.

Important questions remain, however. How does one foment change? How significant a role can such factors as human agency and women's distinctive culture play? Or will such social, economic, and political forces as depression and war determine the future?

If anything, the lesson of this review of women's history has been that human will and women's culture had great weight in the development of American women's history. For instance, in the face of economic and political pressures that eroded Indian women's traditions, their status as producers and traders, and their power within their tribes, they refused to allow themselves to collapse. Instead, they adapted to the market economy by producing new goods that Anglos and others would purchase. They also formed women's associations to fight discriminatory policies and actions. Although outside forces battered them, they resisted and endured.

Hundreds of other women whose names have appeared here similarly defied the demands of dominant institutions. African American women resisted slavery and, when urbanization later overwhelmed them, they created the blues, jazz, and a rich literature. Latinas developed ways to protest labor injustices, then used them as a foundation to demand civil rights, urban reform, and revisions in the family structure. Anglo women protested gender expectations based on domesticity; from Anne Bradstreet to Elizabeth Cady Stanton to Betty Friedan they fought back. Asian American women turned Chinatowns and Little Tokyos into bases from which they learned to preserve their own customs yet adapt to the larger American culture.

Looking at women from a perspective other than their racial or ethnic backgrounds produces similar observations. Lesbian women withstood social pressures by creating "Boston Marriages," and later such groups as Radicalesbians. Hearing-impaired women took their act on the road with such groups as the National Theatre of the Deaf and Gallaudet College Dancers. Religiously oriented women formed the Leadership Conference of Women Religious, Hadassah, and the Center for Women and Religion to achieve their ends. Radical women joined the Socialist and Communist Parties, while rural women participated in such organizations as the Farmers' Alliance and the Populist Party.

Today, as the United States approaches the twenty-first century, these women provide a model and an inspiration. Although numerous Americans fear the future, most recognize that rather than signaling the necessity to quit and turn backward, anxiety only indicates a need to proceed with deliberation and care. Like the hundreds of forerunners who appear in this book, contemporary Americans must confront and resolve the issues.

For instance, more women than men now obtain college educations, while such fields as law and English literature are feminizing. What do such changes mean for coming generations of Americans? How can the United States prepare its youth to accept growing numbers of women in positions of leadership and authority? How can women fortify themselves to avoid the mistakes that men of power sometimes committed? Can they avoid them?

Undertaking to answer these and other questions will benefit not only women but men as well. Clearly, people of both genders must participate. This venture also requires the participation of all types of women and men—those of Native American, Latino, Anglo, African and Asian heritage; gay and lesbian; working class and professional—for they must inhabit together the increasingly globalized world they are shaping.

INDEX

This is a combined index for Volume 1 and Volume 2.
Volume 2 begins with page 173.

Credits in full
Volume 2

Opening illustrations:

Photoessay for Volume 2
Twenty-four pages, A–X, following p. 293

Page A

Top: A young Latina, c. 1890. *Museum of New Mexico,* Neg. #137333

Bottom: Tejanas and Anglos (French) among this class, El Carmen, Texas, ca. 1896. *The Institute of Texan Cultures,* San Antonio

Page B

Top: Inside a frame homestead, Montana, ca. 1900. *Montana Historical Society,* Helena

Bottom: Homestead, Montana, ca. 1890s. *Montana Historical Society,* Helena

Page C

Top: Breaking down cotton stalks, Uniontown, Alabama, 1905. *Library of Congress*

Bottom: A courting couple near Sioux City, Iowa, ca. 1900. *Author's collection*

Page D

Gathering cotton near Dallas, Texas, 1907. *Library of Congress*

Page E

Top: Spring plowing, Mandan, North Dakota, 1906. *State Historical Society of North Dakota,* Bismarck

Middle: Sawmill crew near Pekin, North Dakota, ca. 1897. *Author's collection.*

Bottom: Martha Stoecker in front of her homesteading shack, ca. 1904. *South Dakota State Historical Society*

Page F

Top: Polly Bemis of Warrens, Idaho. Photograph #62-44.7. *Idaho State Historical Society,* Boise

Bottom: California Maidu woman with traditional seed beater for gathering food, early twentieth-century photo. *The Field Museum,* #1835, Hudson photo

Page G

Top: Trimming currency, Bureau of Engraving and Printing, Washington, D.C., 1907. *Library of Congress*

Bottom: A physical education class in the Armory, University of North Dakota, Grand Forks, 1904. *State Historical Society of North Dakota,* Bismarck

Page H

Top: Bertie Lord with coyote she shot, after 1900. *Montana Historical Society,* Helena

Bottom: A teacher with her Flathead Indian pupils in Montana, 1910. *Montana Historical Society*, Helena

Page I

Top: African American pioneer in Mantorville, Minnesota, c. 1905. *Minnesota Historical Society,* from the Dorothy St. Arnold papers

Bottom: Zambrano family and others at baby's funeral in early 1900s, Texas. *The Institute of Texan Cultures,* San Antonio

Page J

Top: Doctors Tai Heong Kong (Li) and Kai Fai Li (see p. iii, above)

Bottom: Washing clothes in a stream near Ft. Pierre, 1911. *South Dakota State Historical Society*

Page K

Top: Working for national woman suffrage. *Library of Congress*

Bottom: Woman suffrage comes early to Oregon—Abigail Scott Duniway, at the polls. *Oregon Historical Society*

Page L

Top: Latina in New Mexico, c. 1915. *Museum of New Mexico,* Neg. #31501

Bottom: Black family among thousands to migrate from the South to northern cities during the early twentieth century. *Library of Congress*

Page M

Top: Working in the dry goods store, Lakota, North Dakota. *State Historical Society of North Dakota,* Bismarck

Bottom: Confirmation Class of 1905 at Temple B'nai Israel, Galveston, Texas. Archives of Temple B'nai Israel, Galveston, Texas; copy from Institute of Texan Cultures, *San Antonio*

Page N

Top: Washing clothes with the aid of a mechanical wringer, Hinsdale, Illinois, 1919. *State Historical Society of Wisconsin,* Neg. #r0177

Bottom: Nancy Hendrickson, planting corn, Morton County, North Dakota, ca. 1918. *State Historical Society of North Dakota,* Bismarck

Page O

Top: Red Cross post card, First World War. *Library of Congress*

Bottom: Kansas showgirls receive a Gideon Bible, 1927. *Library of Congress*

Page P

Top: Creating beauty in the barrio, El Paso, Texas, 1949. *Russell Lee Photograph Collection, The Center for American History, The University of Texas at Austin,* Neg. #3Y185, VN, 14920-34

Bottom: Creole women in Plaquemines Parish, Louisiana, 1939. *Louisiana State Library*

Page Q
Top: Migrant family on the road, 1939. Dorothea Lange photo. *Library of Congress*
Bottom: Cigar factory strike, August 1933. *San Antonio Light Collection, Institute of Texan Cultures*, San Antonio

Page R
Top: Women's Air Force service pilots (see p. 254, above)
Bottom: Riveters in the Long Beach plant of Douglas Aircraft Co., 1942. *National Archives*

Page S
Top: On the way to one of seven internment camps for Japanese Americans, 1942. *National Archives*
Bottom: Welding pipe outlets for a ship in Baltimore. *Library of Congress*

Page T
Top: Emma Tenayuca, union organizer, at age 19. *San Antonio Light Collection, Institute of Texan Cultures,* San Antonio
Bottom: Eleanor Roosevelt greeting Mary McLeod Bethune at a women's dormitory for black war workers, May 1943. *Library of Congress*

Page U
Top: Woman of courage at 15, Elizabeth Echford, during the Little Rock school crisis, 1957. *United Press International*
Bottom: Dolores Huerta signaling to strikebreakers in fields near Delano, California, September 24, 1965. *Harvey Richards*

Page V
Top: Maggie Kuhn at Gray Panther convention, 1977. *Julie Jensen*
Bottom left: Barbara Jordan, Democratic National Convention keynote speaker, 1977. *United Press International*
Bottom right: Joyce Miller, Vice President and Director of Social Services of ACTWU, and first woman on executive council of AFL-CIO. *Office of Joyce Miller*

Page W
Top: National Women's Conference, Houston, Texas, 1977. *Courtesy Jimmy Carter Library*
Bottom: Betty Friedan, Addie Wyatt, and Jean Stapleton lead a march in Chicago for the Equal Rights Amendment, May 1980. *United Press International*

Page X
Top: Astronaut Sally K. Ride aboard the earth-orbiting space shuttle *Challenger*, 1983.
Bottom: University of Texas women's basketball team plays Arkansas. *The Center for American History, The University of Texas at Austin,* UT-Texas Student Publications, Inc. Photographs

P. 340 Poetry copyright Elena Avila, from "Coming Home," p. 148 in *Las Mujeres Hablan: An Anthology of Nueva Mexicana Writers*, edited by Tey Diana Rebolledo, Erlinda Gonzalez-Berry, and Teresa Márquez. Albuquerque: El Norte Publications, 1988.

Glenda Riley is Alexander M. Bracken Professor of History at Ball State University. Formerly, she was professor of history and director of the Women's Studies Program at the University of Northern Iowa. Professor Riley has also served as visiting endowed professor at University College, Dublin; Marquette University; and Mesa State College. In addition to authoring two editions of *Inventing the American Woman*, Professor Riley has written *The Life and Legacy of Annie Oakley* (1994), *A Place to Grow: Women in the American West* (1992), *Divorce: An American Tradition* (1991); *The Female Frontier: A Comparative View of Women on the Prairie and Plains* (1988); *Women and Indians on the Frontier, 1825-1915* (1984); and *Frontierswomen: The Iowa Experience* (1981; 2nd ed., 1994), as well as numerous published articles, reviews, and chapters in edited volumes.

Inventing the American Woman: An Inclusive History, Second Edition

The publisher's editorial and production team for this text consisted of Maureen Hewitt, Lucy Herz, and Andrew Davidson.

Index: Scholars Editorial Services
Typesetting: Bruce Leckie
Cover design: DePinto Graphic Design
Printing and binding: BookCrafters, Inc.